Queering Architecture

Queering Architecture

Methods, Practices, Spaces, Pedagogies

Edited by
Marko Jobst and Naomi Stead

BLOOMSBURY VISUAL ARTS
LONDON • NEW YORK • OXFORD • NEW DELHI • SYDNEY

BLOOMSBURY VISUAL ARTS
Bloomsbury Publishing Plc
50 Bedford Square, London, WC1B 3DP, UK
1385 Broadway, New York, NY 10018, USA
29 Earlsfort Terrace, Dublin 2, Ireland

BLOOMSBURY, BLOOMSBURY VISUAL ARTS and the Diana logo are trademarks of
Bloomsbury Publishing Plc

First published in Great Britain 2023

Cover design: Eleanor Rose
Cover image © Rafael Pereira do Rego

A catalogue record for this book is available from the British Library.

Library of Congress Cataloging-in-Publication Data
Names: Jobst, Marko, editor. | Stead, Naomi, editor.
Title: Queering architecture : methods, practices, spaces, pedagogies /
Marko Jobst and Naomi Stead.
Description: London; New York: Bloomsbury Visual Arts, 2023. | Includes bibliographical
references and index. | Contents: On the uses of queer space thinking / Olivier Vallerand –
Fabulous façades / Ben Campkin and Lo Marshall – Teacher/student : Queer practices
to dismantle hierarchies in studio culture / A.L. Hu. |
Identifiers: LCCN 2022035615 (print) | LCCN 2022035616 (ebook) | ISBN 9781350267046
(hardback) | ISBN 9781350267084 (paperback) | ISBN 9781350267053 (pdf) |
ISBN 9781350267060 (epub) | ISBN 9781350267077
Subjects: LCSH: Homosexuality and architecture. | Architecture–Philosophy. | Queer theory.
Classification: LCC NA2543.H65 Q44 2023 (print) | LCC NA2543.H65 (ebook) |
DDC 720.1–dc23/eng/20220810
LC record available at https://lccn.loc.gov/2022035615
LC ebook record available at https://lccn.loc.gov/2022035616

ISBN: HB: 978-1-3502-6704-6
ePDF: 978-1-3502-6705-3
eBook: 978-1-3502-6706-0

Typeset by Deanta Global Publishing Services, Chennai, India
Printed and bound in Great Britain

To find out more about our authors and books visit www.bloomsbury.com and sign up for
our newsletters.

CONTENTS

FIGURES

Introduction

Marko Jobst and Naomi Stead

Why a book on queering architecture, and why now? There are many possible answers to this question, one of which is that as editors we hoped to produce a book that we ourselves would want to read and in which we would see our own experiences reflected, as queer people engaged with the full breadth of architectural culture: its education, practice, critique, occupation and theorization. We hoped for a book that would reflect our own multifarious engagements, as critical individuals working within this oldest and most conservative of disciplinary traditions – and who have frequently felt the need to creatively resist and subvert, to expand and critique architecture's hegemonies and blind spots, its occlusions and exclusions (Jobst 2017; Stead 2017, 2018, 2019; Gosseye, Stead and van der Plaat 2019; Jobst 2019; Stead et al. 2019; Frichot and Stead 2020; Gabrielsson et al. 2020; Jobst 2021; Jobst and Frichot 2021).

In conceiving this book, we also hoped to see more of what others were doing in this field *now*, at the beginning of the third decade in the second millennium, a time of great crisis in the environmental, social and political realms, which state of crisis has only been exacerbated by the global pandemic that has marked most of this book's production.

So while being cognizant of the history of past scholarly work in this area (Olivier Vallerand, in his chapter in this volume, amply traces the emergence and development of 'queer space theory' through key texts and intellectual events in the 1990s and beyond) – we also wanted to know what practitioners and scholars have to say about queering architecture today – in light of the complex emergences and overlaps, politics and identities, concepts and theories which mark our current condition.

Of course, we are not alone in this desire – a flurry of recent events and publications have begun to illuminate the ongoing political and methodological power of 'queering', as a stance, an approach and a process. To name just a few examples from the past five years, we note the very recent publication of Adam Nathaniel Furman and Joshua Mardell's *Queer Spaces: An Atlas of LGBTQ+ Places and Stories* (Furman and Mardell 2022). Two years before that, in 2020, Olivier Vallerand's *Unplanned Visitors: Queering the Ethics and Aesthetics of Domestic Space* appeared (Vallerand 2020), alongside Regner Ramos and Sharif Mowlabocus's edited volume *Queer Sites in Global Contexts: Technologies, Spaces, and Otherness* (Ramos and Mowlabocus 2020).

The year 2017 was something of a signal moment for publications in the area, seeing the release of Andrew Gorman-Murray and Matt Cook's edited collection *Queering the Interior* (Gorman-Murray and Cook 2017), and Brent Pilkey et al.'s edited volume *Sexuality and Gender at Home: Experience, Politics, Transgression* (Pilkey et al. 2017). In addition, three important journal special issues appeared: Dirk van den Heuvel and Robert Gorny's edited edition of *Footprint* journal on 'Trans-Bodies/Queering Spaces' (Van den Heuvel and Gorny 2017), a special issue of *The Funambulist* dedicated to 'Queers, Feminists and Interiors' (Lambert 2017) and a special issue of *Log* guest-edited by Jaffer Kolb under the theme 'Working Queer' (Kolb 2017).

It is no coincidence that a number of these authors and editors also appear in this volume – the world of scholarly work on queer spaces in and around the architectural discipline is a relatively close-knit one. It is our hope that with this book we have brought together some of these established voices in the field – including Joel Sanders, editor of one of the seminal 1990s texts, *Stud: Architectures of Masculinity* (Sanders 1996) – as well as a range of new and emerging voices in this field.

Whither 'queer'?

At the onset of the 2020s, when this book was conceived, the term 'queer' was in broad and sometimes indiscriminate use within and beyond academia. 'Queer' remains in everyday parlance primarily as a category of sexual identity, operating as one among the terms in the widely accepted, ever-growing acronym – lesbian, gay, bisexual, trans, intersex, asexual – always inviting for more. But it also potentially suggests deviations and variations in these other terms, destabilizing them and multiplying the relations they can forge. So, while 'queer' is commonly used to designate non-standard sexual identities, it is also a term that potentially cuts across all the terms in the acronym, indicating their unruliness and resistance to all kinds of normativity.

But the history of the term and its development are more complex and richer than this usage in everyday parlance allows for. The word has undergone multiple transformations and changes in understanding and application, especially in the context of academic theory and disciplinary discourse. Originally a derogatory term, 'queer' was reclaimed in the 1980s in activist circles, leading soon after to the field-instituting notion of 'queer theory', which was introduced by Teresa de Lauretis in 1990 at the eponymous conference at the University of California, Santa Cruz.

Three decades later, the moniker not only stands for a field of theoretical inquiry that has LGBTIQ+ issues at its core but also surpasses them substantially. It is so well established that it is routinely questioned, in its relationship to activism as well as its adequacy in the face of intersectional frameworks and feminist new materialist theory. Queer remains a category that serves a broad spectrum of purposes but one that can be understood to be too cosily sidled up to academia – too privileged and too rarefied, too much a matter of discourse and not enough of everyday life.

The first decade of the twenty-first century saw repeated questioning of the usefulness of the term – to the point of several announcements of its supposed impending 'death'. This never did arrive, however, since the term and the modes of inquiry and thinking it fosters seem to find ever new uses, however nuanced in their relation to sexuality, broader issues of normativity and anti-normativity, or any other issue with which queer theory was initially associated. As Hannah McCann and Whitney Monaghan write in *Queer Theory Now: From Foundations to Futures*, 'we seek to demonstrate the value of queer theory *now*, and point to some of the ways that students, activists, artists and scholars may continue the project of testing queer theory's limits, shaping it anew for themselves' (2019: 17). Replace 'artists' with 'architects' or 'architectural researchers' in this statement, and a new territory opens. It is one we wish to take up in speaking of queer theory and its ever-shifting present.

In the sequence of approaches to queer theory over the decades, we turn in particular to the transformation of queer into a methodological orientation: from an adjective or noun into a verb. 'To queer' means to unsettle established relations and norms, to act in the oblique, to look askance. This has been the starting point for us as editors and the basis upon we ask how, and whether, the discipline of architecture can be queered – or queered further.

The conception of 'queering' as a process or methodology is certainly not new in the field of queer theory. Many have employed such a conception, including Browne and Nash in *Queer Methods and Methodologies*, in 2010. But it is certainly an approach that has only discontinuously and fragmentarily been applied to architecture as a practice, a discipline and a theoretical and historical discourse. A decade after Browne and Nash (around the time the initial ideas around our anthology were conceived), Amin Ghaziani and Matt Brim pointed out in *Imagining Queer Methods* (2019) that if the term 'queer' was to be celebrated for its elusive, slippery nature, for being resistant to pinning down and far-reaching in its political potency, the question of queer *methods* offered a paradox of sorts, for to establish a method is to impose order, to set out a framework, to construct a logic – in other words, to enact a process not unlike architecture. In this discipline in particular, the question of queering and the implicit destabilizing it invokes seem to run against the imperative for stability and permanence – even if there are many ways in which we can conceive of architecture as being much more than, or even resisting, that conception.

A volume in four (interconnected and overlapping) sections

This volume is formally arranged in four sections constituting its subtitles: methods, practices, spaces and pedagogies. We arrived at this structure in the interest of addressing the multivalence of 'architecture' – understood here equally as a discipline and a practice, a culture and a series of techniques, a body of concepts and a very particular mode of education – all of which can be crossed by 'queer' and associated practices of queering.

The first term, *methods*, carries the vestige of an earlier conception of what this book could be. In the initial stages, our idea was to foreground issues around *writing* architecture and investigate what it might mean to queer architecture specifically through experimental writerly practices. Both of us have written (on) non-standard methods of writing in/of/about architecture, and equally we have both pursued themes related to queer sexuality in various experiments in writing 'otherwise'.

Indeed, both of us have attempted to write architecture as queers: not only to question architecture's practices and material objects but also to question its discourses and the way those are written into existence – their modes and methods, forms and tonalities, their *style*. In the earliest stages of the book, the question of methods was therefore specifically a matter of *writerly* approaches – and this interest remains central to the anthology, slipping in an out of the chapters collected here, sometimes more overtly, at other times less so.

But as we talked about the book and developed its framework further, it became clear that there was also a need to reflect more broadly – on how architecture has been affected by the institution and maturation of queer theory over the past years and decades. Perhaps inevitably, this took us beyond the question of how to queer architectural writing and architecture through writing – and moved the book towards the broader set of concerns that arise when the terms 'queer' and 'architecture' come to bear on each other.

The attempt to systematize these ideas and directions of inquiry resulted in the four terms to be found in the subtitle of this book. If *methods* is the primary term, and one that underpins much of what is at stake in a project like this, *practices* is second, for the history of queer theory is very much the history of performativity, of the art of *doing*, of a particular constructed stance, of actions and activities undertaken. Some of the key foundational texts of queer theory, most famously Judith Butler's *Gender Trouble* (Butler 2002), concerned themselves precisely with gender and sexuality as performed and performative.

There is a long and rich history in architectural thinking and writing that defines our discipline precisely in terms of performance, rather than simply conjunctions of materials and their arrangement into inhabitable forms. If the most obvious subject of architecture is buildings, its other, equally crucial aspect is the activities that happen in them – what has variously been named as their uses, functions or programmes; and likewise the people who undertake such activities. In other words, architecture is equally concerned with *that which takes place* – with site and setting, and also with situation, and what happens in the built environment – inside and out. In this way architectural also spills outside of buildings into the urban realm, where performances of aberrant, forbidden or persecuted sexualities play themselves out most obviously, and sometimes most violently – but where queer individuals can also find freedom and build community, no matter how ephemeral.

The bridge that conceptually connects methods and practices is our structure's third term: *spaces*. It is by now widely acknowledged that architecture is a discipline that manipulates space – even if the term wasn't part of the disciplinary vocabulary before the nineteenth century. The very notion of interior and exterior weds us not only to the question of what happens within spaces, namely their performative aspect, but also to the visibility and accessibility that are integral to histories of sexuality and queer theory. Indeed, Eve Kosofsky Sedgwick's *Epistemology of the Closet* (Sedgwick 2008), one of the foundational texts of queer theory, names that ultimate interiority, the space of privacy and domesticity, of confinement and secrecy, which came to represent the repression of those whose sexuality remained beyond the norm – and likewise the act of rejecting such oppressions by coming out of it.

It is therefore hardly surprising that architectural writing focusing on queer issues is often either centred on domestic interiors and interiority in general, or on the collective, public and largely urban spaces where LGBT+ communities have carved out their communal territories and forged realms of collective existence. Architecture remains implicit in both – for there is no interior without a building, much as there is no city without its multiplicities – and yet, what 'architecture' itself might actually be, remains more difficult to pin down.

'Spaces' is a term employed in this volume to reflect on the perhaps obvious notion of a 'container' of private and public voids in which sexuality resides and enacts itself. But it is also a reminder that there are multiple ways of defining the *mattering* that the discipline we call architecture performs, and that there are still many angles on understanding how this material 'stuff' that composes our built environments can be queered – or perhaps should be understood to be queer already, in ways that are not always obvious.

The final term that we use to structure this anthology, *pedagogies*, reflects not only a desire to acknowledge that education, in its various forms, composes a significant part of what we as editors do but also the ways in which architecture is (or often isn't) taught – to acknowledge issues around sexuality and all manner of 'otherings'. If one major aspect of this anthology is the focus on architectural discourse in its broadest sense, and another the focus on various forms of architectural practice, this final aspect aims to highlight the importance of bringing 'queer' to the formation of the professional architect.

Architectural education varies from one country to the next; it ranges from being affiliated with engineering and sciences – and therefore primarily perceived as a technical discipline – to being understood as closer in spirit to the arts and humanities. This means that schools of architecture vary dramatically in their relationship to the practice of building, even within the same country – either stressing its pragmatic and technical side or focusing more on social and cultural aspects. The education of an architect is also defined in relation to the professional bodies that regulate registration and award licences to practice architecture, and such bodies can shape the range of disciplinary issues and questions that are deemed to be of primary importance. In the cultures where we as editors, and likewise our contributors, operate, there is a tacit understanding that societal relations inform the products of our discipline, and students are taught to take numerous aspects of architectural inhabitation into account, whether through speculative and critical design or through written outputs aligned with historical and theoretical approaches. With them comes the question of sexuality; but the broader question of queering education itself, and what that might presuppose, is rarely tackled in a field such as architecture. This is no doubt part of the work yet to be done.

It is important to point out that the four categories through which we have structured this book are just general tools for systematizing and foregrounding aspects of our inquiry into queering architecture. In all the chapters this volume contains, the four make an appearance: a text located in the section on methods is likely to have aspects that are about space, practice or indeed pedagogy (see Vallerand); a text located within the spaces thematic (Canlı) is also about queering writerly methods and practices of both writing and living. A chapter in the section on practices (Campkin and Marshall) is clearly related to the educational framework the two authors bring to it and also to the various queer and non-queer spaces where the described practice took place, and the concomitant methodological interventions in the realm of urban planning. And on it goes.

This multivalency of themes holds true for each chapter in this anthology. It would indeed be possible to reconfigure the volume differently, so that each chapter came together with a different set of companions – and by doing so, resonate and foreground different ways of reading. But for the purposes of clarity and legibility – and also because this volume is intended for students at all levels of architecture and affiliated disciplines, as well as more advanced scholars and practitioners – we opted for what might appear as a more traditional structure. The project of queering the structures of anthologies such as this one, and indeed queering individual authorship in architecture more broadly, is something to explore collectively in the future.

A diversity of voices, a range of contributions

When it came to inviting and selecting contributors, we were keen to include a mix of emerging and more established voices. It was important to offer a broad range of contributors in terms of professional background – from those who operate within academic structures of theory and pedagogy to those whose work is closer to advocacy or architectural practice itself. The intention here was to reflect the world both of queer theory, with its complex relationship to activism, and of architecture and its many and varied discourses – some closer to the practice of building, others more concerned with architecture's broader cultural, social, political and economic contexts.

In selecting contributors, we also considered the full spectrum of audiences this book is intended for – ranging from students, to researchers, to educators, to practitioners in architecture, as well as those who come from affiliated disciplines, such as design, interior architecture, landscape architecture, human geography, sociology and the arts, to name the obvious few.

In terms of writerly approaches, this also meant that some texts would be more theoretical in the abstract sense and others more personal or based on the writer's own lived experiences – whether in architectural practice or everyday life. We believe that this variety of approaches, to both what is communicated and how, is integral to any project of queering, and queering architecture in particular.

Queer theory itself has been questioned for its supposedly arcane rarefication, its close affiliation with the world of academia within which it emerged, and its subsequent relationship to entrenched discrimination and marginalization on the grounds of class, race, Indigeneity and disability, and the many other attributes which have historically led to exclusion from higher education and its attendant publishing circles. This is mirrored in architectural theory's long and convoluted history since the 1960s, and its complex and often contentious relationship to architectural practice, as well as everyday peoples' experiences of architecture.

In response to these tensions, our approach with this collection has been to aim for a wide range of contributors, one that is clearly not exhaustive but still allows for a spectrum of voices and approaches and modes of research and writing. This spills over into the question of writerly positions, techniques and tonalities – from first-person to third, from highly theoretical to speculative and experiential, from scholarly to literary. As we prepared this anthology and crafted the contributor line-up, we were acutely aware of the need to raise voices which have not been heard in the past – either because they have been actively suppressed or indirectly excluded. The challenge was to include a diverse set of authors with a correspondingly wide-ranging set of positions, whatever those authors' exact relation to the term 'queer' or the problematics that emerge in the cross-sections. In other words, intersectionality is everywhere in these pages, as a number of authors acknowledge. The range of contributors and their focus here are only the starting point for a broader intersectional conversation.

The development of this book came at a time of broader challenges during a world pandemic. A number of early contributors had to pull out due to the pressures in their professional and private lives. There was also the issue of how to fully engage with geographical diversity. Queer theory itself has a problem with its lodgment in the hegemony of the Global North, a pattern which is also true of architecture. Any desire to affirm existing and historically relevant writers and practitioners in architecture risks reconfirming the sites of power from which their work grew (as well as language, as Vallerand points out in his chapter). In practice, this means that while this volume still contains a strong emphasis on North-American, Western European and Australian voices, we have also tried to expand beyond those well-trodden territories and into the Global South.

Expanding inclusivity always comes with its own challenges, and we hope that the question of 'queering architecture' will indeed be taken beyond where we take it here. In turn, and to come back to the title of this volume, the very queering to which architecture is subjected will be a process that only makes sense if the outcome of such a proposed act of queering is indeed radical in terms of disciplinary aims, knowledge and practice.

Contents and discontents: an unruly collection

The contents of this book are as wildly varied and unruly as the concept of 'queering' itself. They also cover the full scope and scale of what can be understood as 'architecture' – which, here, is used as a kind of shorthand for a range of places and activities, ideas and techniques that go well beyond buildings and their design. Certainly many of our authors are interested in buildings: what people and actions they admit and encourage, and which they exclude or reject. But in each chapter the subjects addressed also ooze both outward and inward, expanding in both physical and conceptual scopes to include urban space and urban design and the lived experience of cities, as well as the detailed design and constitution of interiors, as well as online spaces of digital intimacy and connection. The chapters collected here consider histories, theories and practices, addressing queer people, performances, and practices in place. If there is any overriding theme in this highly varied collection, it is perhaps the spatialization of affect: how people connect and share experiences and identities, and how this is enabled or thwarted by the particularities of location.

In beginning the book's first section, 'Methods', Olivier Vallerand commences Chapter 1 by charting a comprehensive account of how 'queer space' has been conceived through a range of theoretical, aesthetic, social, political, relational and ethical challenges to disciplinary knowledge and hegemony in architecture. And just as Vallerand ultimately finds a 'productive messiness' in the concept and convergence of queer and space, Dirk van den Heuvel and Martin van Wijk in Chapter 2 write from an institutional perspective, reporting on ongoing attempts to uncover 'queer evidence' in the archive: namely the traces of queer desires and lifestyles in the National Collection of Dutch Architecture and Urban Planning. Pondering the collection's privileging of certain voices while marginalizing others and opening the possibility of queering a major national collection of architectural documents, the authors consider the cases of three post-war architects, whose house designs can be seen as autobiographical – carrying traces of queer world-making.

In Chapter 3, Marko Jobst excavates the Baroque as equally a style and a discourse, a term and a concept – arguing that it should be understood as intrinsically queer, and hence a vehicle for the further queering of architectural history and historiography. Using the Serbian Orthodox Baroque of Belgrade as an example, Jobst theorizes and locates the 'elusive queerness' that is, he argues, central to this most canonical of architectural terms. The final chapter in the methods section, Chapter 4 by Ece Canlı, uses experimental modes of writing to question the status of the academic writer as authority – showing knowledge and experience to be fragmentary and discontinuous, and reconfigurable through factual-fictional-personal narratives. With a particular focus on the (socio)spatiality of the body and the bodily occupation and disuse of spaces in the built environment, the chapter combines personal and theoretical reflections and situated writing in affective ways.

The book's second section, 'Practices', continues the theme of experimental writing, with Regner Ramos's contribution of Chapter 5: a compilation of different fragmentary essays, voices and approaches, each springing from his website, El Site. Equally a research method and a form of performative writing, the chapter reflects on how ethnographic approaches can gather and celebrate queer experience in the particular context of Puerto Rico and explore the evocative potential of the fragment in expressing 'the spatiality of queerness in the Caribbean'.

The question of what it means to deliberately design a queer artefact to be installed within the context of a major cultural institution is a subject addressed by Timothy Moore and Adam Nathaniel Furman in Chapter 6, which reflects on their collaborative design for 'Boudoir Babylon', a temporary installation at the National Gallery of Victoria. Framing the design intent to produce a space that is 'safe, symbolic and social', Moore and Furman consider the implications of what happens when queer designs are realized in real time and space.

The realities of professional architectural and urban design practice are also a theme of Chapter 7, where Ben Campkin and Lo Marshall take historical planning documents, drawings and disputes as a point of dramatic departure into an amateur drag performance: *Fabulous Façades*. A knowing play on the 1931 New York Beaux Arts Ball, this 'urban studies performance' across three sites in London is equally a research outcome and a personification of long-standing queer venues, and the chapter reflects on the research potential of drag as a practice which 'embraces incongruity, subverts disciplinary hierarchies and conventions, and facilitates collective engagement with the affective terrain of primary sources'.

In Chapter 8, Joel Sanders continues the sub-theme of building regulation and policy in reflecting on his seminal book *STUD*, twenty-five years after its first publication. Sanders traces not only the personal and professional conditions in which the book originally emerged in the wake of the AIDS epidemic but also the shifts in his thinking and practice in the decades since. Focusing in particular on the influence of his later exposure to trans and disability studies, the chapter presents Stalled! – an initiative seeking to shift regulation, design and practice towards greater inclusion in the design of restrooms.

The book's third section, 'Spaces', begins with Chapter 9: Nicholas Gamso's analysis and critique of two moving image artworks installed in Boston's Museum of Fine Arts in 2017. Exploring the effects of the gallery spaces and architectural milieux in which the two works – by artists Mark Bradford and Derek Jarman – were installed, Gamso also examines the effects of darkness, opacity and abstraction, developing the concept of a 'minor architecture' of 'fugitive social interactions' – both in the works analysed and in the queer club and nightlife environments they address.

In Chapter 10, Sarah Nicholus explores queer space in the 'peripheral modernity' of Natal, a city in Northeastern Brazil. Using ethnographic observation and transnational theorizing, Nicholus analyses three 'marginal' spaces: a gay nightclub, an ephemeral gathering of LGBT+ youth and a festival party – using these to frame queer space as 'ephemeral, fluid, flexible, subversive, [and] radically inclusive . . . as it unsettles the colonial logics of capitalism, heteropatriarchy, and white supremacy'. This approach is aligned with Simona Castricum's Chapter 11, which looks at processes of transing and queering in her own creative practice, which fuses architecture and musical performance. Arguing for the need for 'radical design methodologies to critique the dystopias we live in', Castricum argues for a mode of 'world-building' in which critical design tools and alternative design thinking methods work towards a world where trans and gender-nonconforming individuals can flourish and fully engage in public space and civic life.

Naomi Stead's chapter in the volume reflects on the author's experience as a queer parent and practices of reading – in variously queer domestic spaces and of variously queer books. Weaving together gender and sexuality, motherhood and rainbow family, politics and performative reading, the chapter explores 'the spatial and affective connotations of the word "queer"' when encountered in books as emissaries within domestic space.

The fourth section of the book, 'Pedagogies', acknowledges the central role of institutionalized education in embedding architectural cultures and building architectural identities. In Chapter 13, Gem Barton reflects on her own long-standing educational practice, which brings together teaching, research and a practice of speculative spatial design. Exploring in particular the relationships and hierarchies between the disciplines of architecture and spatial design, Barton argues for queer theory in general to be read spatially and offers a manifesto for queer spatial pedagogy. This thematic is continued by A. L. Hu, who looks back to their own architectural education and subsequent practice as a teacher of architecture to question 'long-held norms that stifle students' growth' – calling for the dismantling of normative studio culture based on power differential, hierarchy and competition. Through an account of student peer learning and support as practices of relational care, Hu traces the potential in architectural education for processes of 'becoming' and argues for 'normalizing queer practices of promiscuous care, fluidity, and holding space for emotions to begin queering studio culture'.

Finally in Chapter 15, Colin Ripley explores how architectural education might employ the tools of architecture in its own subversion, in a 'counter-pedagogy' that seeks to resist or counter architecture itself. Using the example of a conceptual drawing project conducted with students, Ripley uses the work of Jean Genet and Gilles Deleuze to 'counter the official pedagogies both of the institution and of the discipline of architecture' – namely, to queer architecture.

The range of the book is broad: from the materiality of buildings and the built environment to the immaterial spaces of digital culture and the internet; from physical places to the experience of people within them; from disciplinary research cultures and methods to architectural history and historiography; from the practices and effects of institutional collection processes to the politics and poetics of queer performance; from planning regulations and procedures to the entangled affects of teaching and learning in architecture; from queer designs to queer occupations; from high theory to the minutiae of everyday lived experience – the volume covers all of these things and more. As editors we celebrate its multiplicity as an indication of the spatial and conceptual multivalence of 'queering' and 'architecture' themselves. We commend it to you, the reader, in the hope you will find it challenging, and stimulating, and affecting, and curious, and queer.

References

Browne, K. and Nash, C. J. (2010), *Queer Methods and Methodologies: Intersecting Queer Theories and Social Science Research*, London and New York: Taylor & Francis.

Butler, J. (2002), *Gender Trouble*, London and New York: Routledge.

Frichot, H. and Stead, N. (eds.) (2020), *Writing Architectures: Ficto-Critical Approaches*, London: Bloomsbury.

Furman, A. N. and Mardell, J. (eds.) (2022), *Queer Spaces: An Atlas of LGBTQ+ Places and Stories*, London and New York: Routledge.

Gabrielsson, C., Frichot, H., Havik, K. and Jobst, M. (eds.) (2020), 'Reading(s) and Writing(s): Unfolding Processes of Transversal Writing', *Writingplace Journal for Architecture and Literature*, 3: 4–9.

Ghaziani, A. and Brim, M. (eds.) (2019), *Imagining Queer Methods*, New York: NYU Press.

Gorman-Murray, A. and Cook, M. (eds.) (2017), *Queering the Interior*, London and New York: Routledge.

Gosseye, J., Stead, N. and van der Plaat, D. (eds.) (2019), *Speaking of Buildings: Oral History in Architecture*, New York: Princeton Architectural Press.

Jobst, M. (2017). *A Ficto-Historical Theory of the London Underground*, Spurbuchverlag Baunach: AADR Publishing.

Jobst, M. (2019). 'Unidentified Emotional Object: When Queer Desire Journeyed to Belgrade', in D. Beljaars, C. Drozynski (eds.), *Spaces of Desire*, pp. 177–88. London and New York: Routledge.

Jobst, M. (2021), 'Writing Architectural Affects', in M. Jobst and H. Frichot (eds.), *Architectural Affects After Deleuze and Guattari*, 228–45, London and New York: Routledge.

Jobst, M. and Frichot, H. (2021), *Architectural Affects After Deleuze and Guattari*, London and New York: Routledge.

Kolb, J. (ed.) (2017), 'Working Queer', a special issue of Log, no. 41.

Lambert, L. (ed.) (2017), 'Queers, Feminists and Interiors', *The Funambulist: Politics of Space and Bodies*, 13 (Sept/Oct).

McCann, H. and Monaghan, W. (2019), *Queer Theory Now: From Foundations to Futures*, London: Bloomsbury.

Pilkey, B., Scicluna, R. M., Campkin, B. and Penner, B. (2017), *Sexuality and Gender at Home: Experience, Politics, Transgression*, London: Bloomsbury.

Ramos, R. and Mowlabocus, S. (eds.) (2020), *Queer Sites in Global Contexts: Technologies, Spaces, and Otherness*, London: Routledge.

Sanders, J. (ed.) (1996), *STUD: Architectures of Masculinity*, New York: Princeton Architectural Press.

Sedgwick, E. K. (2008), *Epistemology of the Closet*, Berkeley: University of California Press.

Stead, N. (2017), 'Closet Case: A Hide and Seek Short Story', *The Funambulist: Politics of Space and Bodies* 13 (Sept/Oct): 14.

Stead, N. (2018), 'Queering Architecture: A Question-Manifesto', in J. Oliver (ed.), *Associations: Creative Practice and Research*, 259–63, Yountville, CA: Melbourne University Press.

Stead, N. (2019), 'The Future (of Interiors) is Queer', in G. Brooker, H. Harriss and K. Walker (eds.), *Interior Futures*, 90–103, California: Crucible Press.

Stead, N., Ednie-Brown, P., Watson, F. and Rhodes, K. (2019), 'Exhibiting the Workaround: Gender, Activism, and Architectural Education', *Journal of Architectural Education* 73 (2): 193–201.

Vallerand, O. (2020), *Unplanned Visitors: Queering the Ethics and Aesthetics of Domestic Space*, Montreal & Kingston: McGill-Queen's University Press.

Van den Heuvel, D. and Gorny, R. (eds.) (2017), 'Trans-Bodies/Queering Spaces', *Footprint* 11 (2): 21.

I

Methods

1

On the uses of queer space thinking

Olivier Vallerand

No space is totally queer or completely unqueerable [. . .].
Queer space is imminent: queer space is space in the process of,
literally, taking place, of claiming territory.

CHRISTOPHER REED (1996)

Definitions of 'queer' vary greatly, from activist to theoretical to mainstream discourses. In turn, theorists, historians and practitioners of architecture have used the concept of 'queer space' to discuss a range of ideas, including aesthetic challenges to formal conventions, political challenges to disciplinary knowledge, architectural practice and design education, calls to include sexual orientation and gender identity in historical discussions of designers and users, and, as the previously stated quote by Reed underlines, attempts to reimagine spaces as layered networks of interpersonal relations shaped by the materiality of buildings and cities (Vallerand 2020b: 16–23). These different impulses have coexisted since the idea of queer space emerged in architectural discourses, but the relatively limited scholarly output around the topic has also meant that the potential points of convergence and divergence between these different approaches have been mostly ignored, leading to discussions of concepts with limited commonality between them, beyond a link to gender identity and sexual orientation. Furthermore, as built examples of queer approaches to design have been very limited, writing and exhibitions have remained a major mode of expression for queer thinking in architecture. This focus on theoretical explorations has sometimes overemphasized abstract understandings of space, away from an embodied experience of the built environment, a critique that has also been addressed to some queer theory (Benavente and Gill-Peterson 2019; Green 2002, 2007; Namaste 2000; Oswin 2008; Seidman 1997).

In this chapter I explore how different approaches to queer space intersect, to untangle how theorists and practitioners link ethics and aesthetics, queer political activism and queer theory, along with formal and social critiques. Building on the idea that challenges to traditional forms of designing or writing highlight the social normativity of those forms, many have sought to propose new ways of thinking about how people experience space. However, in writing as in designing, balancing formal and social critique is sometimes challenging and one risks diminishing allied, but different, points of view while trying too forcefully to make a point. I thus argue here for a renewed focus on identifying the objectives behind queer approaches in architecture to assess their limits and, by extension, more productively use those limits. The objective is not to frame some approaches as more successful than others but rather to present some of the questions that come from studying these texts and projects in their sometimes contradictory objectives or disconnection from everyday struggles and to celebrate the messiness that sustains much queer space theory in architecture.

Throughout the text, I use 'queer space' and 'queer space theory' as they are the terms that have been mostly used since the 1990s, even if discussions were often limited to specific groups such as gay men. Using 'space' rather than 'architecture' also opens up a broader field of meanings as well as links to parallel discussions in geography, planning or interior design. Furthermore, 'queer architecture' has been used to discuss specific aesthetic decisions that only form one stream of queer space discourses (Holder 2017; Messina 2019). Thus, my use of 'architecture' here refers to the disciplines devoted to the design, history and theory of the built environment, while 'queer space' refers to approaches that think about the intersection of gender, sexuality and the built environment, both to study it and to (attempt to) design it.

Defining queerness in architecture: from the personal to the communal?

In their introductory essay to the exhibition *Queer Space* at the Storefront for Art and Architecture in New York, curators Beatriz Colomina, Dennis Dollens, Eve Kosofsky Sedgwick, Henry Urbach and Mark Wigley asked: 'And likewise, with "space": do we mean physical space? Or do we mean the space of discursive practices, texts, codes of behaviour and regulatory norms that organize social life?' (Colomina et al. 1994). This question, as well as questions about who navigates these different spaces, hid behind most of the late 1980s to early 1990s first wave of thinking about the idea of queer space. The exhibition underlined the competing impulses at play: held in 1994 to make visible the contribution of gay and lesbian people to the built environment as a celebration of the twenty-fifth anniversary of the Stonewall Riots, the curators were also trying to define an emerging field in a more theoretical way. In her call for 'Queer Space Manifesto/Proposals' included in the exhibition catalogue/poster, Sedgwick (1994), a pioneering queer theorist, asked: 'What makes space queer? How to give queer space a history and a future, a powerful presence?' The curating team thus positioned their understanding of queer space as being directly tied to a tradition of manifestos or written proposals to rethink and reframe how we design, inviting the artists, historians, geographers and architects who participated to use a variety of approaches that echoed different understandings of queer spaces. The commemorative signs inserted throughout Manhattan by the historians-led collective Repohistory to highlight LGBTQ people and events or the photos of houses inhabited by gay and lesbian people collected by Mark Robbins and Benjamin Gianni were for example juxtaposed with the early explorations of thermosensitive paint by Jürgen Mayer H. (Vallerand 2020a, b). However, if at first the projects seem to oppose visual representation and theoretical exploration, they share an interest in how (queer) personal and communal identities are hidden throughout ordinary landscapes, as layers within symbolic understandings of urban, suburban and non-urban environments that blur how private and public are often understood. They strive for a definition of queer space that supports an ethical project that contests understandings of space as being either queer or not, in some cases using tools focused on the aesthetics of space.

As the *Queer Space* exhibition also highlights, queer space discourses in architecture emerged in the context of a strong interest in continental philosophy, psychoanalysis and critical theory by architects. For example, Mark Robbins was one of the first architects to build on feminist interest in psychoanalysis to explicitly associate an eroticized male body with representations of architecture (Robbins 1992), in part to expose and challenge how feminine bodies have historically been objectified by architects in both visual representations – to 'decorate' photos of architectural spaces – and discussions of buildings – for example in the association of architectural orders with gendered bodies. Similarly, the oft-cited *Sexuality & Space* (1992), edited by Beatriz Colomina, heavily relies on psychoanalytic readings of architectural spaces and representations, for example in the numerous references made to the phallic shape of skyscrapers. If often celebrated as one of the first edited collections about sexuality and its relation to architecture, most chapters rely on an essentialist and binary reading of gender and sexuality that does not acknowledge the challenges made by contemporaneous queer theorists to gender and sex categories, limiting its potential for the development of a queer understanding of architecture. While queer theorists like Judith Butler (1990) were attempting to understand how normative understandings of sex, gender and sexuality intersect to produce a 'heterosexual matrix', a norm that appears 'natural' but is in fact invisibly constructed to define everything as heterosexual until proven differently, the texts in *Sexuality & Space* often focus on the difference between women and men rather than trying to understand how this difference is constructed or how its construction might impact our understanding of the built environment.

In recent years, Colomina has acknowledged how *Sexuality & Space* built on an earlier generation of gay and lesbian studies and feminist theory and has suggested that the word 'queer' could be equated with the idea of 'perverting' the study of architecture (Kotsioris 2020), without, however, explicitly discussing the potential of queerness to challenge binary readings. The book *Sexuality & Space* followed an event held at the Princeton School of Architecture, where a group of students and faculty were also developing texts and projects that three decades later still constitute core works about queer space in architecture, for example, Joel Sanders's exploration of masculinity in the edited collection *Stud* (1996), John Paul Ricco's explorations of 'minor architecture' inspired by Gilles Deleuze and Félix Guattari's writings (Ricco 1994, 1998), Jürgen Mayer H.'s installations around thermosensitive paint and data-protection patterns (Mayer Hermann 1999) or Henry Urbach's exploration of the closet and clubs (Urbach 1992, 1996).

In parallel to the *Queer Space* exhibition, other design-related events were held in 1994 to celebrate the twenty-fifth anniversary of the Stonewall Riots. The Organization of Lesbian and Gay Architects and Designers (OLGAD), founded in 1991, planned a Design Pride in New York City that included *A Guide to Lesbian & Gay New York Historical Landmarks*, a foldout historical map with similar goals to Repohistory's project,[1] and *Design Legacies*, an exhibition and booklet celebrating the legacy of designers who had died of AIDS. These initiatives show the focus of the organization: far from proposing to identify a queer theory of space and architecture, they were trying to make visible the contribution of gay and lesbian architects and designers (note the apparent absence of bisexual or trans people in the titles, typical of the 1990s, despite the presence of some bisexual or trans people in the map), about offering role models and eventually breaking down assumptions about queer designers.

The focus of *Design Legacies* on AIDS also highlighted the importance of the epidemic in early queer space thinking, something that Colomina noted when looking back at the *Queer Space* exhibition and *Sexuality & Space* book (Kotsioris 2020). The tense relations between sexual and gender minorities and governmental institutions around the epidemic framed the development of queer activism by groups like ACT UP and Queer Nation and the parallel emergence of queer theory in academic circles. In architecture, the spectre of AIDS arguably made writing about queer space urgent in the first place and discussions about the disappearance or transformation of cruising spaces – heavily targeted at the time as vectors in the spread of HIV – were an important focus of queer space writing in the 1990s, almost always explicitly building on personal narratives of the experience of sexualized spaces. The written mapping of bathhouses and sex clubs thus becomes an important motif, as in the writings of Ira Tattelman (1997, 1999, 2000) or John Paul Ricco (1994), in what seems to be an attempt both to preserve the memory of these most-often invisible social spaces and to underline the importance of the visceral experience of space in opening up new understandings of how the body interacts with the built environment. For example, in 'Spatial Rubbing: The Zone', a discussion of a Los Angeles sex club, Henry Urbach (1993: 95) not only describes his own exploration of the club but also broadens the discussion to reflect on how 'a queer community takes responsibility for itself to ensure physical, communal, and erotic survival: this is the lusty dance, the onward march of a proud, endangered tribe'. This expansion of the personal to the communal mirrors not only Urbach's exploration of the closet in 'Closets, Clothes, Disclosure' (1996) but also a general interest in the enmeshing of personal and communal – 'private' and 'public' – in queer space theory. If sexual orientation and gender identity are often discussed as something personal or private, these texts highlight how the communal experience of self-identification brings safety. By looking at sexualized spaces, queer space theorists try to understand how the privacy of sexual intimacy translates into a gradient of spaces – from bathhouse rooms to public parks – where queer people find themselves and create relations, pointing to the relevance of these spaces at a time where they are targeted.

Similar questions frame architectural critic Aaron Betsky's *Queer Space: Architecture and Same-Sex Desire* (1997). Like his *Building Sex: Men, Women, and the Construction of Sexuality* (1995) from two years earlier, *Queer Space* takes an historical approach that seeks to challenge the gendered construction of the disciplines of architecture and interior design and to make visible marginalized examples from the past or to reclaim canonical figures – mostly homosexual men, with only brief mentions of Julia Morgan and Elsie de Wolfe – whose sexuality has previously been ignored. Betsky (1997: 5–6) explicitly notes that his book is about 'spaces with characteristics we might call queer' because they emerged in the 'cultural condition [. . .] experienced by homosexual men in the Western world in the twentieth century', positioning his work within an understanding of queer spaces as being spaces designed by or for queer people or used mostly by queer people. Bringing his argument to the 1990s, Betsky frames *Queer Space* with an introduction and closing chapter that not only celebrate night clubs and anonymous gay male cruising spaces but also lament their transformation. Describing for example the dream-like experience of Studio 54 parties, Betsky's writing merges the historical and ethnographic experience, framing a definition of queer space that alternates between a historical look at its association with non-heterosexual figures and personal accounts expanding on an aesthetic and sensorial experience of space shared with other men he knew.

Around the same time, scholars from outside of architecture also explored how queer thinking could impact understandings of architectural, urban and rural spaces. For example, the collection *Queers in Space: Communities | Public Places | Sites of Resistance* (Ingram, Bouthillette and Retter 1997b) brought together diverse contributors using landscape, planning, and urban and social geography lenses to present a much broader range of people and experiences, while still using 'architectural' language such as the 'emerging architecture of queerscapes' (Ingram, Bouthillette and Retter 1997a: 15) or references to Bernard Tschumi's concepts of crossprogramming, transprogramming and disprogramming. Importantly, and in a more balanced way than previously, the book takes into account lesbian and bisexual women and explicitly addresses gender and race, moving away from the focus on the experience of gay white men present in much queer space discourse from architects. Trans and nonbinary people are still barely discussed, reflecting the era, but the book offers more nuanced understandings of gender that show a focus on a different kind of visibility. Instead of envisioning queer space as being used specifically by queer people, the title *Queers in Space* underlines how it attempts to understand the layered use and experience of space where queer and non-queer people coexist in space, and how resistances, tensions and transformations define queer space. Furthermore, from the beginning, the editors frame the book and its discussion of queer theory as being specifically built on a 'grounded' experience of the built environment, as made explicit by the title of the introduction – 'Lost in Space: Queer Theory and Community Activism at the Fin-de-Millénaire' – and their explanation of the objectives of the book:

> We titled this anthology *Queers in Space* because the phrase connotes being 'out there floating', disconnected and separated from the planet. Although people who experience marginalization might like to be more 'grounded', inequity in access to public space continues. For minorities, including people marginalized through (homo)sexuality, these forms of 'uneven development' have often compounded their sense of isolation and rootlessness. (Ingram, Bouthillette and Retter 1997a: 6)

By focusing on isolation, a lack of community, the editors underline a difference between some of these early approaches, a focus either on individuals who exemplify 'the gay designer' or 'the gay client', or communities that experience spaces in non-normative ways. Beyond the objects of inquiry, this also suggests different objectives behind queer space thinking: Is thinking about – and defining – queer space another intellectual tool to theoretically talk about architecture or is it a way to underline – and respond to – how the built can inflict harm? I do not necessarily think that this question needs to be answered one way or the other, but it asks queer space thinkers to position themselves in relation to a critical look at the discipline. Discussing sexuality and gender in relation to architecture without also thinking about the social class, race or gender of who is talking about queer space silences the privilege that allowed queer space thinkers to even be able to discuss such questions in the early 1990s. How can we understand the ways in which architecture impacts non-white queer people if non-white voices do not even have a place at the table in architectural discourse? Similarly, how can we think about non-male queer architects if men take up most of the bandwidth of architectural conversations or leadership (Vallerand 2019)? If these questions might not have been evident in the intellectual context of the 1990s, they cannot be – and have not been – ignored in recent years.

Looking beyond a definition

The editors of *Queers in Space*, as with others at the time and since, understand their project not only as a tool to define and frame a conversation but also as an inspiration for 'a new generation of theoretically grounded activists to consider queerer geographies and designs. Thus these pages contain not a single manifesto but the rough beginnings of many' (Ingram, Bouthillette and Retter 1997a: 12). In architecture, unfortunately, their call to think in more sophisticated ways about the relation of gender, sexuality and the built environment took some time to be heard, leaving the topic ignored by all but a few historians, theorists and practitioners over the next two decades (Adams 2010a, b; Bonnevier 2005, 2007a, b; Ricco 2002; Stead and Prior 2007). This did not happen only for queer studies, as feminist or critical race studies of architecture and design were also kept on the margins, despite efforts in the previous decades to show the importance of these discussions in challenging the discipline (Ahrentzen 1996; Barton 2001; Burns 2012; Lokko 2000; Rothschild and Rosner 1999). This unfortunately means that while other disciplines were refining and developing sophisticated understandings of gender and sexuality, architecture and design were still stuck in an overwhelmingly cis male – as well as white and able-bodied – paradigm. Prompted by broader societal discussions – like #metoo, Black Lives Matter or, in the case of LGBTQ issues, debates around marriage or the use of public restrooms – queer space theory, like feminist and critical race theories, has made a comeback over the last few years in both academic and mainstream architectural publications, with some of it obviously building on work developed over the previous decade, but which had yet to be published. Like the 1990s wave of queer space thinking, contributors to this new phase build on a variety of objectives but, importantly, often seek to include a more diverse group of people beyond the gay men that overwhelmingly populated the 1990s interpretation of queer space, even if this more diverse representation does not automatically always mean more sophisticated approaches.

Some of these publications are once again coming from a relatively theory-heavy academic context. For example, *Log* published a special issue guest-edited by Jaffer Kolb in 2017 under the theme 'Working Queer'. The issue included a range of approaches, from an interview with Betsky discussing the impact of his book (Kolb and Betsky 2017), to a discussion of a project by Andrés Jaque focused on how queer refugees navigate space through the use of digital media (Jaque 2017), to highly speculative formal written experiments such as '2,497 Words: Provincialism, Critical or Otherwise' by Michael Meredith (2017), a reflection on discourse and writing, or 'Noncon Form' by Annie Barrett (2017), an attempt to queer the work of Gordon Matta-Clark, Herzog & de Meuron or OMA. Many of the articles in the special issue are, however, highly theoretical discussions that have little to do with an embodied experience of architecture, raising again the question of how theory can engage the issues from which queer activism originally emerged, linked to questions of health, wellness and – literally – life and death. Furthermore, the articles are written by authors from a relatively narrow circle of elite US institutions, almost the same ones as in the 1990s. How would these questions be approached elsewhere or in less privileged contexts? This – and related criticism addressed to queer theory as a whole – would need more than a chapter to be discussed, but practices such as MYCKET, discussed later, have attempted to address this by stepping aside from academic institutions to expand the reach of queer space thinking beyond these limited points of origins.

Two other special issues appeared in 2017. Based in Delft, the Netherlands, the academic journal *Footprint* published 'Trans-Bodies / Queering Spaces', exemplifying both the wider geographical diversity of current queer space thinking – away from the North-American focus of the 1990s – and a shift to the experience of trans people (Gorny and Van den Heuvel 2017). The thirteenth issue of *The Funambulist*, a spatial-activist magazine led by Léopold Lambert, themed 'Queers, Feminists & Interiors', also showed geographical diversity and a focus on trans experiences but did so with a much more politically involved exploration of everyday lives and spaces. This visibility of trans people in architecture had begun a few years earlier, notably with philosopher and curator Paul B. Preciado's (2012, 2014, 2017, 2018) Foucault-inspired discussions of the technologically informed relation of trans bodies and architectural spaces and representations. Similarly, Canadian poet and scholar Lucas Crawford has worked on the development of a 'trans theory' of architecture by enmeshing an exploration of Diller Scofidio and Renfro's work with a personal narrative that underlines the highly subjective experience of space highlighted in much queer theory, merging form and content in publications such as a book based on his PhD dissertation (2015) and a poetry book (2018). In architecture, as in other fields, this new visibility of trans people in the 2000s–2010s was fuelled in part by the internet offering a platform to connect and project their voices. Trans and nonbinary people have also paradoxically become more visible as they have become the new target for conservative forces following major legal victories for gay, lesbian and bisexual people in many countries, as highlighted by recent battles around public restrooms.

The architectural aspect of 'bathroom battles' has made it the topic of much queer space thinking in recent years, for example, in QSPACE's *Coded Plumbing* (2017). This was an initiative by a group of emerging architects and Columbia University students who created an installation offering a public forum to 'unravel plumbing codes and design standards' (QSPACE 2017) and rethink what we assume as the 'correct' way to design and regulate restrooms. Gaining even more visibility and leading to changes to building codes, the Stalled! project, developed by a team led by trans historian Susan Stryker, legal scholar Terry Kogan, and architect Joel Sanders, used historical and legal writing to support design studies with the explicit goal of challenging building codes and design norms around 'privacy', to be more inclusive of trans and nonbinary people, and also those with different bodily abilities, cultural habits, religious beliefs, or family obligations (Sanders 2017b, 2018; Sanders and Stryker 2016). The initiative was also an opportunity for Sanders (2017a) to reflect on his position as a cis-male architect, discussing in articles and lectures his personal shift in thinking about sexuality and gender, from an early focus on the gay male experience of space to a desire to explore the broader potential impact of work on gender identity to transform the built environment.

If the focus on Sanders's own intellectual journey in many of his texts and talks about Stalled! reads problematically in its centring on a cis experience when discussing spaces designed with trans people in mind, Sanders's interest in designing more inclusive public restrooms is exemplary of queer space thinking that focuses on gender and sexuality as a design factor to rethink the everyday experience of the built environment. The 2018 'Intersections' series of *Urban Omnibus*, an online publication by the Architectural League of New York, similarly presents content about LGBTQ experience that focuses on the preservation and management of the built environment, investigating how it can benefit or harm people, including around issues like rising rents or safe space (Moore 2018). Importantly, these recent discussions echo earlier queer space thinkers' challenges to the perception of spaces as being either public or private, expanding beyond the analysis of domestic spaces or cruising grounds to actively challenge assumptions around the safety of spaces depending on one's self-identifications and propose transformations to these spaces.

If inclusivity initiatives around public restrooms focus on the ethical side of queer space thinking – the impulse to design spaces that limit the harm done to, in this case, trans people – a deliberate attempt to explore how queer ethics and queer aesthetics intersect is present in the work of MYCKET, a Sweden-based queer feminist collective merging formal and social experimentations, writing and making, built work and performance. The collective was formed in 2012 by Katarina Bonnevier,[2] Thérèse Kristiansson, and Mariana Alves Silva (later joined by Ullis Ohlgren and Anna Märta Danielsson), choosing a name that highlights their interest in blurring divides, in proposing transformations beyond merely being critical (Bonnevier, interview with author, 2018). MYCKET is a Swedish word, which means 'much, a lot', underlining their maximalist approach to queering the rigidity of architecture and their interest in excess as a queer feminist tactic (Bonnevier 2017). Through their focus on aesthetics, they look to highlight how norms are manifested in spatial and material design and to challenge these norms through design, to create reparative spaces rather than paranoid spaces (Bonnevier, interview with author, 2018), an idea borrowed from Sedgwick (1997). Their research-based practice focuses on the design of performative spaces where personal relations are explored, including the role played by architecture in the experience of intimacy and eroticism, materialized for example in *The Club Scene* series of projects (2012–16). Designed over thirteen 'acts', *The Club Scene* restages salons, clubs, and other meeting spaces significant for queer and feminist activism, exploring a wide variety of spaces geographically and historically by paying close attention to discursive impulses and the representation of spaces in archives (Bonnevier, Kristiansson and Alves Silva 2017). Building from these temporary installations and performances, MYCKET have worked between 2016 and 2020 on the planning and construction of 'The Ball Cap', a new public space for dance and movement in Råslätt, a suburb outside of Jönköping, Sweden. Collaborating with community members during the process, the project, like Stalled!, exemplifies the potential that recent queer space practitioners have sought to achieve, an exploration of how thinking about gender and sexuality open a door to creating spaces that are more inclusive in a broad way. In doing so, they have also combined their queer thinking with feminist methodologies developed for example by Matrix Feminist Design Co-Operative (Dwyer and Thorne 2006; Grote 1992) or muf architecture/art (Shonfield et al. 2001).

Celebrating a spectrum of understandings and approaches?

MYCKET's work summarizes an important aspect of queer thinking in architecture, a desire to closely link personal desires and narratives with a theoretical understanding of the built environment and its history that Bonnevier (2005: 165) announced in one of her first published texts: 'before we proceed, comes my confession: I still have a need for heroines in architecture. And I have a crush on Eileen Gray. This nonconformist architect and designer awakes my desires and dreams, like a triumphant mirror sending sparkles to my own everyday life and professional practice in the male-dominated and heteronormative regime of architecture'. Bonnevier's words underline how queer thinking is deeply embedded in an embodied experience that necessarily impacts its development and reception.

In 2020, Lucas Crawford attempted to publish an opinion piece in the *Journal of Architectural Education* titled 'Five Reasons I Won't Share Washrooms with Cisgender People', an ironic discussion of reasons given to restrict trans people's access to public restrooms. Surprised by the executive editor's demand that the text's 'language needed to be toned down for the readership of *JAE*' after the guest editors reassured him that the *JAE* 'could accommodate creative and provocative writing in style and content', Crawford reframed the text for the digital venue *Platform*, ending with a postscript reflecting on the power assigned to different discursive venues in the context of the architectural discipline and asking readers: 'What kind of architectural criticism would you write, read, or otherwise help to generate?' Are queer discussions appropriate when they present abstract theoretical explorations or when they address the history of gender and sexual minorities without acknowledging their author's subjectivity, but not when they express the everyday frustrations their writers experience when navigating the built environment? Quoting Crawford (2020) again:

> For whom does architectural criticism exist and who is regarded as a potential writer of it? A trans poet so fed up with xenophobia that they might curse in order to get through, viscerally, to the reader? Sex workers? Taxi drivers? [. . .] Until the gatekeepers of architectural criticism rethink the social outcomes of their preferred styles, tones, and prioritized readers, an issue on Othering is window-dressing at best and a farce at worst.

It is illuminating that, notwithstanding its aesthetic and theoretical qualities, *Cruising Pavilion* (2018–19), an exploration of cruising spaces used by gay men exhibited in the context of the Venice Biennale, a renowned gallery in New York, and a national architecture centre in Stockholm, can be celebrated in magazines and newspapers around the world 'despite' its sometimes-explicit character, while a call for trans inclusion is rejected by one of the leading architectural journals because of its explicitness. This situation underlines the still limited position of queer discussions in architectural institutions such as *JAE*, but, in the context of a special issue on 'Othering', it also certainly does not answer long-standing questions about who exactly is allowed to be represented in queer space thinking when an opening is made to such discussions.

The privileging of Euro-American-centric cis white gay male perspectives – starting with my own – is slowly being challenged by a more broadly inclusive and intersectional perspective to include lesbian, trans, and nonbinary perspectives from around the world. However, the high visibility of a cis white male architect like Joel Sanders in Stalled!, a project developed for trans and nonbinary people, when other trans-led initiatives had already existed for many years, raises questions about how much this evolution is actually really impacting how the discipline works. Similarly, the Anglo-Saxon origins of queer theory have led to an overwhelming focus on the experience of queer people from English-speaking countries. As a native French speaker, this has been particularly visible to me – and somewhat ironic considering the roots of queer theory in thinking developed by French theorists. If my research on queer space has been welcomed in English-speaking circles and I have been able to position myself within networks of knowledge in the English-speaking North-American, European, and Australian contexts, the opportunities to do so in French-speaking settings has remained limited until very recently. However, writing in other languages, bringing experiences from other cultures, can transform thinking about how gender and sexuality intersect with the built environment. Cultural expectations about gender norms, sexuality, intimacy, domesticity, and many other social issues vary greatly around the world and impact how questions presented through queer space theory will be received. Furthermore, as an emerging generation of queer theorists coming from non-English-speaking countries has argued, in some sense, the notion of translation is essential to queer thinking (Baer and Kaindl 2018; Epstein and Gillett 2017; Savci 2021). The richness of perspectives that come from cultural and linguistic differences is essential to an exploration of gender and sexual categories opened up by queer theory, but in many ways, the architectural and design disciplines are still stuck in a Western-centric – if not Anglo-Saxon-centric – framework that also frames its (limited) engagement with gender and sexuality. However, some practices like MYCKET are making openings toward a transnational dialogue, while politically engaged publications such as *The Funambulist* are making deliberate efforts to include Asian, African, or Middle Eastern voices.

This chapter has by necessity been only a brief survey of the growing number of works seeking to explore the potential of queer space thinking to rethink spatial design – of 'queering architecture', as the title of this anthology suggests. Almost by definition, queer space thinking seeks to challenge something, but these challenges are not always easy to define or to make impactful. Is this 'something' power structures – in direct relation to queer theory – or is it aesthetical norms? Is it about designing spaces that take into account a broader range of uses and a larger group of users, is it about designing spaces that are less harmful to people who have been and continue to be marginalized from both accessing the profession and accessing its services, or is it about getting away completely from what we think of as 'architecture', moving toward the importance of the personal and communal embodied experience of the built environment, taking inspiration from the reframing presented by queer geography? 'Queer space' as a concept is messy, and it is this messiness that makes it so productive in its constantly evolving shape, in the uncomfortable questions it inevitably raises and in the difficult answers it forces us to seek. However, I believe that at its core is a desire to create a more inclusive built environment, or at least to challenge the status quo of a still very conservative discipline rooted in heteronormative frameworks. A challenge is that, while theoretical abstraction and aesthetic or formal experiments can often be used to shine a light on ethical concerns and vice versa, the balancing act is quite difficult and sometimes results in relatively unproductive debates around the best approach to be taken.

It could be said that the fact queer space theory emerged at a point where the architectural discipline was highly invested in theory per se has overemphasized one side of its development and partially erased the importance of the reaction to the AIDS epidemic, as well as the struggles experienced by LGBTQ people every day. In recent years, the visibility of the #metoo movement or legal battles around public restrooms have reignited an interest in the topic, and this has again led to both design-based initiatives such as Stalled! and more theoretically informed symposiums such as 'Stand by Your Monster and Some Queer Methods' at Princeton (2017) or 'A Queer Query' at SCI-Arc (2020). Some thinkers and practitioners such as MYCKET have deliberately and explicitly discussed and experimented with this ethics/aesthetics spectrum of architectural discourses and practices. By embracing the messiness of queer space theory and its unclearly defined objectives, MYCKET successfully create spaces, both metaphorically and physically, for a diversity of people to explore and create environments in which they feel safer and comfortable to express their self-identifications. But MYCKET also point to another challenge to the queering of the architecture and design disciplines: while still keeping ties with the academic world, they have deliberately sought to explore other venues, to develop work outside of the elite academic locations of much queer space thinking, and to actively engage the people being discussed. These questions about who exactly is represented in queer space thinking might be the most important to explore in the future. If queer theory – and by extension queer space theory – has often focused on challenges to binary understandings of gender identity and sexual orientation instead of the visibility of queer figures that earlier gay and lesbian studies explored, it might be worth asking if we should not take a step back to think about who has been represented in queer space theory, to think about how class, race, and gender have framed many of these discussions, and to take concrete steps to change how those with voices in the architectural discipline relate to the people using the spaces they design or think about.

Notes

1 The map eventually led to the development of the New York City LGBT Historic Sites Project (https://www.nyclgbtsites.org/) and a 2018 special issue of the academic journal *Change Over Time* dedicated to LGBTQ heritage,

covering topics such as types of properties related to LGBTQ history, photo-documentation of lesbian nightclubs, critical uses of photography, and strategies for sustaining diverse heritage. See the introduction to the issue by Lustbader (2018).

2 Bonnevier's PhD dissertation (2007a) celebrates the challenges to social norms enacted through spatial interventions by architect Eileen Gray and authors Natalie Barney and Selma Lagerlöf in the early twentieth century by developing her own formal interpretation of their work.

References

Adams, A. (2010a), 'The power of pink: children's bedrooms and gender identity', *FKW // Zeitschrift für geschlechterforschung und visuelle kultur*, vol. 50, pp. 58–69.

Adams, A. (2010b), 'Sex and the single building: the Weston Havens House, 1941–2001', *Buildings & Landscapes: Journal of the Vernacular Architecture Forum*, vol. 17, no. 1, pp. 82–97.

Ahrentzen, S. (1996), 'The F word in architecture: feminist analyses in/of/ for architecture', in T. A. Dutton and L. H. Mann (eds.), *Reconstructing architecture: critical discourses and social practices*, University of Minnesota Press, Minneapolis, pp. 71–118.

Baer, B. J. and Kaindl, K. (eds.) (2018), *Queering translation, translating the queer: theory, practice, activism*, Routledge, New York and London.

Barrett, A. (2017), 'Noncon form', *Log*, no. 41, pp. 141–4.

Barton, C. E. (ed.) (2001), *Sites of memory: perspectives on architecture and race*, Princeton Architectural Press, New York.

Benavente, G. and Gill-Peterson, J. (2019), 'The promise of trans critique: Susan Stryker's Queer Theory', *GLQ*, vol. 25, no. 1, pp. 23–8.

Betsky, A. (1995), *Building sex: men, women, architecture, and the construction of sexuality*, William Morrow, New York.

Betsky, A. (1997), *Queer space: architecture and same-sex desire*, William Morrow, New York.

Bonnevier, K. (2005), 'A queer analysis of Eileen Gray's E.1027', in H. Heynen and G. Baydar (eds.), *Negotiating domesticity: spatial productions of gender in modern architecture*, Routledge, London and New York, pp. 162–80.

Bonnevier, K. (2007a), *Behind straight curtains: towards a queer feminist theory of architecture*, Axl Books, Stockholm.

Bonnevier, K. (2007b), 'Out of the Salon: with Natalie Barney towards a critically queer architecture', in J. Rendell, J. Hill, M. Fraser and M. Dorrian (eds.), *Critical architecture*, AHRA Critiques: Critical Studies in Architectural Humanities, Routledge, London and New York, pp. 200–5.

Bonnevier, K. (2017), 'The revue of STYLES', *Architecture and Culture*, vol. 5, no. 3, pp. 353–69.

Bonnevier, K., Kristiansson, Trs and Alves Silva, M. (2017), 'Artifacts introduction speech', *Architecture and Culture*, vol. 5, no. 3, pp. 455–62.

Burns, K. (2012), 'A girl's own adventure: gender in the contemporary architectural theory anthology', *Journal of Architectural Education*, vol. 65, no. 2, pp. 125–34.

Butler, J. (1990), *Gender trouble: feminism and the subversion of identity*, 1st ed., Routledge, New York and London.

Colomina, B. (ed.) (1992), *Sexuality & space*, Princeton Papers on Architecture, Princeton Architectural Press, New York.

Colomina, B., Dollens, D., Sedgwick, E. K., Urbach, H. and Wigley, M. (1994), 'Something about space is queer', in B. Colomina, D. Dollens, E. Kosofsky Sedgwick, C. Patton, H. Urbach and M. Wigley (eds.), *Queer space*, Storefront for Art and Architecture, New York.

Crawford, L. (2015), *Transgender architectonics: the shape of change in modernist space*, Ashgate, Farnham, Surrey.

Crawford, L. (2018), *The high line scavenger hunt*, University of Calgary Press, Calgary, AB.

Crawford, L. (2020), 'Five reasons I won't share washrooms with cisgender people', *Platform*, https://www.platformspace.net/home/five-reasons-i-wont-share-washrooms-with-cisgender-people.

Design legacies: a tribute to architects and designers who have died of AIDS, (1994), Design Pride '94, New York.

Dwyer, J. and Thorne, A. (2006), 'Evaluating Matrix: notes from inside the collective', in D. Petrescu (ed.), *Altering practices: feminist politics and poetics of space*, Routledge, Abingdon, pp. 39–56.

Epstein, B. J. and Gillett, R. (eds.) (2017), *Queer in translation*, Routledge, London and New York.

Gorny, R. A. and van den Heuvel, D. (2017), 'New figurations in architecture theory: from queer performance to becoming trans', *Footprint*, vol. 11, no. 2, pp. 1–10.

Green, A. I. (2002), 'Gay but not queer: toward a post-queer study of sexuality', *Theory and Society*, vol. 31, no. 4, pp. 521–45.

Green, A. I. (2007), 'Queer theory and sociology: locating the subject and the self in sexuality studies', *Sociological Theory*, vol. 25, no. 1, pp. 26–45.

Grote, J. (1992), 'Matrix: a radical approach to architecture', *Journal of Architectural and Planning Research*, vol. 9, no. 2, pp. 158–68.

Holder, A. (2017), 'Five points toward a queer architecture; or, notes on 'Mario Banana No. 1', *Log*, no. 41, pp. 155–60.

Ingram, G. B., Bouthillette, A.-M. and Retter, Y. (1997a), 'Lost in space: queer theory and community activism at the Fin-de-Millénaire', in G. B. Ingram, A.-M. Bouthillette and Y. Retter (eds.), *Queers in space: communities | public places | sites of resistance*, Bay Press, Seattle, pp. 3–16.

Ingram, G. B., Bouthillette, A.-M. and Retter, Y. (eds.) (1997b), *Queers in space: communities | public places | sites of resistance*, Bay Press, Seattle.

Jaque, A. (2017), 'Grindr archiurbanism', *Log*, no. 41, pp. 74–84.

Kolb, J. (2017), 'Working queer', *Log*, no. 41, pp. 63–6.

Kolb, J. and Betsky, A. (2017), 'The end of queer space?', *Log*, no. 41, pp. 85–8.

Kotsioris, E. (2020), '"The queering of architecture history has yet to happen": the intra-canonical outlook of Beatriz Colomina', *Architectural Histories*, vol. 8, no. 1, p. 22.

Lambert, L. (2017), 'Queers, feminists and interiors', *The Funambulist*, no. 13, pp. 10–13.

Lokko, L. N. N. (ed.) (2000), White papers, *black marks: architecture, race, culture*, Athlone Press / University of Minnesota Press, London, UK and Minneapolis, MN.

Lustbader, K. (2018), 'LGBTQ heritage', *Change Over Time*, vol. 8, no. 2, pp. 136–43.

Mayer Hermann, J. (1999), 'Data-protection pattern family', *Assemblage*, vol. 38, pp. 42–7.

Meredith, M. (2017), '2,497 words: provincialism, critical or otherwise', *Log*, no. 41, pp. 169–75.

Messina, R. (2019), 'Adam Nathaniel Furman: "Nowadays you can be a gay architect, but you can't do queer architecture"', *Frame*, https://www.frameweb .com/article/nowadays-you-can-be-a-gay-architect-but-you-cant-do-queer- architecture.

Moore, J. R. (ed.) (2018), *Intersections*, Urban Omnibus, The Architectural League of New York, https://urbanomnibus.net/series/intersections/.

Namaste, V. K. (2000), *Invisible lives: the erasure of transsexual and transgendered people*, University of Chicago Press, Chicago.

Oswin, N. (2008), 'Critical geographies and the uses of sexuality: deconstructing queer space', *Progress in Human Geography*, vol. 32, no. 1, pp. 89–103.

Preciado, B. (2012), 'Architecture as a practice of biopolitical disobedience', *Log*, no. 25, pp. 121–34.

Preciado, B. (2014), *Pornotopia: an essay on Playboy's architecture and biopolitics*, Zone Books, New York.

Preciado, P. B. (2017), 'Trashgender: urinate/defecate, masculine/feminine', *The Funambulist*, no. 13, pp. 15–17.

Preciado, P. B. (2018), 'The architecture of sex: three case studies beyond the Panopticon', *The Funambulist*, no. 19 (supplement), pp. 1–16.

QSPACE (2017), *Coded plumbing*, November 17, http://qspacearch.com/coded -plumbing.

Reed, C. (1996), 'Imminent domain: queer space in the built environment', *Art Journal*, vol. 55, no. 4, pp. 64–70.

Ricco, J. P. (1994), 'Coming together: jack-off rooms as minor architecture', *A/R/C, Architecture, Research, Criticism*, vol. 1, no. 5, pp. 26–31.

Ricco, J. P. (1998), 'Fag-o-sites: minor architecture and geopolitics of queer everyday life', Ph.D. thesis, University of Chicago, Chicago.

Ricco, J. P. (2002), *The logic of the lure*, The University of Chicago Press, Chicago.

Robbins, M. (1992), *Angles of incidence*, Princeton Architectural Press, New York.

Rothschild, J. and Rosner, V. (1999), 'Feminisms and design: review essay', in J. Rothschild (ed.), *Design and feminism: re-visioning spaces, places, and everyday things*, Rutgers University Press, New Brunswick, NJ and London, pp. 7–34.

Sanders, J. (ed.) (1996), *Stud: architectures of masculinity*, Princeton Architectural Press, New Jersey.

Sanders, J. (2017a), 'From Stud to Stalled! architecture in transition', *Log*, no. 41, pp. 145–54.

Sanders, J. (2017b), 'Stalled!: transforming public restrooms', *Footprint*, vol. 11, no. 2, pp. 109–18.

Sanders, J. (2018), 'Noncompliant bodies, accommodating space', *Urban* Omnibus. https://urbanomnibus.net/2018/03/noncompliant-bodies-accommodating-space/

Sanders, J. and Stryker, S. (2016), 'Stalled: gender-neutral public bathrooms', *The South Atlantic Quarterly*, vol. 115, no. 4, pp. 779–88.

Savci, E. (2021), *Queer in translation: sexual politics under neoliberal Islam*, Perverse modernities: a series, Duke University Press, Durham, NC and London, UK.

Sedgwick, E. K. (1994), 'Wanted: queer space manifestos / proposals', in B. Colomina, D. Dollens, E. Kosofsky Sedgwick, C. Patton, H. Urbach and M. Wigley (eds.), *Queer space*, Storefront for Art and Architecture, New York.

Sedgwick, E. K. (1997), 'Paranoid reading and reparative reading; or, you're so paranoid, you probably think this introduction is about you', in E. K. Sedgwick (ed.), *Novel gazing: queer readings in fiction*, Duke University Press, Durham, NC, pp. 1–37.

Seidman, S. (1997), *Difference troubles: queering social theory and sexual politics*, Cambridge University Press, Cambridge.

Shonfield, K., Dannatt, A., Ainley, R. and Muf (2001), *This is what we do: a Muf manual*, Ellipsis, London.

Stead, N. and Prior, J. (eds.) (2007), *Queer space: centres and peripheries*, University of Technology Sydney, Sydney.

Tattelman, I. (1997), 'The meaning at the wall: tracing the gay bathhouse', in G. B. Ingram, A.-M. Bouthillette and Y. Retter (eds.), *Queers in space: communities | public places | sites of resistance*, Bay Press, Seattle, pp. 391–406.

Tattelman, I. (1999), 'Speaking to the gay bathhouse: communicating in sexually charged spaces', in W. Leap (ed.), *Public sex/gay space*, Columbia University Press, New York, pp. 71–94.

Tattelman, I. (2000), 'Presenting a queer (bath)house', in J. A. Boone, M. Dupuis, M. Meeker, K. Quimby, C. Sarver, D. Silverman and R. Weatherston (eds.), *Queer frontiers: millennial geographies, genders, and generations (Queer frontiers editorial collective)*, The University of Wisconsin Press, Madison, WI, pp. 222–58.

Urbach, H. (1992), 'Peeking at gay interiors', *Design Book Review: DBR*, no. 25, pp. 38–40.

Urbach, H. (1993), 'Spatial rubbing: the zone', *Sites*, no. 25, pp. 90–5.

Urbach, H. (1996), 'Closets, clothes, disclosure', *Assemblage*, no. 30, pp. 63–73.

Vallerand, O. (2019), 'Where are the lesbian architects? Visibility and its challenges', *The Plan Journal*, vol. 4, no. 2, pp. 327–43.

Vallerand, O. (2020a), 'Messing up the domestic: queer bodies expanding architectures', *Somatechnics*, vol. 10, no. 3, pp. 397–415.

Vallerand, O. (2020b), *Unplanned visitors: queering the ethics and aesthetics of domestic space*, McGill-Queen's University Press, Montreal and Kingston.

2

Queer encounters in the archive

Misplaced love letters and autobiographical homes

Dirk van den Heuvel and Martin van Wijk

Introduction

This chapter contains a report-cum-reflection of the ongoing research into queer voices and architecture at Het Nieuwe Instituut in Rotterdam. In general terms, our inquiry concerns the question of how to articulate a queer reading of the archive, which in our case is the Dutch National Collection of Architecture and Urban Planning. It is quite a challenge to push a collection that is organized and protected by the financial and institutional frameworks of Dutch heritage law beyond its stringent disciplinary logics, let alone to aim for forms of cross-pollination between the propositions of queer theory and the established curatorial practices of a collection of architecture and urban planning.

Our multi-vocal authorship reflects queer studies' understanding of queerness and queer identities as performative and relational, in line with the pioneering work of Judith Butler. We are two authors who self-identify as gay and queer, but who are of different generations and come from different fields and practices, namely architecture and archival research, on the one hand, and art history and gender studies, on the other hand. One author is also the supervisor of the other: the former is more reflective and aims to unpack and historicize the subject material, whereas the latter seeks an activist approach situated in the latest queer theoretical scholarship. In line with such different positions, which we'd like to think of as generative and transformative to the ways in which we produce and situate our knowledge, we choose not to settle for a single definition of queer. After all, almost as a note of warning to ourselves, not only are queerness and queering contested terms and transitional, ever-shifting concepts themselves, they are currently also being mainstreamed, mostly in Western countries, by multinational industries and straight media, and within academia and cultural institutions. Our own position working from within a national institute reflects this mainstreaming, too.

Hence, in the context of this chapter, our understanding of queering in relation to the national architecture collection and its archival dossiers oscillates between unlocking hidden LGBTQ+ histories, identifying historic cases previously overlooked or suppressed and writing their stories on the one hand and the more political act of resisting the heterosexist logics of the archive and the discipline of architecture on the other hand. What we present is a brief discussion of the current state of our research, including a selection of related materials and actors.

Queering the collection

We started our current research by simply asking what sort of archives in the collection can be directly linked to a queering of the collection. Could we identify archives or materials that have been produced by queer actors, or involve queer subjects, which have been overlooked until now, misrepresented, even straightwashed or erased from the archive? And – bearing upon the important question of visibility – who is included in the archive, what sort of traces are there and what sort of untold stories?

Before diving into these questions, however, let us first briefly address the place from which we are writing, the institute that maintains the Dutch National Collection of Architecture and Urban Planning. Het Nieuwe Instituut is a heritage institution for architecture, design and digital culture that was created in 2013 from a merger between three separate cultural institutions, each of which was dedicated to one of the aforementioned three fields. The institute aspires to stage thought-provoking exhibitions in its four gallery spaces, to instigate explorative research projects and to entertain a lively discursive programme of events, lectures, (de)tours, seminars and summer schools. Under the leadership of its foundational director Guus Beumer, Het Nieuwe Instituut embraced an ambitious and broad range of questions, which impacts the future of the creative industries and knowledge production: from eco-feminism in relation to the built environment to more-than-human knowledge, from material investigations into the status of the digital and its infrastructures to working with copies and copying technologies in the creative world of design.[1]

In contrast with the institute's quest for innovation, or even disruption of established categories and practices, the National Collection of Architecture and Urban Planning can be regarded as a heavy-weight, conservative agent of continuity, the sediment of more than a century of design practice and its professional disciplines. The collection consists of over 800 separate archives, sometimes quite small yet precious, such as the one of avant-garde artist and architect Theo van Doesburg, sometimes very large, documenting the complete professional history of ground-breaking architectural firms, as in the case of the Rotterdam office of Van den Broek and Bakema. It holds a vast array of all sorts of drawings, models, photos, slides, audio-visual materials, correspondence and book collections, as well as recently acquired born-digital archives. As a collection of archives, it has its own history, which goes back to the late nineteenth century. Initially established as a grassroots, profession-driven amateur collection, it was elevated to the status of a national collection in the 1970s, which brought new income, resources, special care and responsibilities, but most of all, institutionalization: it became part of the institutional apparatus or *dispositif*, to use Michel Foucault's term. The collection of architecture archives was now fully integrated into the bigger system of knowledge production and power distribution, a system through which architectural discourse is articulated and, crucially, human agency, subjectivity and identity are produced.[2]

The collection can therefore be viewed as an index of this dynamic of power and knowledge and how it intersects with sociocultural privilege and aspiration: typically, the dominant authors that populate the Dutch national collection are male, white and heterosexual. To queer such a collection, in search of dissenting positions outside the established heteronormative canon, seems almost an impossibility, since the collection and its caretakers embody the very institution. Obviously, the system of access and acquisition, with its numerous filters, thresholds, gates and gatekeepers, has resulted in the privileging of certain voices while marginalizing others. Hence, to queer the national collection and its archives raises profound questions, not only about the various holdings and their histories but also about our own institutional practices within Het Nieuwe Instituut. At stake is the crucial issue of who and what is represented by the national collection, and for whom and to what end it exists, especially so in relation to notions of democracy, an open society and the associated legitimacy of cultural politics and institutions in a country like the Netherlands.

Our own investment in identifying, recovering and (re)writing the experiences of gay architects is motived by our desire to redress the erasure of a queer past from the archive. The Cuban American theorist José Muñoz wrote about this absence of recorded queer experience as follows:

> Queerness has an especially vexed relationship to evidence. Historically, evidence of queerness has been used to penalize and discipline queer desires, connections, and acts. When the historian of queer experience attempts to document a queer past, there is often a gatekeeper, representing a straight present, who will labor to invalidate the historical fact of queer lives – present, past, and future. (Muñoz 2019: 65)

We see this difficult relationship between queerness and historical evidence immediately reflected in the national collection of Dutch architecture. Conventionally, the sexual identities of the subjects included in the archive have always been left unmentioned. Established as a professional archive by and for architects, the main focus of the archives at Het Nieuwe Instituut was and still is geared towards monographic documentation of the architectural works and the design process. As a rule, biographical data is only sparsely present, and hence, what one could call circumstantial evidence that points to queer lives and desires is quite rare. Naturally, this omission of personal data does not affect queer subjects exclusively, yet the erasure of queer lives is related to a heteronormativity that still dominates architectural practice and discipline and is especially effective since it remains implicit and mostly uncontested. At least one case can also be described as a form of self-erasure, which we will highlight in the next section.

A first exploration of possible LGBTQ+ presence in the collection of Het Nieuwe Instituut brings out promising beginnings of new stories. At the same time, however, these are also problematic, since they reconfirm practices of marginalization. Especially in terms of intersectionality, the archive shows itself as, indeed, an index of power dynamics. It is possible to identify a set of architects who are cis-male gay men, yet, lesbian women seem absent. They are doubly invisible, twice outsiders, so to speak. Women are already heavily underrepresented in the collection, let alone lesbian women.[3] An internal inventory from January 2022 counts 642 male authors against 30 female ones.[4] But even this figure can be regarded as too positive a conclusion, since most of the included women are there because they are part of a married couple or an office collective. Regarding the heteronormative binary of male-female, it must be mentioned here that nonbinary or transgender people are missing from the archive altogether.[5] In the case of the identified gay men who are included in the collection – albeit covertly – it appears as if we are looking at the curious and difficult position of outsiders who are insiders at the same time.

Our report builds on a number of earlier initiatives that have explored LGBTQ+ representation in the collection of Het Nieuwe Instituut, starting in 2015 with the institution's participation in the meetings of the national 'Queering the Collections' network.[6] These relatively informal meetings inspired the first queering architecture event at Het Nieuwe Instituut in 2016,[7] and two evening programmes organized as part of the *Dwars door het Archief* series, which combined archival research with public conversations.[8]

More recently, the series has been followed up by the Collecting Otherwise initiative, which focuses on developing alternative methods for acquisition, classification and distribution of cultural heritage to ameliorate the historical gaps in the collection.[9] Another collaborative research project that runs parallel to our current research is 'The Critical Visitor', a five-year research project which brings together academic partners and twelve Dutch cultural institutions, among them Het Nieuwe Instituut.[10] The project aims to develop intersectional approaches for rethinking and retooling accessibility and inclusivity in heritage institutions, combining two PhD projects in archival studies and museology with three work packages of field labs, archival interactions and a public event series called 'The Queer Salon'.[11] All these initiatives are bound together by a shared commitment to contest and transform institutionalized practices by exploring alternative avenues, something which we see as a collaborative work in progress. It is therefore important for us to acknowledge that the knowledge shared through these activities informs our own ongoing effort to generate institutional transformation.

Queer encounters

In the following part we offer a selection from the Dutch national collection of three cases of gay architects: Onno Greiner, Dick van Woerkom and Wim den Boon. All three were active practitioners in the post–Second World War period and designed in the modernist tradition. Identifying these architects has been a process of triangulation, of reading and re-reading the archive. In a way, our queer reading of these archives is also an inquiry into the ways in which identity, sexuality and queer affection have been codified or reproduced through the archive. The double coding of the material, its implicit dimensions and connotations, requires what we have coined a 'special agent', someone who has both access to the archive and is familiar with the codes of queer and gay culture. In our case, senior archivist Alfred Marks has played a key role in flagging certain archival material in the collection as 'queer' or 'gay' through his own earlier queer explorations of the national collection. We have supplemented this archival research with oral histories and personal testimonies, such as a radio interview and conversations with surviving partners, family members and contemporaries.

   In their personal lives and each in their own way, Onno Greiner, Dick van Woerkom and Wim den Boon resisted expectations around gender and sexuality of their time, engaging in same-sex relationships in various degrees of openness. Amidst the archival material that documents buildings and design processes, we found traces of these queer desires and lifestyles, such as misplaced love letters, or juridical correspondence, newspaper clippings, personal photo albums with intimate and nude self-portraits and snapshots of unknown young men. Some of these materials and objects seem to have entered the archive by accident and feel somehow misplaced or unintendedly included, their contents hinting at incomplete records of queer histories that inevitably elude us. This ephemeral quality is what Muñoz drives at with his notion of queer evidence, which can be thought of as 'trace, the remains [of queer acts], the things that are left, hanging in the air like a rumour' (Muñoz 2019: 65). Muñoz's notion of queer evidence provides one of the possible keys for reading queerness which may help us to locate queer desire and intimacy in the archives and lives of Onno Greiner, Dick van Woerkom and Wim den Boon.

To further triangulate the lack of personal data and evidence, we have chosen to focus on the design of their own homes as a form of autobiography. It helps us to imagine the way these three architects navigated their world and times and succeeded in creating a place for themselves. At this point, we'd like to stress this research is still unfinished, and we present the following as incomplete evidence, as a form of approximation that acknowledges the 'unknowability' of queer futures and queer history writing.[12]

Onno Greiner

Onno Greiner (1924–2010) followed in the footsteps of his father, the Amsterdam School architect Dick Greiner (1891–1964). In a 1993 interview on national radio Greiner talks about his difficult relationship with this dominant family figure, being conflicted between wanting to distance himself from him while at the same time seeking his recognition. His long-suppressed homosexuality is an obstacle in this father-son relationship, according to Greiner himself. The interview does not cover the possible impact of his sexuality on his work; being gay and coming out are only discussed in terms of private life, not professional activities. Architect and researcher Andrea Prins, who authored a monograph on Greiner, argues that Greiner might have sublimated these profound personal insecurities into a kind of reassuring architecture, buildings in which one can always find direction, where one doesn't get lost. She summed this up with the word 'orientation' (Prins 2016: 15), thus suggesting how sexual orientation might be inscribed by and in spatial experience, how human bodies are situated in and move through space, as well as time.

Greiner is best known for his theatres and cultural centres, yet he also built himself a beautiful, restrained modernist patio house in the Amsterdam suburb of Amstelveen, which is hardly known (Figures 2.1 and 2.2). The interior of the patio home is generously spacious and has a certain monastic quality because of the use of bare and raw materials – natural slate, spruce wood and white plaster. If these materials and the lack of ornament codify a space as 'ruggedly masculine', as argued by Joel Sanders (1996: 14), the patio home invites us to reflect on the ways in which gender identities, in particular masculinity, is constructed through architectural codes and conventions. Greiner's partner, who still lives there, talks of lively parties with friends and how the house is also a very private space, so that you can walk naked

FIGURE 2.1 *Patio garden of the private home of Onno Greiner, which he built for himself. Greiner sits on the right. The garden design is by Mien Ruys. (Collection Het Nieuwe Instituut, GREO_61018f1-54a.)*

without fear of any of the neighbours looking in.[13] Indeed, the house is hidden from the street rather than facing it, which is quite uncommon in the Netherlands. The spatial layout of this private home enables multiple ways of moving through the different spaces. Much like Eileen Gray's E.1027, analysed by Katarina Bonnevier, Greiner's patio dwelling with its hidden cupboards and closets is a 'house filled with secrets . . . [which] hides and reveals simultaneously' (Bonnevier 2005: 162), and thus creates both a certain specificity and ambiguity in terms of the spatial relationships.

Dick van Woerkom

Speaking of an insider, Dick van Woerkom (1924–87) was one of the co-founders of the current national collection. He was the chief curator of the precursor institution, the Amsterdam-based *Documentatiecentrum voor de Bouwkunst* (Documentation Centre for Architecture). Although the archive contains scarce personal material, there is a tragic tale with orientalist undertones to be discovered in small clues that hint at his unhappy relationships with two young North African men (Boone 1995). A reused envelope previously sent to his lover in Algeria and a wandering note about a

FIGURE 2.2 *Onno Greiner, cluster of patio houses, Amstelveen, 1961–72, Axonometric drawing. (Collection Het Nieuwe Instituut, GREO_61018t7-2.)*

conversation with his other companion point to this; they are little more than glimpses of a hidden love life. Interestingly, there is also legal correspondence between his lawyer and the Dutch Immigration Service about a residence permit for the first partner, a young Moroccan man. Six months later, this relationship was superseded by one with the partner from Algeria, who moved in with van Woerkom in 1978. For the most part, however, questions about the nature and duration of these relationships remain unanswered. According to one of his friends and former employee at the Documentation Centre for Architecture, Dick van Woerkom kept his private and professional life strictly separated, without exception.[14] He would not invite colleagues into the private sphere of his own home for instance. His case fits a pattern of self-erasure by homosexual architects, who would destroy all their personal correspondence and documents before the acquisition process. It reminds us of Sharon Marcus's words that the production of gay history is often 'complicated by the privacy, secrecy, shame, and fear that inhibit people from leaving detailed records of their sexual lives' (Marcus 2005: 201).

In contrast to the lack of personal data, van Woerkom's archive holds a wonderful series of so-called paper architecture schemes, houses for real and fictional clients, such as an artist, a musician and a photographer. This design series was very much in the spirit of De Stijl and the New York Five, radically minimalist and in search of an autonomous formal language of a free-flowing space captured inside neutral grids with red, blue and yellow colour accents. Hardly anyone knew van Woerkom had produced these from the mid-1970s onwards until the end of his life. In 1987 he presented them in a special exhibition devoted to his work which he had organized himself. He died shortly after its opening.[15]

His archive at Het Nieuwe Instituut is filled with these domestic designs. There are precious pencil drawings and also numerous idea sketches he scribbled on the back of meeting minutes, envelopes and other papers lying around. One series from these studies is wholly devoted to a house for himself. It presents a most complicated, cubic structure, almost four houses in one, with multiple entrances and interlocking spaces and stairwells (Figure 2.3). Van Woerkom used these design exercises to further the universalist ideas of De Stijl and modern architecture, aiming to be purer than the original avant-garde masters. Another – queer – reading suggests that this autobiographic domestic space is also a subversion of the nuclear family dwelling, something which also becomes clear in some of his other designs for forms of communal living (Figure 2.4). We would like to suggest

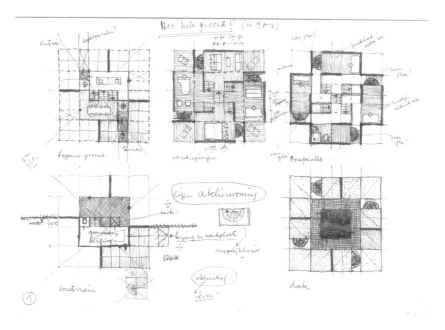

FIGURE 2.3 *Dick van Woerkom, own studio house, sketches, undated.* *(Collection Het Nieuwe Instituut, WOEX_303-15.)*

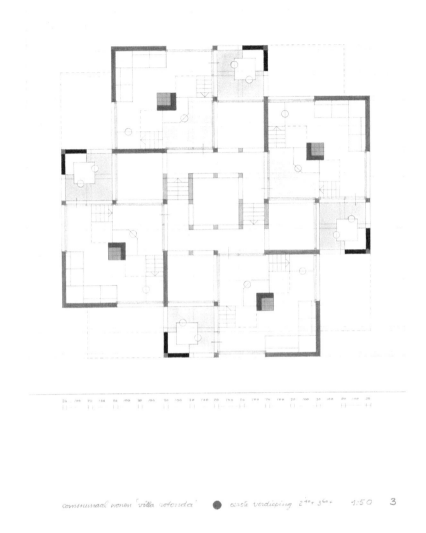

communaal wonen 'villa rotonda' ● *eerste verdieping* 2ᵈᵉ+ 3ᵈᵉ+   *1:50*   3

FIGURE 2.4 *Dick van Woerkom, communal living 'Villa Rotonda', first floor, undated. (Collection Het Nieuwe Instituut, WOEX_347-3.)*

that these house designs articulate a desire for forms of belonging beyond the heteronormative.

Wim den Boon

Last but not least, the most radical of the three was Wim den Boon (1912–68), an interior and furniture designer and an architect of a handful of private houses. After the Second World War he was active in the foundation *Goed Wonen* (Good Living), which propagated strictly functionalist design. However, he was forced to leave this organization since his articles were too zealous and uncompromising in tone (Vöge 1989: 17). From the archive, an image emerges of someone who loved to kick over sacred cows and who cultivated a huge aversion to anything bourgeois, which can be seen from the preserved newspaper clippings about so-called Teddy Boys or greasers and anarchist Provos. With his leather gear, moped and greased hair, he appears as a textbook example of this youth culture himself, despite his middle age. His anti-bourgeois nature is mirrored by the renovations he carried out. The 'before' and 'after' photos give the impression that den Boon exalted the modern and minimalist interior as a means of liberating people from stifling bourgeois conventions.

The many travels he ventured on speak equally of a longing for freedom: in his youth he cycled to Southern Europe and later in his life he drove on a moped via France, to see the buildings of Le Corbusier with his own eyes, and Spain (Gaudí), along the coast of North Africa and back via Italy, where he took an interest in architecture of the fascist period. There are also canoe trips along the Rhône and around Corsica. These trips across rugged natural landscapes have been captured by him in beautiful photo albums and written reports – den Boon was an outstanding photographer and writer. His travel accounts to the Mediterranean also testify to a fascination for vernacular architecture of the Mediterranean, in particular the Maghreb countries. 'The most primary and abstract architecture is the most human. [. . .] The Arabs naturally have this in them', he wrote.[16] This highlights the problematic ethnographical, othering gaze firmly inscribed in the tradition of Dutch modern architecture, to which den Boon was no exception.

Den Boon lived a double life, as we learned through the stories of his nephew.[17] He hardly participated in family life, and his own brother purportedly did not know he was gay until after his death. There are stories about parties in den Boon's tower room he rented in The Hague, which was raided by the police. While the archive does not reveal anything about den Boon's sexual orientation and practice, there is a lot of equivocal material in the archive, especially in the personal photo albums. A recurring motif in the albums is the posed self-portraits in leather motorcycle clothing. The enigmatic title of one of his albums betrays his anti-bourgeois stance: 'The respectable lies of the official decency' (Figure 2.5). The pictures are quite intimate and personal, as den Boon exposes himself literally and figuratively, appearing as a kind of superman, clad in leather or wholly nude, riding a motorbike or enjoying canoeing holidays and hiking tours in the wild (Figures 2.6 and 2.7). Clearly, here he was his own man, unlike when around his family or in professional life.

In the 1960s den Boon designed a series of highly original fantasy houses, most unusual within the circles of Dutch functionalism and modern architecture. They were exercises without clients, such as the Narrow House

FIGURE 2.5 *Wim den Boon, title page from private photo album, 'The respectable lies of the official decency', undated. (Collection Het Nieuwe Instituut, BOOQ_fa 12-2.)*

(Figure 2.8). The section betrays some autobiographical aspect is at work here; we see for instance the kind of sports car he loved to drive, and a canoe as well. The designs are purely speculative, and they share some commonalities: in all of them, due to the absence of doors, the spaces flow into each other, different functions are separated by height differences and stairs, and the relationship between inside and outside (private and public) is designed in a most unusual way, not aiming for modernist transparency but rather for protection and control of the interior spaces from the outside, as if to create a safe space for a non-compliant way of life beyond bourgeois falsehood.

Concluding remarks

History looms large over the archive. Its fixed categories and canonical exercises cast long shadows over the subjects and materials, especially so in the case of marginalized queer lives. In this chapter, we have started to recover the incomplete histories of Onno Greiner, Dick van Woerkom and Wim den Boon through the traces of queer desires and lifestyles that haunt their archives.

FIGURE 2.6 *Wim den Boon, clad in leather, private photo album, undated.*
(Collection Het Nieuwe Instituut, BOOQ_fa 12-12.)

We have tried to highlight the work of perusing the dossiers and documents
and the indispensable process of triangulating these with sources and voices
from outside the archive. Such re-re-readings also need to aim for the
revaluing and reconnecting of biographical ephemera to the monographic,
disciplinary approach, which still dominates architecture and architecture
history today, and which is in need of serious reassessment. In addition, we
have underscored the crucial role of what we have coined 'special agents',
the archivists and curators who are themselves both insiders and outsiders.
Working from within the institutional confines, they are able to trace the

FIGURE 2.7 *Wim den Boon, canoeing in nature, private photo album, undated.* *(Collection Het Nieuwe Instituut.)*

double coding, to read against the grain and to help find those narratives that deviate from the established canon.

All this brings us back to the challenge of narrating historical queer experience from the archive, which conjures up the very question of methodology itself. At this point we might turn again to our divergent positions and perspectives as co-authors with different backgrounds and academic pedigrees.

One of us suggests that the work to be done is riddled with paradoxes which are often hard to straddle. To start with, he posits that it is not possible to fully abandon history, that it remains necessary to situate queer lives by careful historicizing and contextualizing – to try and understand them as being embedded in a specific place and time. This raises concerns from the other one, who warns of bringing back the fantasy of a fully transparent and neutral recovery of history, notwithstanding his appreciation of history as situated and embedded. This author is less interested in the positivist undertaking of historical analysis, in approaching historical queer experience through empirical data collection if you will, and more so in unsettling the

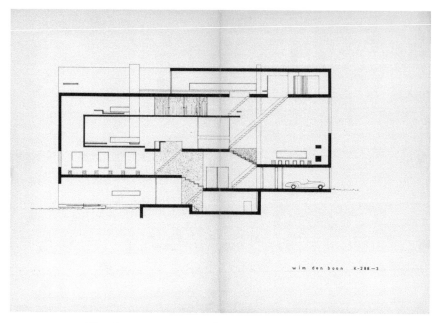

FIGURE 2.8 *Wim den Boon, Het Smalle Huis, fantasy house, undated,* c.1960.
(Collection Het Nieuwe Instituut, BOOQ_k288-1.)

notion of evidence altogether. To him, mere evidencing is not enough to
redress the epistemological erasure of queer existence.

Our first author agrees with this but also protests: situating and
historicizing is not the same as empirical data collection, on the contrary.
He once again argues that queer experience and concepts should not be
understood as something a- or trans-historical, and that room should be
left for yet unknown, future interpretations the moment new materials
are uncovered and other connecting stories emerge. According to this
author, narrating a queer past requires better care and understanding,
while realizing that the curatorial work undertaken will remain an
approximation and incomplete and, paradoxically, will always produce
a new object, as it were, through which the historical narrative is made
visible and palpable. The second author responds by posing that the key
question at hand is how contemporary queer thought might enable us to
narrate queer experience differently, and how it may help us to develop
alternative, queerer modes of engaging the archive. Behind all this, the
two agree, lies a shared desire and aspiration: to locate and narrate queer
world-making practices that let us dream of, imagine and enact queerer
ways of being in the world.

Notes

1   For an overview of the activities of Het Nieuwe Instituut one can visit the website: hetnieuweinstituut.nl; or see the book publication: Brendan Cormier, *Expansive Bodies. Contesting Design at Het Nieuwe Instituut*, nai010 publishers, Rotterdam 2021.

2   See for a history of this process of institutionalization: Sergio M. Figueiredo, *The NAi Effect. Creating Architecture Culture*, nai010publishers, Rotterdam 2016.

3   There is one open and out lesbian urban designer in the collection: Riek Bakker (b 1944), but with a very small file of three panels of a competition design for Parc de la Villette in Paris, dated 1982. Bakker's archive is still with the office she co-founded, Bureau B+B, in Amsterdam. A recent acquisition of the professional, female network 'Vrouwen Bouwen Wonen' also has queer lesbian people involved, yet this archive has been researched thus far from a feminist perspective and less from a queer one.

4   Internal document '1. Matrix Archieven Werkbestand, Download 13–1', 13 January 2022.

5   Open and out trans presence in architecture is of relative recent date, and is admittedly still rare, although Uwe Bresan and Wolfgang Voigt have included a trans woman planner in their historical overview of German LGBTIQ+ persons: Hildegard Schirmacher (1924–2015), see Uwe Bresan and Wolfgang Voigt (eds.), *Gay Architects. Silent Biographies from the 18th to the 20th Century*, Wasmuth and Zohlen, Berlin, 2022. Trailblazers in the field today are Paul Preciado and Lucas Crawford, while Simona Castricum features in this volume.

6   The initiative, instigated by the Dutch Gay and Lesbian archives IHLIA in Amsterdam, goes back to a symposium in 2015, organized by IHLIA, the Amsterdam Museum, the Reinwardt Academy for heritage studies and COMCOL, ICOM. The Queering the Collections network was hosted by Het Nieuwe Instituut in 2021, 31 March, in the framework of the project 'Collecting Otherwise'. For more information, see Riemer Knoop and Lonneke van den Hoonaard (eds.), *Queering the Collections. Tips & tricks voor het nog zichtbaarder maken van gender- & seksuele diversiteit in musea en collecties*, IHLIA and Reinwardt Academie, Amsterdam 2016. IHLIA stands for: Internationaal Homo-Lesbisch Informatiecentrum en Archief. Its history goes back to 1978, when the Dokumentatiecentrum Homostudies was established in Amsterdam.

7   'Queering Architecture' 15 September, 2016. Archivist Alfred Marks provided the specific queer selection of documents from the collection. Speakers included among others Jasmine Rault, who analysed Eileen Gray's work as an example of Sapphic modernity and the late Henry Urbach, one of the pioneers of queer theory in architecture. For an online report of the seminar, see https://collectie.hetnieuweinstituut.nl/en/activities/queering-architecture

8   'Through Queer Eyes' 15 September, 2016, and 'Queer Houses and Places' 26 September, 2019. 'Dwars door het archief' literally translates as 'athwart

the archive'. The talks were moderated by the collection department and its archivists and curators, and take a specific societal view on the collection materials, which can lead to surprising selections and combinations. Past editions focused on a range of topics, among others: feminisms, squatting practices and colonial legacies. Curator Hetty Berens has called it an 'acupunctural' approach that allows to further explore the resources of the collection. See for an online report of both 'queering' events: https://collectie.hetnieuweinstituut.nl/en/activities/through-queer-eyes, and: https://collectie.hetnieuweinstituut.nl/activiteiten/queer-houses-and-places

9   The Collecting Otherwise working group exists of a multidisciplinary and international team, who come together on a monthly basis to question the archival gaze using a work-in-progress method. The first iteration (2021) has looked into feminist and genderqueer spatial practices, resulting in the acquisition of the archive of the women's association 'Vrouwen Bouwen Wonen' (Women, Building, Dwelling). The current focus (2022) is on decolonizing methods, with a natural interest in the many traces of remaining, of historical relations with the former Dutch colonies in the Caribbean, and the former Dutch East Indies. Involved colleagues are among others Setareh Noorani, Delany Boutkan, Carolina Pinto, Federica Notari and Harriet Rose Morley. See the web magazine: https://collectingotherwise.hetnieuweinstituut.nl/en

10 Eliza Steinbock, associate professor of Gender and Diversity Studies at Maastricht University, brought the network together, with Hester Dibbits of the Reinwardt Academy and Erasmus University, and one of us, Dirk van den Heuvel, as co-organizers. The team is completed by Noah Littel and Liang Kai Yu as PhD candidates. The project has received a grant from the Dutch national science organization NWO as part of their Smart Culture programme for the creative industries.

11 The Queer Salon series are conceived as open to the public and are hosted by Het Nieuwe Instituut. They are recorded and published online. Due to the Covid-19 pandemic, the first Queer Salon with a keynote lecture by Olivier Vallerand took place online on 11 February, 2021. It can be viewed at https://jaap-bakema-study-centre.hetnieuweinstituut.nl/en/activities/queer-salon

12 In the spirit of the queer novelist Alan Hollinghurst, esp. *The Stranger's Child* of 2011; see also the interview with him in the Oxonian Review: https://oxonianreview.com/articles/an-interview-with-alan-hollinghurst

13 Conversation with Paul Rueckert, 5 February, 2022.

14 Conversation with Frank den Oudsten, 13 May, 2022.

15 Van Woerkom's archive was brought to the national collection by the architectural historian Bernard Colenbrander, after van Woerkom had passed away of heart failure. Colenbrander was the right hand of van Woerkom at the Documentation Centre for Architecture and acted as the executor of van Woerkom's estate. Van Woerkom had a disturbed relationship with his family, none of whom were still in contact with him at the time of his death. Conversation with Bernard Colenbrander, undated.

16 Travelogue North Africa, June–July 1954, Collection Het Nieuwe Instituut,
    BOOQ a21.

17 Conversation with Arie den Boon, 1 April, 2022.

References

Bonnevier, K. (2005), 'A Queer Analysis of Eileen Gray's E.1027', in H. Heynen
    and G. Baydar (eds.), *Negotiating Domesticity. Spatial Productions of Gender in
    Modern Architecture*, 162, Abingdon: Routledge.

Boone, J. A. (1995), 'Vacation Cruises; or, The Homoerotics of Orientalism', *PMLA*
    110 (1): 89–107.

Bresan, U. and W. Voigt (eds.) (2022), *Gay Architects. Silent Biographies from the
    18th to the 20th Century*, Berlin: Wasmuth & Zohlen.

Cormier, B. (ed.) (2021), *Expansive Bodies: Contesting Design at Het Nieuwe
    Instituut*, Rotterdam: nai010 publishers.

Figueiredo, S. M. (2016), *The NAi Effect: Creating Architecture Culture*,
    Rotterdam: nai010publishers.

Knoop, R. and L. van den Hoonaard (eds.) (2016), *Queering the Collections: Tips
    & Tricks voor het nog zichtbaarder maken van gender- & seksuele diversiteit in
    musea en collecties*, Amsterdam: Reinwardt Academie.

Marcus, S. (2005), 'Queer Theory for Everyone: A Review Essay', *Signs* 31 (1): 201.

Muñoz, J. E. (2019), *Cruising Utopia: The Then and There of Queer Futurity*, 10th
    anniversary ed., New York: New York University Press.

Prins, A. (2016), *Onno Greiner (1924–2010). Een zoektocht naar helderheid en
    geborgenheid*, Hilversum: Uitgeverij Verloren.

Sanders, J. (ed.) (1996), *Stud: Architectures of Masculinity*, New York: Princeton
    Architectural Press.

Vöge, P. (1989), *Wim den Boon. Binnenhuisarchitect (1912–1968)*, Rotterdam:
    Uitgeverij 010.

3

Queering architectural history

Anomalous histories and historiographies of the Baroque

Marko Jobst

Inflection zero: 'Yet to Happen'

What does it mean to queer architectural history? Is it to approach the implicit heteronormativity of architecture as a discipline, and then subject it to acts of queering whatever form they may take in relation to history? Or is it to queer the discourses that constitute the discipline, the historiographies that give architecture its textual form, render it intelligible? Or is it, perhaps, to attempt to understand certain extant historical buildings as themselves queer – in some essential yet routinely overlooked way? And if any, or all, of the above were possible, what would be appropriate methods for such a project?

In this chapter, I will suggest that one way of queering architecture is by queering its histories and historiographies through acts of bringing into visibility modes of queerness that are intrinsic to them yet remain suppressed. This implies not only that 'queer' is already present both in architectural historiographies and historical architectures themselves but also that the queering of architecture via its historical and theoretical discourses is inseparable from the question of the writerly forms such discourses assume, and the ways in which the normative and normalizing tendencies in writing architecture might, and should, be challenged.

. . .

In 2020, architect and academic Evangelos Kotsioris conducted an interview with the renowned historian of architecture Beatriz Colomina, the author of seminal books such as *Sexuality and Space* (1992), the first edited volume to introduce the term 'sexuality' prominently in architecture, and *Privacy and Publicity: Modern Architecture as Mass Media* (1994), a highly original – disruptive even – reading of modernist architectural practices. In the interview, Colomina suggested that 'the queering of architecture history has yet to happen' and Kotsioris foregrounded the issue by making it the title of the article – despite it being only one of several ideas that the interview covered. As Colomina put it, to queer the history of architecture would mean 'not just to add queer architects to the history of modern architecture, but to queer the history itself. It's actually much queerer than we think, and that's much more interesting' (2020).

Colomina's use of the term 'queer' here is clearly broader than the question of sexuality, if related to it. It implies anything and everything that subverts norms, expectations, or even propriety. But it also seems to be a question of bringing to the surface what is inherently present, showing that architecture itself – and, importantly, ways in which its histories are constructed – is much stranger than we tend to think. On this reading, architectural histories, and by implication the discipline's historiographies, are intrinsically queer: they hide all manner of oddities, anomalies, and perversions. As a result, Colomina refers to her approach to history as 'intra-canonical', in that it tends to look at canonical works of architecture closely in order to subvert them, and our expectations of them.

In this spirit, I put forward in this chapter a way of queering architectural history and historiography via one of its more central, or indeed canonical, terms: the Baroque. I want to note not only that the Baroque has been essential to modern architectural historiography (a point which has, after all, been made by numerous authors) but that the Baroque should also be seen as intrinsically queer, and thus a perfect vehicle for queering architectural history itself.

The 'intra-canonical' approach that Colomina describes is akin to 'queer' through its subversion of norms and the normative. Meanwhile, the architectural canon, composed as it is of key architects and works deemed to have set the norm in various periods and historical locations, is mirrored in a set of canonical texts, terms and concepts that have been normalized over time – even if routinely redefined or critiqued. In having a closer look within ('intra') the canon of architectural history – the Baroque specifically – I will also reflect on its attendant historiographies. Various aspects of this re-evaluation of the Baroque have been covered extensively in the past couple of decades, yet to my knowledge never by centralizing Baroque's intrinsic 'queerness'.

Colomina's notion of the intra-canonical also resonates with French philosopher Gilles Deleuze's queer-coded approach to the history of philosophy by 'taking an author from behind and giving him a child that would be his own offspring, yet monstrous' (Deleuze 1995: 6). In both cases, the claim is that the queer was inherent in the normative; it just needed to be brought overtly into the world. The anomalous child Deleuze speaks of must belong to the philosopher whose work he transforms from within, and everything Deleuze aims to draw out of the work should already be present in it. I take this to be one of the more interesting challenges when attempting the project of queering architectural history in ways that are not a question of adding queer architects to the cannon: less an issue of imposing a reading than *uncovering* what it already present, yet not recognized – uncovering it in a subversive, and decidedly queer way.

Inflection first: queer Baroque

Baroque: exuberant, excessive, perverse, kitsch; overly emotive in a way that suggests artifice; highly decorative, dramatic in its attempts to move what remains immobile, spatially convoluted if not always complex; prone to the creation of illusions, visual and other. And in its more contemporary iteration: multi-layered in a way that surpasses the combination of media that characterized even its initial phase, delirious in its potential, once again found to be unsound, easily given over to problematic ideological positions. Linked to sensation either way. But also, a term invented after the body of work it describes has passed into history, a concept with philosophical implications, a pure invention of writing, of historiography, of discourse. An illusion.

At its most basic, Baroque is taken to refer to the art and architectures of the seventeenth and eighteenth centuries in the European context initially but subsequently also far beyond it. In this period, the classical formal and spatial idioms established during the Renaissance were transformed into something unexpected, strange and often wild. As such, the Baroque remains first and foremost a name for a style – it is indeed inseparable from the very notion of 'style' as a historiographical category – but one that was neither conceived as such nor called 'the Baroque' at the time the works it designates were produced. The routinely recounted history of the emergence of the term refers its likely origins to the artisanal realm of jewellery and places deformation at its core. *Barroco*, on this standard reading, was used to describe an imperfect, asymmetrical pearl, a formal equivalent of all manner of distortions and malformations the art and architectures of those two centuries were deemed to have performed.

It would only be in the second part of the nineteenth century that the recuperation of the Baroque from overtly negative readings took place, and even then, indirectly and in the context of the Renaissance as the norm and ideal from which its works were still perceived to have deviated. This would continue into the twentieth century by cutting across the dominant current of architectural modernism, until Baroque influences, issues and ultimately citations reappeared with the Postmodern in one form, and then in the twenty-first century even more radically so through the various iterations of so-called Neobaroques. In this most recent manifestation, the term was revived in the context of new technologies, multimedia and all manner of creative practices that saw the Baroque as the undercurrent of modernism.

In other words, the Baroque was and remains a historiographical invention, one that has provoked a broad range of readings and interpretations over time. And yet, it never veered from the essential notion of being a *distortion of normative and normalizing ideals*. As such, it should be of particular interest to any project that uses the term 'queer' as the starting point for troubling art and architectural history. As Monika Kaup puts it, 'the baroque was born deviant – a mongrel by birth: The original meaning of baroque – the nonclassicist use of classical forms – encapsulates the baroque's quintessential deviance and its hybridizing mode of innovation. The baroque contests the norm, not by discarding it but by bending and deforming it' (Kaup 2019: 152).

Baroque: the deviant bender.

. . .

Importantly for this project of bringing 'baroque' and 'queer' into close proximity, in the introduction to *Rethinking the Baroque* Helen Hills suggests that we should be 'thinking of baroque as a "conceptual technology" that does not simply allow retrospective understanding but actually provokes new forms of historical conceptualization and interpretation' (2011: 3). It is not, in other words, just a category that emerged in art and architectural historiography and remains, on some readings, integral to its character; it is a set of practices and techniques that actively instigate new ways of seeing and thinking.

Hills's own chapter in that edited volume, titled 'The Baroque: The Grit in the Oyster of Art History', emphasizes the Baroque's relation to disruptive approaches to historiography. It troubles 'the smooth waters of a linear historicism' (2011: 11) – note the rippling, undulating imagery here – and leads to the notion of a 'productive' Baroque, which Hills identifies in the works of Walter Benjamin, as well as Deleuze. Productive, in that it is not a retroactive classificatory category but an active, constructive tool employed in the creation of novel meanings.

In an extensive overview of the emergence and uses of the term, Hills details the range of interpretations of art and architecture of the seventeenth century that aligned the Baroque with the 'bizarre', 'decadent' and 'perverse' – even before the term was put to the various other uses recognizable to this day. In Quatremère de Quincy's interpretation, for example, the works of the period in question were 'destructive of nature's order and forms'; they were no less than 'vice' itself (Hills 2011: 13). This clearly derogatory, moralizing and deeply normative terminology aligns the Baroque very closely with all that can be understood to be 'queer' in some way. The art and architectures of a period that only later acquired its name were soon after declared to be malformed, undesirable – in short, perverse; while the term 'Baroque' would carry with it these negative connotations, retaining them even through the most affirmative of interpretations.

The Baroque – however defined and to whatever period it may ultimately be applied – was, and remains, that piece of grit Hills identifies in the title of her essay. At its core, it remains associated with perversion, rarely an interruption of the given course of development that might, even inadvertently, lead to something to which value can be assigned, let alone an object of sensual appreciation: an irregular pearl.

. . .

The Baroque is a term to be found at the core of modern architectural historiography. Andrew Leach opens *What Is Architectural History?* with a quote from Heinrich Wölfflin's *Renaissance and Baroque*, pointing at the lasting importance of the concepts and questions developed in that seminal volume (2010: loc 134). Several years later, in *The Baroque in Architectural Culture*, Leach, John Macarthur and Maarten Delbeke expand on this, claiming that if Wölfflin's book was 'one kind of founding document for the modern historiography of architecture, then the baroque quickly figures in that field's core problems' (2015: 1). The authors identify these as 'questions of how architecture changes its appearance, function and meaning over time; and of how to present realized works of architecture as moments within processes of change' (2015: 1). As the authors show, Baroque would be integral to the development of the discourses on space, perception and subjectivity, all of which marked dramatically the modern historiographies of architecture. As they write, '[t]he modern construction of the baroque as an historical subject offered a privileged view on the artifice of history itself' (Leach et al. 2015: 3).

Let's take this proposition regarding artifice to a slightly more extreme position. The Baroque, in architecture specifically, is the key problem that gave birth to architecture's own modern historical discourse, and Leach, Macarthur and Delbeke focus on its importance – its veiled presence – in the formation of modernism and its historiographies. What seemingly couldn't be further apart – modernism's reasoned paring down of principles and Baroque's sensuous exuberance, whether we speak of form or broader values – is shown to be carried, like that speck of grit that allows an anomalous pearl to form, from one set of historical values and manifestations of architecture to another.

But more than that: the suggestion that one of the core problems of architecture is that of change, and its moments of arrest over time, potentially unfolds a different problem, that of the establishment of architectural norms and principles, which is also bound to be the process of their surpassing, transformation and abandonment. This twisting out of an ideal shape and past it, this movement away from any externally imposed point of stasis, is at its core the question of instability of meaning in architecture, of the relative nature of its productions and its understanding of itself – as a practice, a discipline or, at its broadest, an approach to becoming in and with the world.

This, though, is also the gist of what we understand as queerness: unstable, always on a quest for meaning, always aware of its limitations and contingencies, a loose set of provocations and positions that allow them to question norms and apparent certainties. Most of all, it is an impure interruption that can be found even in most unlikely places. Or especially there: as a hidden, troubled, and troubling undertow that reveals the lie of a perfect form.

. . .

But the questions of historiographies, whether they be disruptive or not, are also closely tied to the very forms of their discourse. As Gregg Lambert writes in *The Return of the Baroque in Modern Culture*, these critical discussions around the Baroque – its etymology, status as a historical category or the numerous interpretations of it that have been ongoing for a century now – remain unable to conclude with certainty 'whether, or not, the baroque ever existed as a definite historical or cultural phenomenon, but only found existence in "the non-place of language", that is, in the rarefied air of academic debates belonging to art history and aesthetic criticism' (2004: 5). Referring specifically to Severo Sarduy's point that all the studies of the Baroque seem to have to start with the definition of the term, Lambert wonders if

> the critical literature on the baroque could itself be considered as a distinct genre, a literary form defined repeatedly by its discursive conventions, by which we could characterize the works of baroque criticism by the repetition of form, or by certain conventions that appear to underlie the identification of baroque works. If this were true, there would be very little difference between the work of baroque criticism and the form of the novel, or a story that begins routinely with the phrase 'Once upon a time . . . '. (2004: 5)

In other words, there is something of a loss of contour expected to separate architecture in its identifiable material forms from the discourses used to describe and understand them. Instead, constructions fold from the realm of the textual and into the realm of the built, then unfold again, transformed. This itself presents an uneasy analytical smear, potentially deceptive, a mirage: an act of destabilizing architecture that cuts to the core of its desire to acquire disciplinary certainty by always pointing at its material manifestations, its solid and earnest utilitarian outcomes. It is potentially the tension present in all the discussions of the role of theory in architecture versus its practice, since the 1960s at least; and if the Baroque is found at the centre of architecture's historiography, it might also be at the crux of the discipline's uneasy relationship with literature – and modes of writing more broadly.

Regarding Eugenio d'Ors's notion of 'baroque eon' specifically, Lambert notes that it is 'open and in perpetual revolt' rather than a matter of linear histories and notions of progress. D'Ors saw the Baroque not as a specific historical moment but a stage in the development of any number of periods, locating that which can be deemed 'baroque' in the general movement away from the ideal, stable, perfect and the norm; it is a perpetual return to disturbance, obliquely positioned in relation to historical time. Consequently, d'Ors's 'baroque eon', on Lambert's reading, implies 'the excavation of the "states of exception" that have been elided from any official history' (2004: 8). As a result, the Baroque finds its way into the writing of both modern and postmodern authors 'for whom these states of exception represent the re-telling or the excavation of a completely *Other* history – unofficial, censored, repressed or colonized' (Lambert 2004: 9).

In short, d'Ors's 'baroque' is that which repeats itself, finds itself as a movement away from the ideal, not only in the seventeenth and eighteenth centuries but also in all the movements that shift the balance past idealization and normalization. It is a disruption, an inflection away from the straight line. This 'revolt', as Lambert would call it, is where the understanding of the Baroque aligns itself once again with the queer – not only through the question of its otherness but through that very potential to react against dominant and domineering narratives of stability and perfection.

. . .

One of these 'other' histories Lambert notes is traced by Mabel Moraña in 'Baroque/Neobaroque/Ultrabaroque: Disruptive Readings of Modernity', where she offers a summary of the most widely used etymological understanding of the term, turning it into an image of the style:

A foreign particle becomes implanted into the corporeal substance of a mollusk, and it is slowly surrounded by layers of nacre that develop into a pearl. Nevertheless, if in the process of its formation, the emerging jewel finds irregularities in the interior walls of the oyster, its potential circularity is disrupted. Imperfect, pathological, that deformed pearl evokes a sphericity never achieved: its slightly monstrous body is affirmed in the nostalgia of totality and perfection. The baroque pearl is a melancholic, transubstantiated, imperfect being, saturated by matter. It is, at the same time, hybrid and palimpsest, a deformity conceived through the transgression of its own limits – something new, that results from the defensive struggle exercised by the body that received the challenge of heterogeneity. As the product of a contradictory dynamics of absorption and resistance, the baroque pearl combines, in its process of formation, both the norm and its exception. (2005: 241–2)

Imperfect, pathological, deformed, monstrous; nostalgic, melancholy, palimpsestic and hybrid; deformed, transgressive, heterogenous, resistant – with exceptions re-introduced into norms as disruptors. In just one short paragraph, Moraña offers a set of adjectives that reverberate with all manner of queerings. The author, of course, is writing about 'American Baroque' and the processes of colonization and transculturation that are inextricable from it. Yet the description and its attendant interpretations offer an image applicable beyond those particular colonial dynamics between Europe and the American continent into which Baroque was introduced, where it underwent hybridizations, and where it keeps thriving, as is apparent from the wealth of publications on the subject (see Zamora and Kaup 2010). If Lambert is right about the strange nature of Baroque discourse and its intrinsic links to 'other' histories – and Moraña's description mirrors that proposition with poetic exuberance worthy of the topic – then the question is what other *Other* Baroque histories we should be looking for.

To that effect, Moraña is on a quest for '*the logic of baroque disruption*, that is, its epistemological operational capacity', and her aim is to 'read the Baroque as the allegorical reproductibility of the struggles of power' (2005: 242–3). This 'logic of baroque disruption', the 'epistemological operational capacity' of discourse, she discusses in the context of the American continent, the histories of its colonization and the dichotomy – and possible surpassing – of the European, Catholic Baroque through the transformations it underwent in the 'New World'. But the logic of disruption Moraña describes – I am tempted to say sculpts, considering the highly saturated language she uses – is also deeply analogous with processes of queering. It reveals how that which we have named 'the Baroque', unstable and semi-fictitious as it perpetually remains, resonates with queer discourses in ways that haven't been fully explored.

And it is perhaps unsurprising that it is in the context of the histories of the American world that a conjunction between the terms 'Baroque' and 'queer' can most easily be found, in the writings of Néstor Perlongher for one and also a number of others across the region. Yet, this is already the so-called Neobaroque, for which many names exist in this regional context, but all of which remain wedded to the twin issues of coloniality and Catholicism. Is there a broader discussion to be had, one that takes the original period of the Baroque into account as well?

. . .

In *Universal Baroque*, Peter Davidson insists on seeing the Baroque as 'supraconfessional and genuinely international' (2007: 2) and claims that resistance to this understanding came primarily from nineteenth-century nation-state thinking retrospectively applied to the style, coupled with its associations with revived Catholicism (2007: 5). But in a crucial couple of paragraphs, he moves further, making a reference to the Baroque as essentially 'queer':

In the achievement of the stupendous, categories are bound to become fluid, things are (literally and in the arts of illusion) inevitably going to flow into each other, so that with magnificence and decorum comes an element of the deliberately astonishing, a pleasure in the astonishing, something that might elicit the English words 'flouting' and 'flaunting'.

This is something perceptible in certain lights [. . .] as *queer*. The pleasure of the cabinet of curiosities is also a pleasure in queerness, in juxtaposition, in an investigation of the surreal poetry of an expanding perception of the world, in the continuous arrangement of discontinuous objects as though they were connected. (2007: 11)

The use of 'queer' here is intriguing, much as it remains unqualified, perhaps deliberately so. Do we speak of the queer in that quaint, politically seemingly neutral sense of the strange, unusual, weird? Or is this a reference to the term's more contemporary use, with meaning inextricable from questions of sexuality and the political framing of what it might mean to stake out a socially aberrant position? Considering that Davidson also uses the term 'camp' further on in the text (2007: 21) – a term Mark Booth, incidentally, traces to seventeenth-century Versailles (1999) – perhaps the link to aberrant sexualities is not that accidental after all.

This brings us back to the original art and architectures of the seventeenth century and what bloomed from them, but also past the questions of discourse, terminology or literature. For Davidson, the queer is present at the very outset in what we will subsequently classify as Baroque creativity, in the way that it operates as a series of juxtapositions of meaning and sensation. The continuity across 'discontinuous objects' he writes of belongs to the works themselves – even before it is one of Baroque discourse becoming indistinguishable from material manifestations, as mentioned earlier.

For Lambert, Baroque is pure discourse, and he opens doors for all that is 'other', including that which we may label as 'queer'; for Davidson, that otherness has been in the Baroque all along, precisely as an essential queerness, engrained in objects and spaces of the period. Which is to say: a queerness essential to architecture.

Inflection second: queering (the writing of) history

In the introductory chapter for *After Queer Studies: Literature, Theory and Sexuality in the 21st Century*, Tyler Bradway and E. L. McCallum draw attention to various forms of 'periodization, genealogy, history, linearity, and causality' used when considering the notion of queer time (2019: 6). Referring to the first text in their anthology – which, serendipitously, if perhaps unsurprisingly, is concerned with early modern literature – they ask whether a text that might be labelled as 'queer' is one that 'represents same-sex desire, one written by an author whose biography indicates same-sex erotic attraction, or one that has to be read against the grain to expose its queerness' (2019: 12).

The answer they offer is drawn from the first chapter in their volume. In it, Bradway and McCallum claim, the author Stephen Guy-Bray is

> urging readers to presume all texts as queer. If this stance is made possible by queer theory, Guy-Bray demonstrates how early modern representations of sexuality prefigure and even exceed contemporary notions of queerness. In this respect, the literary archive preserves a future for queer readings to come. (2019: 12)

Now, if we transpose this to the realm of architecture and reframe for buildings with no obvious – which is just another way of saying 'suppressed' – links to same-sex desire or 'queer' authors, then reading against the grain becomes crucial for the project of queering architectural history. It presupposes understanding the queer as a dispersed, diffuse field of signs, meanings and affective investments, embodied in material environments and the desires that circulate in and through them, invited or not, sanctioned or not.

Or, to paraphrase Bradway and McCallum: the architectural archive, composed as it is of all the architectures of the past that persist in material form as well as their attendant discourses and historiographies – as the case of the Baroque demonstrates – is *always already queer*, and exceedingly so. To think of architecture as an archive that can be read in queer ways and therefore queered anew is to invite new understandings of what an archive is, what it contains and what and how might have been deposited in it – as well as the ways in which these complex layers might subsequently be revealed.

This is precisely the task of architectural historiography, as Beatriz Colomina suggests; but it is predicated on seeing all architectural objects as repositories of queerness accumulated over time. Each building, on this reading, is a physical manifestation of queer histories, a complex and often obscure, yet always invaluable container for that 'future for queer readings to come' that Bradway and McCallum identify. *Each and every building* – not just those that 'represent same-sex desire' by carving out spaces for LGBTIQA+ communities and allowing them to thrive, or those that are designed by authors 'whose biography indicates same-sex erotic attraction' – and every single architectural artefact against whose 'grain' we need to work to expose its innate queerness is part of this archive. And only by seeing it as such can we begin to queer architectural history – and its modes of historiography – in ways at which Colomina hints.

. . .

In *The Shapes of Fancy: Reading for Queer Desire in Early Modern Literature*, Christine Varnado points out that queerness remains always inextricably wedded to questions of desire, yet in ways that are 'more capacious', as she puts it, than we tend to think (2020: 8). Desire is never attached to human bodies alone; it is always already 'staged' – the spatial/ architectural imagery is certainly worth noting here – with the aid of objects, clothes, instruments, ornaments and all sorts of prosthetic extensions of the human body that alter 'the shape of desire in the scene' and bring us together with all that lies beyond us in complex affective constellations (Varnado 2020: 9). As a result,

> Queerness, in this larger dramatic and structural sense, is that which crosses, that which sits athwart, that which thwarts and torques existing categorizations. Queerness uses the materials to hand in surprising and inventive ways to transmit desire (not always successfully); it flouts expected timelines and trajectories of proper development; it spins into backward motion, or stands stubbornly still; it upends expected orders of similitude and difference; it generates weirdness and excess, wallows in the degraded, and emphasizes its own artifice. (2020: 9)

This is a rich description of all manner of operations that can be associated with the term 'queer', foregrounding the notion that queerness circulates through all sorts of material environments to and from and across human bodies, in what might be understood as the question of 'affective networks'. But also, not for the first time in a text of this kind or in relation to the period it concerns itself with, queerness and its operations appear remarkably baroque in Varnado's writerly rendering. They unfold across phenomena and discursive registers, strange, excessive and keen to 'wallow' in that which is marked as degraded.

Desire has been written in the context of architecture and its histories and theories in any number of works. And yet, the very site of desire being brought side by side with queerness – and in the context of the period in which what we designate as 'the Baroque' was formed – seems worth retaining as part of this anomalous discursive pearl in the making. If Bradway and McCallum's take on Guy-Bray allows for the intensification of the architectural archive until it is saturated with queerness, Varnado's approach lends the notion of an equally all-pervasive desire. It is, in other words, not only that all of architecture carries with it relentless and relentlessly suppressed modes and manifestations of queerness; it is also that the deep and broad reach of the archive portrays architecture as filled with sexual desire to the brim. And while the concept of desire can itself be understood to operate beyond the realm of sex – the work of Deleuze and his collaborator Félix Guattari is exemplary here once again – it is precisely *sexual* desire that is at stake.

If all architecture holds on to the realm of *queerness* and gives it complex form by folding and unfolding it, closeting and then differently closeting it once more, all of architecture should also be understood as the realm in which queer *desire* perpetually slips in and out, oozing and infusing, slippery and viscous and always on the verge of that degraded bliss.

. . .

Considering the question of affect, which is integral to the story of desire that Varnado presents, Heather Love writes in *Feeling Backward: Loss and the Politics of Queer History* that the texts she is interested in are ones that represent

> significant points in a tradition of queer experience and representation that I call 'feeling backward'. These dark, ambivalent texts register these authors' painful negotiation of the coming of modern homosexuality. Such representations constitute a crucial 'archive of feeling', an account of the corporeal and psychic costs of homophobia. In their work, I pay particular attention to feelings such as nostalgia, regret, shame, despair, ressentiment, passivity, escapism, self-hatred, withdrawal, bitterness, defeatism, and loneliness. These feelings are tied to the experience of social exclusion and to the historical 'impossibility' of same-sex desire. (2009: 4)

This notion of an 'archive of feeling' and its embodiment of 'impossible desires' allows me finally to approach the task of queering architectural history through a concrete example in the third section of this chapter – by tracing queerness, sexual investments and affective orientations in buildings in order to subvert their official, (hetero)normative narratives. Queering architectural history becomes not only a matter of architecture being understood as a non-human embodiment of queerness, and that queerness always carrying with it sexual desire, but also presupposing architecture as the site of affective relations that are far from overtly and obviously affirmative.

Or, differently put: if reading architecture against the grain to unveil its innate queerness is the main thrust of this project, then affects, feelings and emotions forged in the process should not be pushed too quickly towards the spectrum of resolutions and affirmations. This, I would maintain, is already the starting point for the question of modern architectural historiography, whose roots keep taking us back to the Baroque, as Leach, Macarthur and Lambeke point out, and Lambert takes to one possible extreme when approaching Baroque historiography as literature and fiction. And it is with this final point in mind that I will swerve towards the concrete example of a building, one that carries an archive of my own feelings, some of which can be found in my separate text 'Belgrade Baroque',[1] written in a more literary, genre-evading, queer-loving manner.

Inflection third: queer(ing) Belgrade Baroque

The Cathedral Church of St. Michael the Archangel in Belgrade (*Saborna Crkva Arhangela Mihaila*), Serbia, is a building that couldn't seem further away from any overt notions of queerness. It is an Orthodox Christian church completed in the middle of the nineteenth century, located on an important site of previous churches serving the Serbian community and a potent symbol of the country's increasing independence after centuries of Ottoman rule (Vujović 1996). It can be found in numerous prints, paintings and photographs that were made after it was consecrated in 1845, and it remains an important historical monument in the context of Belgrade to this day. In fact, despite its modest size and relatively unremarkable appearance, it is still a building that dominates the views and representations of central Belgrade's silhouette from its location at the top of the sloping hill overlooking the river Sava near its meeting point with the Danube.

What distinguishes the building is its belfry: the church was conceived in a broadly neoclassical style that combined various period elements, with the belfry clearly displaying its late Baroque lineage. Perceived as the style that would modernize the country's artistic and architectural productions by ushering it away from the heritage of Ottoman rule and into alignment with Central and Western Europe, this form of late Baroque was carried down from Vojvodina, the province north of the Danube that would have formed part of the Austro-Hungarian Empire and lay, for the most part, beyond the reach of the Ottoman Empire. As such, this northern region had an art and architectural history defined by a continuity with Western European and Catholic Christian traditions, and it was here that the transformation of the Baroque into a style used for Serbia's Orthodox Christianity would have taken place, influenced by educational and artistic links to Ukraine in particular and, more broadly, Russia (Jovanović 2012). In that sense, the northern Serbian – and more broadly all Orthodox Christian – Baroque belongs to the still theoretically underexamined trajectory that takes the Baroque, as that 'supraconfessional and genuinely international' style Peter Davidson declares (2007: 2), beyond the realm of Catholicism and into Christian Orthodoxy – a discourse to which Jelena Todorović has made numerous valuable contributions in the context of Serbian art history (see for example 2006, 2017).

In other words, Serbian Baroque of the nineteenth century had a long and convoluted trajectory of development through Orthodox Christianity via numerous regions and across a couple of centuries before it even arrived in Belgrade; and it is a history laden with meanings and interpretations, more convoluted and ambiguous than any developed in the Catholic countries of Europe, or indeed on the transatlantic journeys the style would have taken to arrive to the Americas. As such, Orthodox Christian Baroque was *anomalous* from the very beginning, revealing historical contingencies that went into its making, labelling and sets of associations and affective charges it carried. It is decentred in terms of geography and confessional affiliations, while the myriad inflections and meanings the style carried with it are further 'othered' in the context of Serbia, and Belgrade specifically.

For south of the Danube, where Belgrade lies, the history of the Baroque is still stranger (and paler) than in Vojvodina – even before the arrival of its nineteenth-century iteration embodied in that belfry. The Jesuits would have been present in the city since the seventeenth century, having arrived during one of the several brief exchanges of ownership of the city between the Austrian and Ottoman empires, ushering in elements of Baroque art and culture mostly through the establishment of educational facilities in the city, that is in fairly limited ways. The most substantial, yet utterly elusive, period of Baroque influence and manifestations in the arts and architecture of Belgrade would only arrive during the period of Austrian rule in the early eighteenth century (1717–39) when, in an effort to make the city an important frontier post against the Muslim Ottoman world, Austria developed a series of Baroque urban plans, buildings and contemporary fortification designs, aiming to re-fashion the irregular Ottoman city (Popović 2011). The goal was to bring it in line with the geometrical principles of Baroque urban design coupled with stylistic characteristics manifest in individual buildings, most notably the sizeable Barracks of Charles Alexander of Württemberg. But these plans weren't executed, and the biggest mark on the city was left in the form of contemporary fortifications designed by Nicolas Doxat de Démoret, conceived in keeping with Sebastian Vauban's influential principles of (Baroque) fortification design.

Almost none of this Baroque Belgrade remains. In a more surreal turn of events, as part of the terms of surrender back to Ottoman rule in 1739, it was agreed that Austrian forces would demolish what they had built – the new fortifications to begin with. As for individual buildings, some would be repurposed, some in part demolished, leaving only a single possible example of the architecture of the period of Austrian rule still standing in Belgrade today (and even that one is contested), as well as a few prominent elements that survived in the fortifications.

Which is in part why to speak of a 'Belgrade Baroque' is to speak of something that really doesn't exist, and likely never did – not in any substantial way at least. And yet, as the eponymous exhibition organized by the Belgrade City Museum in 2019 showed (alongside recent publications unaffiliated with it, e.g. Bikić 2019), the interest in this period and the style that gives it its name doesn't wane. If anything, it keeps attracting attention precisely for its spectral character. It could even be said that seventeenth- and eighteenth-century Baroque *haunts* Belgrade to this day: as an unrealized Western European future and a perpetual reminder of an aspiration to escape the Ottoman past by looking westward.

Equally, that nineteenth-century incursion of late Baroque into Belgrade after it had become independent from Ottomans once and for all – embodied in the Cathedral Church of St. Michael the Archangel – would remain similarly elusive, for by the final couple of decades of the century the pan-European national projects would have been in full swing, and with them Serbia's own. As elsewhere, the quest for nationally specific artistic and architectural idioms would result in the re-examination of the country's pre-Ottoman past, specifically via the question of the Orthodox Christian faith, understood in opposition not only to Islam but also to Catholicism. It is at this point that medieval Serbian churches were investigated anew, leading to a modern architectural historiography that stressed links to Byzantium, as well as Serbian cultural distinctions from it. As Aleksandar Ignjatović demonstrates in plentiful detail (2016), this 'Serbo-Byzantine kaleidoscope' would spill into the twentieth century, defining religious architectures of Serbia to this day, as can be seen in the monumental Temple to Saint Sava which was begun in 1935 and is yet to be completed.

The Baroque, understood now not as an international, modernizing style but a specifically Catholic one, would become an inappropriate stylistic choice for the Serbian Orthodox faith and the national identity in which religion plays a central role. Orthodox Christian Baroque became itself an anomaly, impure and malformed, if understandable in terms of how it came to be. In other words, in the context of Serbia the style became slightly, uncomfortably, yet distinctly *perverse*. It remains so to this day.

This leaves the Cathedral Church of St. Michael the Archangel, with its prominent Baroque spire, in the awkward position of being a building of national historical significance, yet one that displays stylistic characteristics more closely associated with the nations of Croatia and Slovenia – those predominantly Catholic former provinces of the Kingdom of Serbs, Croats and Slovenes, which became the Kingdom of Yugoslavia, and then the Socialist Federative Republic of Yugoslavia after the Second World War, together with Bosnia and Hercegovina, Montenegro and Macedonia. The dissolution of that country in the 1990s, with its rabid nationalisms, further deepening of religious and confessional differences, and violent and bloodied insistence on national and historical distinctions, only exacerbates the issue of the way in which the Baroque should be perceived.

As a result, that insignificant Baroque spire – insignificant when observed against a plethora of more exuberant examples, be they European, American or even Russian – remains etched into the sky above central Belgrade like an uneasy, lushly moulded question mark. It is sacred because of its religious function and history, and in its association with that important moment of liberation from the Ottoman Empire; and yet, thanks to the style that is so prominent in its form, it perpetually disturbs its own normative status and ideological functions *from within*. The spire alone destabilizes and deforms dogmatic notions of what a Serbian church should look like, and what is worth foregrounding in Serbian national histories and what should be submerged. It is *of* the nation, yet not of its agreed-upon iconographies; it is *of* religion, yet formed in a language that speaks of another, antagonized confession (Catholicism), even if one equally Christian. It is, in short, consistently and stubbornly *Other* – reminiscent of the otherness of the national self, of identity as such, and of historical and stylistic outcomes which it reveals to be relative. It is a *queer little spire* that can never be erased from the silhouette of Belgrade, since it was there right when the city was forging itself once more as the capital of a free, self-governing country.

Of course, most of this history of the Baroque in Serbia can be examined without recourse to the notion of queerness. Anomalous, problematic, perverse even – any of these terms, which I have used throughout this chapter, would have sufficed to make a similar point: that in the history or Serbian architecture, and the architecture of Belgrade specifically, the Baroque occupies a complex, unresolved place, in part as a result of the history and characteristics of the Baroque in general, in part due to the style's relationship to Orthodox Christianity, and in part due to the specific historical circumstances that define the region.

But if our aim is to *queer architectural histories and historiographies* – and so much of queer history in its material and spatial manifestations remains either confined to a veritable labyrinth of closets or has been downright erased – then the issue becomes one of re-establishing queerness where it is least supposed to reside. This is the realm of all that is normative – and heteronormative in particular – as would be the case with Orthodox Christian religion and its architectures, in this particular example; it is the realm of the historical cannon, especially when said canon is one whose ideological underpinnings are deeply discriminatory and repressive; and it is the question of disturbing the methods of historiography that support such normative constellations and constructions, queering them by introducing aspects of aberrant sexuality, illicit practices and echoes of lives suspended between free access to sanctioned epistemological methods and knowledge-creation that perpetually carries with it traces of otherness. Such an epistemological 'logic of disruption' (Moraña 2005) will need to be utilized alongside all the other weapons in the arsenal we are building – if we want architectural history to reveal itself as the irregular pearl it already is.

Note

1 https://journals.open.tudelft.nl/writingplace/article/view/4350

References

Bikić, V. (ed.) (2019), *Barokni Beograd: Preobražaji 1717-1739 (Baroque Belgrade: Transformation 1717–1739)*, Belgrade: Archaeological Institute.

Booth, M. (1999), 'Campe-Toi! On the Origins and Definitions of Camp', in F. Cleto (ed.), Camp: Queer Esthetics and the Performing Subject, 66–79. Edinburgh: EUP.

Bradway, T. and E. L. McCallum (eds.) (2019), *After Queer Studies: Literature, Theory and Sexuality in the 21st Century*, Cambridge: Cambridge University Press.

Davidson, P. (2007), *The Universal Baroque*, Manchester: Manchester University Press.

Deleuze, G. (1995), *Negotiations, 1972–1990*, New York: Columbia University Press.

Hills, H. (ed.), (2011/2016), *Rethinking the Baroque*, London and New York: Routledge.

Hills, H. (2011/2016), 'The Baroque: The Grit in the Oyster of Art History', in H. Hills (ed.), *Rethinking the Baroque*, 11–36, London and New York: Routledge.

Ignjatović, A. (2016), *U Srpsko-Vizantijskom Kaleidoskopu (In the Serbo-Byzantine Kaleidoscope)*, Belgrade: Orion Art.

Jovanović, M. (2012), *Barok u srpskoj umetnosti (Baroque in Serbian Art)*, Belgrade: Dereta.

Kaup, M. (2019), 'Antinomies of the Twenty-First-Century Neobaroque', in J. D. Lyons (ed.), *The Oxford Handbook of the Baroque*, 148–83, Oxford, England: OUP.

Kotsioris, E. (2020), '"The Queering of Architecture History Has Yet to Happen": The Intra-Canonical Outlook of Beatriz Colomina', *Architectural Histories* 8 (1), 22.

Lambert, G. (2004), *The Return of the Baroque in Modern Culture*, London: Continuum / Bloomsbury Publishing.

Leach, A. (2010), *What is Architectural History?* Cambridge: Polity Press, loc 134.

Leach, A., Macarthur, J. and Delbeke, M. (2015), *The Baroque in Architectural Culture 1880–1980*, London and New York: Routledge.

Love, H. (2009), *Feeling Backward: Loss and the Politics of Queer History*, Cambridge, MA: Harvard University Press.

Moraña, M. (2005), 'Baroque/Neobaroque/Ultrabaroque: Disruptive Readings of Modernity', in N. Spadaccini and L. Martín-Estudillo (eds.), Nashville, TN: Vanderbilt University Press.

Popović, D. (2011), *Beograd u XVII veku: Od 1717. do 1739. (Belgrade in the 18th Century: From 1717 to 1739)*, Belgrade: 3D+.

Todorović, J. (2006/2019), *An Orthodox Festival Book in the Habsburg Empire: Zaharija Orfelin's festive greeting to Mojsej Putnik (1757)*, London and New York: Routledge.

Todorović, J. (2017), *Hidden Legacies of Baroque Thought in Contemporary Literature: The Realms of Eternal Present*, Cambridge: Cambridge Scholars Publishing.

Varnado, C. (2020), *The Shapes of Fancy: Reading for Queer Desire in Early Modern Literature*, Minneapolis: Minnesota University Press.

Vujović, B. (1996), *Saborna Crkva u Beogradu (The Cathedral Church in Belgrade)*, Belgrade: Narodna Knjiga.

Zamora, L. P. and M. Kaup (eds.) (2010), *Baroque New Worlds: Representation, Transculturation, Counterconquest*, Durham and London: Duke University Press.

4

Notes from transient spaces, anachronic times[*]

An architextural exercise

Ece Canlı

1

Still. My fingertips are forced to sculpt these words[1] by the fault current of thoughts flowing[2] out of my skin,[3] yet there is a screeching distance unfolding between my senses and the sensible, called time.[4] I cannot but behold as it unfurls like a palimpsest: beneath every passing instant resurfaces a memory,[5] overlapping with an earlier reminiscence and joining to the very instant that has just elapsed. This snowballing medley of recollections follows me everywhere I walk now, like a cloud of spectres projected on the walls[6] of this place, called home.[7] Home, a sequel to many other homes.

---

[1] This text offers an amalgamation of personal and theoretical reflections on (socio)spatiality, material reconfigurations of the body in built environments and the politics of corporeal segregation, recounted from the perspective of design and queer[i] materiality. Taking a critical look at various human-made environments, it discusses how normatively designed spaces are inhabited by 'different' bodies differently and how some of these bodies get disoriented or punished when not fitting in these spaces. As a counter-narrative, it simultaneously sketches out possible frictions in the use and disuse of these spaces, which would carve out

other forms of co-existence in material surroundings. In doing so, however, instead of writing *about* spatial design by assuming words and things as discrete phenomena, this material-discursive[ii] exercise embarks on writing *through* designed spaces, letting matters and discourses simultaneously organize each other in order to 'proliferate, spread and generate unforeseeable effects [and affects], far beyond the intentions of the architect' and of the writer (Gabrielsson et al. 2019: 5). In this form of writing, the narrator (me), together with the reader (you), traverses, absorbs and disgorges these places, as a diffracted method of rethinking spaces we design and are designed for.

[i] While the term 'queer' still predominantly refers to bodies whose genders, sexualities, desires, emotions and ways of being resist hetero-cisnormativity and challenge binary confines of identities, the theory, expanded by intersectionality, decolonial thought and other fields of inquiry, arrived at a more nuanced understanding of queer as 'embodied and discursive complexity' (Bryant 2015: 263). This understanding urges that gender, sexuality and other identity categories, including race, ethnicity, class and and ability, are not mutually exclusive but interlaced axes of a bigger matrix of power, deeply rooted in patriarchy and ongoing forms of colonial capitalism. My take on queer(ing) is thereby not only about 'challenging bodily restrictions as well as normative spaces' (Schalk and Reisinger 2017: 344) but also about unsettling, interrupting and and undoing the apparatuses of this matrix. I see it as a political potential and a dissident form of world-making, like a skeleton key that slowly accesses each axis to rot the hegemonic machine *ab intra*.

[ii] I consider design and architectural practices as material-discursive phenomena, since 'the relationship between the material and the discursive is one of mutual entailment' in such a way that words and languages reproduce matters while materiality configures discourses – so the meaning emerges (Barad 2003: 822). This premise brings forward the importance of *writing through space* as a political practice and a method which constructs, deconstructs and and transmits the very real material effects and synaesthesia – just like design practices themselves (Frichot 2010; Crawford 2015).

[2] This leaking current oozes out in different directions and, inevitably, interrupts the flow of writing, while generating a new typology in the architecture of the text and the performance of reading. Such textural configuration consists of two discrete yet interdependent parts: body text and footnote. The body text consists of several diary entries written in the first person, registered from a specific time and place the author occupies.[iii] The entries explore poetic and literary dimensions of writing, by navigating through various factual and fictional spaces evoked by the author's memories,[iv] experiences and and second-hand knowledge, all

of which offer 'a critique to the humanist tradition of objectivity, while encouraging the author to discuss one's own subject-position, including one's own sexuality, in a specific space and time' (Pilkey, Scicluna and and Gorman-Murray 2015: 130). In the meantime, these merely subjective contemplations are exhausted by footnotes to give theoretical accounts of certain spaces, concepts and and histories. By employing this structure, the text aims to confront the norms of academic writing where the body text hosts formal, chronological and and analytical information often supported by renowned authorities, while the footnote remains a marginal site for supplementary information, personal reflections and and lesser-known sources. In this text, the status of the 'disseminator of knowledge' is relegated to the periphery, while the peripheral itself is scattered as kaleidoscopic pieces of information which prima facie seem discontinuous and unrelated, yet interconnect each other in a fractal way and together form a multifaceted comprehension of queerness and spatiality – like puzzle pieces. This literary, performative and and material-discursive method is central to the text's contribution to the ongoing endeavour of queering architectural configurations.

ⁱⁱⁱ The diary fragments were written between June 2020 and March 2021 during coronavirus lockdowns which informed the tone of the text and further emphasize the importance of time-, space- and and context-specificity of writing.

ⁱᵛ I draw from similar techniques that were used by other queer feminist scholars, including Audre Lorde, who called it *biomythography* – referring to the fusion of history, biography and myth and Gloria Anzaldúa, who wrote *autohistorias*, giving theoretical-narrative accounts of herself between prose and poetry, fantasy and reality. Such form of theorizing – writing-as-researching, writing-as-walking, writing-as-inhabiting – is yet another method to grasp our affective relationships with our designed environments.

³ The endeavour of writing *through* designed spaces entails starting off with the skin which is not only the primary matter that demarcates the boundaries between one's body and the space but itself a 'bodyscape' – an affective aperture between bodies and worlds. In the last decades, while architectural and affect theorists have mainly challenged the conventional reading of the skin as the mere container and exoskeleton of the body just like a façade of a building,ᵛ queer feminist scholars have discussed 'the fleeting yet persistent surface of the skin as the product of interrelations' (Kokoula 2017: 16). Feminist scholar Sara Ahmed (2004: 90) explains this interrelation with the notion of 'stickiness', which is not an inherent quality of a skin or a surface but 'an effect of the histories of contact between bodies, objects and signs'. This suggests that the iterative proximities and contacts between surfaces (of bodies, objects, words, spaces) generate material-discursive signs like derogatory

names or spaces that exclude certain bodies, which, in time, adhere to
and thicken the skins of these bodies (Kokoula 2017). In these conditions, although these seemingly ontologically different entities are considered inseparable and intermingled[vi] (Stafford and Volz 2016; Kokoula
2017), their social, functional and symbolic status become solidified.
This concept also disavows the assumption that gender, sexuality, race
and other identities precede our material surroundings and that design
is just a neutral add-on, proving instead that identities and materialities
are co-created and co-solidified in a constant entangled act of sticking.
My premise here is that undermining this misconception is contingent
upon rethinking the skin-body as penetrable, diffusive and processual,
which changes shape in constant 'becoming' to be never fully crystallized
and completed, just like an unfinished space that is open for unexpected
modifications (Stafford and Volz 2016; Kokoula 2017). Thus, taking into
account spatio-corporeal knowledge of queer and trans* bodies who are
not only 'transient figurations 'of' a material milieu [. . .] in permanent
reconfiguration' but also the agents of transformation of these milieus is
a start for a radical reconceptualization of architecture (Gorny and Van
den Heuvel 2017: 6).

[v] Analogy between the body and building or 'body-as-house' still prevails in mainstream architecture, comparing skins to walls, veins to
conduits, windpipes to vent pipes, orifices to doors and with today's
smart home technologies, brain to hardwired systems. However, this
human-machine-architecture configuration continues to speak from a
rather modernist functionalism and discards what this technosomatic
translation begets.[a] Today the romantic 'body-as-home' discourse is
proved partial, as the privileged experience of 'feeling at home in one's
skin' is contingent upon this body's legitimacy and acceptance by society and law – thereby upon its gender, sexuality, race, class and other
traits (Bryant 2015; Crawford 2015).

[vi] The entanglement of skin (body), architectural space and
technologies calls out philosopher Paul Preciado's (2012: 122)
renowned paradigm shift called 'pharmaco-porn-power' vis-à-vis the
nineteenth century's 'biopower', a term Foucault coined to explain
how gendered, sexualized and racialized subjects were reproduced
through not only punitive, corrective and surveillance technologies
from statistics to demographics to public hygiene but also spatial
distribution and disciplinary architectures (i.e. hospitals, asylums,
schools, prisons, barracks etc.) Preciado (2012: 125) argues that
from the Cold War era onwards, biopower's spatial distributions that
used to reinvent bodies (including homo/heterosexuality, criminality
and otherness) have transformed into pharmaco-porn-power in
which architecture and bodies do not only reproduce each other but
also diffuse into one another through 'biomolecular' and 'somatic-

semiotic-technical' apparatuses as the new currencies of sexual, racial and gendered subjects with DNA samples, cells, endocrinological techniques and chemical prostheses. In this regime, architecture turns into 'liquid' places which are not only inhabited by us but live within us organically, operating from within, through atoms, molecules and electrons. In this dystopic formulation, however, lies not only submission to such techno-power but also resistance. The tools and possibilities of Preciado's 'pharmacopornographic' era, with its surgical and endocrinal tools reclaimed by trans* activism and employed to play with the body's transient, flexible and uncanny nature, open doors for manipulating the body and its given sexual, social and reproductive abilities. The possibility of bodies in constant transformation and in transition can also propose a 'radically embodied conception of architecture' by disrupting the stability of architectural construction (Gorny and Van den Heuvel 2017: 4). In this approach, architecture can at least 'survive as critical practice and micropolitical action' (Preciado 2012: 130).

[a] Poet and scholar Lucas Crawford's (2015) critical look at plumbing as a metaphor for genitalia-based hygiene in modernist architecture unravels how this gender-unnatural construction is inescapably linked to trans* bodies.

[4] Temporality's co-dependent, contingent and yet erratic relationship with spatiality suggests that although the prevalent orchestration of time in modern societies – predicated on enforced productivity accomplishment and linearity – dictates an artificial synchronization between chronological time and the expansion of space, bodies that do not follow this normative spatiotemporality might experience time and space differently, in an inverse proportionality or even in dissonance. The chronotope of capitalist and patriarchal modernity draws a temporal continuum of heterosexual coupledom, marriage, reproduction and palliative death, accompanied by a prolific career, car, house, land and stocks (Halberstam 2005; Freeman 2010). While queer temporalities rupture this 'chrononormativity' (Freeman 2010) by syncing out of normative family-, home- and world-making models, today's 'self-neutralizing straight time', along with efficiency-oriented currency and obsession with presentness, goes beyond the question of intimacy and reproduction (Halberstam 2005; Muñoz 2009). Our material surroundings (i.e. workplaces, building estates, public facilities) are designed increasingly for continuous circulation to prevent 'losing time'[vii] and to compartmentalize time into genders, ages and abilities, against which queer temporality can resist with 'asynchrony, anachronism . . . delay, ellipsis . . . hysteron proteron and pause' (Freeman 2010: xxii).

[vii] The idea of 'catching time' reached its peak with the pandemic-driven virtual dependency which has made us squeeze much more online activity in a single time-space configuration than ever before,

demanding more rush, less leeway and unconditional 'availability' to be present in more than one place at once. It is concerning how this new 'normalized' time-lapse imposed by 'institutional forces come to seem like somatic facts' (Freeman 2010: 3).

[5] I consider these superimpositions (gathering different times – past, present, future – in one single space; and different spaces – interior, exterior, imaginary – at a time) an important method to theorize and practice designing. Anachronistic amalgamations can break the progression-oriented linearity of history and turn the chronopolitics of spatial experiences into patchworks, which can expose the interrelation between bodies, spaces and events that are oftentimes deemed sporadic.

[6] While the raison d'être of a wall, akin to skin,[3] is to constitute the body-scape of a building and capture the otherwise hovering air into a definitive volume for sheltering, securing and providing for its inhabitants, walls can also immure bodies indefinitely into solidified airs (e.g. penitentiaries and detention centres) or they can leave them unguarded (e.g. borders and homelessness). Just like dividing a space into compartments, erecting a wall in a field – like frontiers and barricades with barbed wires – also means that some bodies experience the materiality of these walls more than others – like queers, trans* and differently abled bodies, immigrants, sex workers, drug addicts and elderlies (Ahmed 2017; Preciado 2017). Moreover, some of these walls are deemed rather intangible and even non-existent since they are reduced to a mere metaphor. Sara Ahmed (2017) calls them 'brick walls', against which an individual bangs their head every time they come to an impasse in tackling institutional (i.e. academia, profession, politics, law) hegemonies that enforce heteronormativity, whiteness and unacted diversity. However, these physical, social and political barriers are omnipresent and the more walls thicken and proliferate like skins, the harder it gets for bodies to suffuse into spaces organically; which means that pondering on walls entails not only reifying them but also dismantling[viii] them symbolically, discursively and literally.

[viii] Queer scholar Jack Halberstam (2018, 2020), drawing on the works of anarchitects from the 1970s, propounds that 'collapsing' serves as a potential queer method; not the outcome of it but the very moment of a structure being about to fall. Such collapse is a rather active one, which gives space for contemplation and reconciliation between the moment of suspension and total dismantlement.

[7] The question 'what makes a house a "home"?' has long concerned architects and designers, especially those who sought to drift from standardized and functional understanding of domicile to affective customization that yields attachment, safety and 'belonging'.[ix] This seemingly innocuous pursuit prevails today yet still promotes (hetero) sexualization, cisnormativity and nuclear family as a continuation of

the twentieth century's domestic arrangements. Precisely due to this overcharged yet tamed intimacy confined in cohabitation, for some, home signifies not only a haven but also unsafety, abuse, danger and a place one fears to go to (Anzaldúa 1987; 2002; Halberstam 2018). Then the question shifts to 'what makes a home for those who cannot fit in and wish to elude those household structures exposing them to repression, rejection and violence?' – *or what is queer about home?* In most cases, misfitting bodies venture out to grow, sometimes for such a long time that 'home' becomes the search itself. From a couch 'situated in the "public" space of friends' private homes' to squats, for moving bodies – or bodies in motion – 'in-betweenness' becomes both a condition of homemaking and a form of homecoming[x] (Bryant 2015: 282). That various forms of cohabitation, kinship, intimacy, care, belonging and ownership emerge throughout such transitions[xi] is itself a queer response to today's incessant real estate industry that keeps consolidating upper-middle-class prosperity, corporate wealth, land handover and displacement of marginalized communities. On the other hand, the idea of bodies in a constant refuge and flux as a counter-narrative should not be romanticized, since this is not to deny that nonconforming bodies too need access to housing, settlement and comfort.[xii] Nor does inhabiting a house necessarily mean complying with heteronormativity and conservatism; instead complex dynamics of domesticity allow non-normative occupants – including polyamorists, sex workers, bachelors and diasporic families – to experiment with different arrangements of intimacy, friendship, partnership and parenthood, through new spatial and sexual arrangements (Pilkey, Scicluna and Gorman-Murray 2015; Bryant 2015).

[ix] Scholar Jason Bryant (2015: 263) suggests that 'like "home", we can imagine queer as a concept of be/longing. For, to "be" queer is to be just who one is. And to "long" is to imagine, to pine for or to claim agency as a creative practice.'

[x] This concept of home as 'provisional, impermanent and mobile' (Byrant 2015: 274) also confirms that 'homes can move, as we do'[b] (Ahmed 2006: 9).

[xi] On the other hand, for forcedly displaced immigrants, asylum seekers and ethnic minorities, living in constant transition might be a turmoil, as they can be stripped of rights to housing, schooling and healthcare anytime. Similarly, gender-nonconforming and queer folks are at disproportionally higher risks of experiencing homelessness, due to not only familial and occupational rejections and the lack of financial support thereof which plunge them into criminalized lines of work but also landlords' refusal to rent rooms (Bryant 2015; Canlı 2017).

[xii] It is important to note that access to housing does not entail possession, although the successful inducement of neoliberal capitalism to

house ownership, property income and mortgage futures indicates otherwise. I question though whether it is possible to talk about 'queering housing' without taking into account that 'wealth, most significantly in the form of home ownership, supersedes income as an indicator of disparities between [especially] racial groups' and underpins unequal distribution of resources (Tuck and Yang 2012: 24). Construction – and renovation – of inherited houses on inherited lands (largely seized from Indigenous peoples), which has become the hallmark of the urban and rural landscape of the twenty-first century, means also inheritance of (mostly white and affluent) heteropatriarchal family traditions which marks a paradox with the endeavourendeavour of queering. Can we practice, then, housing that is not predicated on 'middle-class prosperity', 'a (tax) shelter for the rich', and 'new modes of exploitation' (Halberstam 2018)?

[b] As Butler (2014[1992]: 187) aptly suggests, 'a house is the people you walk with.'

2

My feet shuffle over the doorsill, entering into the bleakness of the 6000Kelvin fluorescent lights attached to the mirror that exposes every single wrinkle settling in my skin.[3] The reflection, gloss and dampness of this 3 m^2 room conjure another place of contrast; that 6 m^2 boiling container[8] where my twenty-year-younger self is meeting her first aberrant carnal desires. In the abyss of the mirror, I see my mother's twenty-year-younger unapproving eyebrows and silver tongue looming in my crow's feet, piercing right through my eyes – 'you are grounded!' This bathroom[9] now stinks[10] of a heap of uncleansed yet this time docile intimacies; some glued on metal fixtures, some reverberated off the tiles, some slipped through the air well.

[8] Such ephemeral space, as host for diverse bodies and intimacies, posits a twisting alternative to the traditional bourgeois home as the nest of heterostatic sexual intimacy. A dull matchbox-size container, activated only seasonally, can create a temporary sanctuary out of stifling aluminium finishings and pinhole windows, for two bodies dissolving together. This act of temporal place-making can be considered a production of 'fictional, metaphorical and exceptional spaces within an actual place for a brief span of time' *for, by* and *through* queer bodies (Schalk and Reisinger 2017: 345). Moreover, it is the very condition of heteronormativity that forces these bodies to construct such physical, virtual and imaginary spaces and build provisional homes in which they can 'be/long' (Bryant 2015). These transient, one-off and inherently queer spaces[xiii] can also be considered palimpsestic since each experience

is inscribed on another, as the place absorbs the memories[5] of its hosts and the way their traces 'remain to mark certain spaces for others – to their delight or discomfort – to discover' (Reed 1996: 64). The challenge of a counterhegemonic designer/architect is then twofold: the first is to undertake the impossible task of 'designing' such transient spaces that remain ephemeral and accessible to bodies who cannot afford 'spa tourism'; the second is to turn fixed places into not-taken-for-granted transitory spaces.

[xiii] I am cautious about using the term 'queer space', as its meaning has been altered, contested and denied over times and geographies. From the 1990s on, while queer space – from clubs, pubs, cabarets, bathhouses and parks – has been used to refer to sites of pleasure and affinity where marginalized genders and sexualities can find refuge and socialize, it has also been deemed an oxymoron, since a 'queer space' is 'imminent' (Reed 1996; Gorny and Heuvel 2017). What intrigues me in this discussion is not 'whether certain spaces can be called queer or not' or 'whether we can design queer spaces by using dominant architectural methods',[c] which has the tendency to reduce the potential of 'queer spaces' into a design project. Nor do I suggest that we can 'put some places to queer use' 'by relying on a container conception of space' instead of considering the 'interrelational reciprocity between embedded configurations of bodies and matter' (Gorny and van den Heuvel 2017: 1). I am rather interested in the 'transformative potential of queerness in relation to architecture [which] resides in its call to envision space as a collective and layered environment constantly being reperformed' (Vallerand 2018: 143). This potential indicates less of a 'permanent, stable and material' space and more of an 'expanded strategy for interrogating' places to 'challenge behaviours, rules, expectations and situations framed by the built environment' (Pavka 2020).

[c] Audre Lorde's (2007[1984]) oft-quoted maxim 'the master's tools will never dismantle master's house' is relevant to architecture today more than ever.

[9] In this case, a private 'home' engenders another private space within: a bathroom guaranteeing that one's faeces and urine are securely flushed away. Bathroom, as a promise of 'moving the dirt away', materialized through infrastructural configurations ranging from sewage systems to plumbing and flushing as the hallmark of the nineteenth-century European bourgeoisie fortified by industrial design, has been a significant place for reproduction of bodily hygiene and purity (Cavanagh 2010; Penner 2013). The entrance of the modern European bathroom into the public sphere[xiv] resulted in sex-segregation of these spaces based on biological dimorphism, which has been constitutive of and constituted by heterosexual masculinity based on 'imperative separation of genitality

and anality, of urine and shit' (Preciado 2017: 16). Preciado (2017: 16) argues that the entire architectural arrangement of bathrooms (i.e., urinals, stalls, mirrors) is to reproduce not only the essential anatomical difference between women and men but also gender roles, by stressing that 'whereas the bathroom of women is a reproduction of domestic space in the middle of a public space, the men's bathrooms are a fold of public space intensifying the eyes of visibility, where the erect position reaffirms public space as a masculine space'. This space, then, is the locus of surveiling, disciplining and 'fixing' bodies that appear, sound and behave outside the binary disposition of heterocissexuality, where trans*, gender-nonconforming and visibly queer bodies are frequently exposed to gender policing, harassment and violence (Cavanagh 2010; Bender-Baird 2015). In recent years, sanitary sex-segregation which compels people to use only public bathrooms that match their genders assigned at birth has sparked a number of manifestations, boycotts, public debates and design solutions for 'gender-neutral' queered[xv] bathrooms worldwide. On the other hand, there is a risk in limiting the queer potential of sanitary practices to gender-neutrality. It is important to be cognisant that the very ethnocentric and bourgeois conceptions of purity, hygiene and whiteness reified by design (infra)structures cannot be reduced to isolating stalls or changing pictograms on bathroom doors. One needs also to delve into systemic problems such as the experience of consecutive uses of these public bathrooms by multiple users; gaze, control, access, prevailing standardizations; '"pure" functionality of unadorned architecture' that passes 'as normal and harmless as the normative, straight, white, able and middle-class', and these places' 'disciplinary, individualizing and interiorizing force' (Crawford 2015: 62–5). Taking on different bodily parts and movements (i.e., squatting, standing, stretching, sitting, opening, closing) and imagining that these 'individual' and private faeces eventually merge with the others' and flood together through sewers and pipes can be good ways to demystify both dirt and genitalia. As Preciado (2017: 15) provokingly asks: 'why not inquire whether one will urinate or defecate and if so, is it diarrhea? Nor is anyone interested in the colour or the size of the fecal matter'.

[xiv] This techno-spatial refinement was disseminated not only in public space but all across the world, especially to [ex-]colonies as a project of 'tidying up' the 'innately dirty natives', even if the climate, rainfall patterns, cultural habits and 'ways of peeing' differed in these territories (Penner 2013). Those who benefited from this 'sanitary imperialism' (Penner 2013: 34) have been settlers, upper-class natives, white, abled and heterocissexual bodies, while the nonconforming rest has remained linked to 'dirt, disease and public danger' (Cavanagh 2010: 7). Setting normative bodies apart from those 'filthy others' by design (i.e., differentiated water closets, signs and placements), which

has been the 'normal feature of colonial sanitary arrangements', has immensely mingled sex-based segregation with race-based segregation not only during the Jim Crow laws in the U.S. but also today in various countries such as South Africa (Penner 2013: 256).

[xv] It is also postulated that public bathrooms and stalls are highly sexualized and already 'queer' spaces where cruising, congregating and sexual intimacy take place; however, these acts mostly occur temporarily under perilous conditions after which the space remains heterostatic.

[10] In such 'publicly privatized' places, visual appearance is the main facet that triggers 'social anxiety', while other sensory information – olfactory and acoustic – are wished away as if these senses are not part of the same bodyspace ecology (Preciado 2017: 16). This contradiction is firmly linked to the spatial management of hygiene inherited from modernism which aims at reducing any optical interaction with the dirt to a minimum, to the extent that the body is treated as ontologically different not only from its surrounding spaces but also from its own bodily waste. However, while the intention of 'dispatching the dirt and making it invisible' prevails, the idealization of the flush, as sending the dirt to the land 'away' is finally demystified, since we now see and read that our collective waste gets together and 'goes to the Pacific Ocean or the wastewater treatment facility' (Morton 2013: 32; in Kokoula 2017: 14). This bodily waste being diffused first into the bathroom, then into the ocean, then to air and to food once again stresses the 'constant and uncontrollable nexus of interdependences between the body and its surrounding space' (Morton 2013; in Kokoula 2017: 14), thereby the connection between physical spaces and larger infrastructural arrangements causing environmental injustice. Moreover, shelving or crowding out the 'dirt' to places where it is not seen is akin to sending away people who are treated as 'shit' (Crawford 2015) – not only trans* bodies using 'wrong' bathrooms but also those 'who are not worth being visible', so doomed to outskirts, ghettos and prisons. A queer take on architecture is, then, that of ontological design: not merely concentrating on the final outcome as separate, but reconsidering the infra-/supra-structural connections between things that design us back.

3

Standby. Stacked with shadowy figurines, unfinished sketchbooks and sundry other bric-a-bracs,[11] this dusky corridor[12] lies ahead of me to be crossed, while billions of whirling dust particles twinkle shyly, blur my sight, stick to my tongue and drift me off to the kitchen.[13] A visceral shortcut. A gastric expansion. I land in an as-hollow-as-my-stomach kitchenette somewhere North, where my fifteen-year-younger and expatriated self is trying to prove herself 'cool', embarrassed with her cabinet of spices, pickle-stained worktop and sun-dried victuals dangling around and exposing her 'roots'. But waywardness[14] overrides coolness. I open the cupboards wide. I let the gaze and the dust penetrate. I dive into the sink brimmed with dishwater and let myself flood.

[11] The idea that a space is considered 'designed' not due to its sheer structural composition – its surfaces and substructure – but to its coalescence with artefacts, colours, textures[xvi] and paraphernalia through which we orient[xvii] ourselves in the world entails a multi-layered approach to spatial design. If signs stick to bodies and matters simultaneously and rhizomatically, it means that normativity is thoroughly embedded not only in spaces but also in every single material configuration filling them (i.e., clothes, furniture, consumer goods, sanitary products and electronic devices). This complex designer siege obliges us, then, to start 'queering' with artifacts, by transfiguring, undesigning, reversing, re-appropriating or misusing them (Canlı 2017).

[xvi] In discussions around gendered, sexualized and racialized objects, it is more common to address either mere functionalism that reinforces strict anatomical differences between man and woman or the symbolism of visual codes, from colours (i.e., pink/blue, black/white) to forms (i.e., straight/amorphous, square/circle). Both of these approaches overlook the importance of texture, which is just 'as thoroughly imbricated in gender and sexual norms' and in the processes of 'gendering and sexualizing of the haptic' (Crawford 2020). Crawford draws our attention to textures being perniciously gender-charged (i.e., soft/hard, smooth/shaggy), as they emerge only through a tangible touch or a 'suggestion of contact' of (normatively or non-normatively) gendered bodies. Just like Sara Ahmed's (2004) bodies and objects that together become sticky[3], textures are 'palpable only in becoming', only in relationality, only through contact. It becomes particularly important in architectural texts that delineate spaces by using textures, which create real 'haptic stimulus' and 'synaesthesia'[ii] that go beyond the 'sensory limits of textuality' (Crawford 2020; Frichot 2010). This is to say, it is not only the material things we touch and get touched by that shape our textural memories but also their verbal, textual and discursive characterizations which circulate in our tactile world.

[xvii] In her work on queer phenomenology, Sara Ahmed (2006) describes orientation as being directed toward objects, spaces and bodies, as finding our way in the world and feeling at home. She observes that not only how we move but also 'how "what" we think "from" is an orientation device'. Thus, how this device can orient certain bodies (i.e., white, male, upper-class, able) better, thereby place them in the

world safer than others is the crux of the matter (Ahmed 2006: 4). That 'the experience of space and location is not the same' (hooks 2000: 205) for certain bodies means that these bodies are less oriented or 'disoriented', as they cannot fit and find themselves in the 'designed' world. Yet, for a queer body, this state of unremitting disorientation is also a place of imagination and creativity, since it entails a continuous redirection, experimentation and rearrangement of material and socio-spatial conditions.

12 Although corridors are mostly instrumental attachments between two distinct and central points – as places of *passing*, their 'in-betweenness', being neither the point of departure nor arrival, opens up for possibilities that convey both the extension and the clarity of tunnel vision. In worlds where privacy is a privilege, corridors serve as sites of intimacy, socialization and interaction (i.e., tenement houses, dorms) (Hartman 2019); in worlds where settlement in seized lands is inconceivable, they serve as bridges. For Anzaldúa (2002: 1), bridges, as 'liminal spaces between worlds' are thresholds 'to other realities, archetypal, primal symbols of shifting consciousness' where transformations take place. For her, some people – like queers, the colonized, women and outsiders – not only 'pass by' but 'live in' these bridges, which means a 'constant state of displacement'; thus, despite their discomfort, ambiguity and vulnerability, they can also become a 'home' that is dislodged and estranged. Moreover, even though bridges, which she considers as *borderlands*, signify compassion, reconciliation and 'a promise to be present with the pain of others without losing themselves to it', they change and decay, therefore a collapse is inevitable and acceptable (Anzaldúa 2002: 4). Queer and non-complying bodies can experience these zones as transient spaces where the private and the social intermingle and transparency merges with opacity. All in all, regardless of whether they are called corridors, hallways, borderlands or margins, such decentralized positions 'provide a glimpse of a methodology that dislocates the colonising traversals of thresholds' (herising 2005: 146). A corridor, as a metaphorical and literal tool to rethink spatiality, enables receiving the knowledge of those who come from outside and producing knowledge within one's own locus, thereby having multiple perspectives about the materiality of oppression (Anzaldúa 1987).

13 The kitchen, as yet another keystone of modernism, has long been – and for many, still is – one of the main loci for the reproduction of monogamous heterosexuality, female domesticity, servitude and invisible labour. Even more, for certain bodies such as enslaved and racialized women, the kitchen has been a site of heartbreak and trauma and 'contained a "whole social history", not only of racism and servility, but sexual use and violation' (Hartman 2019: 206). On the other hand, it has also been a place for these women and 'othered' bodies to congregate and claim

their agency, integrity and power. Thus, without erasing such cruel spatial memories of the past but learning from them, can we see the kitchen as a zone of reclamation and resistance? Indeed, for many activists in different times and spaces – from 1980's *Kitchen Table Press* run by Audre Lorde and Barbara Smith to today's queer diasporas in Western cities – kitchens and especially kitchen tables, have been crucial sites where mobilization, empowerment and disobedience take place, especially in times where marginalized bodies are increasingly denied access to public spaces and public deliberation due to gentrification, disenfranchisement and xeno/trans/homophobia (Haritaworn 2015). Such a contextual transposition and appropriation of an otherwise burdensome space is a way of queering, a method not merely for design, but for survival.

[14] Waywardness, as being 'away' from the 'ward'; 'ward' as 'in direction to', 'tendency towards' or being 'oriented'.[xxi] Waywardness signifies digressing from the 'designed' path, going astray or disusing the common path. The wayward body is a body that goes against the odds and the norms; that is 'willing to get in the way' of 'problems', thereby deemed wilful (Ahmed 2017: 66). On the other hand, waywardness is also 'the paradox of cramped creation, the entanglement of escape and confinement, flight and captivity' (Hartman 2019: 227). Being wayward within one's material surroundings means 'the directionless search for a free territory', 'a *beautiful experiment* in how-to-live', and a fugitive survival strategy (Hartman 2019: 228). It is a queer disposition, an insurgent method – like that of this text – through which the wilful designer/architect/thinker/theorist can undertake to retrieve what has long been silenced, marginalized and demolished.

4

Inside out. The last sunbeams of the day fall on my beloved plants and turn this room into an amber-green haven, like those summer cafés on the peripheries[15] where my families who are bound 'not by blood but affinity' feel 'home'.[7] I would be that reckless if this rainbowish gamut of colourcolours casting on my carpet wasn't as confined[16] as those rainbow flags fluttering 6,000 miles away, where the other half of my heart beats. I would, if the silhouettes of those unreachable miles, hours and bodies didn't become my new *ombromanic* wallpaper. I would, if the windows of my terrace were so transparent[17] as to show me a horizon other than the infinite landscape of the tower cranes. I would, if in was out.

[15] Periphery is not only a phenomenological concept, but a spatio-political category, as its existence depends entirely on centrality, while the conditions of those on the periphery (i.e., bodies, objects, spaces,

ideas and desires) depend on the gestures of those in the centre. What the majority of architectural practices operating in the centre today do is reinforce this dependency and enlarge the gap between these two hierarchal positions. Spatial underpinning of segregative practices such as gentrification, privatization and criminal justice system functions like a huge social centrifuge which constantly pushes already marginalized bodies to further margins; to suburbs, urban ghettos, outskirts and out of sight. Beside such socio-material peripheries, there are also epistemic ones that bodies from 'other' worlds hail from, vis-à-vis the centrality of Euroamerican epistemology, as 'the downtown' of academic knowledge production. Even in the context of relatively marginal subject matters, such as 'queering architecture'. the vast majority of theoretical and empirical research, as well as features and articles in renowned architectural magazines originate in and thereby speak of 'First World' metropolises. It is not that gender, sexuality and identity-based spatial struggles and reflections do not take place elsewhere, but that they remain either 'too marginal' or face the obstacle of lingua franca and the whiteness of citational practices (Ahmed 2017). To resist creating monocultures and thickened skins,[3] by neither denying nor romanticizing marginality, it is important to remember that they are 'both sites of repression and sites of resistance' (hooks 2000: 207). Hence, instead of striving to reach and appeal to the centre, a counterhegemonic endeavourendeavour of thinking and 'writing *through* architecture'[1] is to apprehend and nurture the knowledge of the periphery as a form of marginal 'textural orientation' (Crawford 2020).

[16] Although 'confinement' has become an everyday condition for masses during the pandemic, for many ordinary citizens it also meant 'being confined at home'.[7] This emergency-driven temporary confinement has, however, overshadowed the other urgency-driven structural confinement of masses, namely, prisons.[xviii] Recent decades have witnessed an increasing number of incarcerations worldwide, which were not mounted in direct proportion to crime rates but to heavier law enforcement and criminalization of marginalized groups, including queer and trans* bodies, racial and ethnic minorities and under-class populations. The issue of 'queer incarceration', a term that refers both to the imprisonment of queer bodies and to their interminable criminalization before, during and after they are put behind bars, has thus become more relevant than ever. While the brutality of prisons and detention centres is by many still not regarded as a 'design problem', designers, architectural firms and private-public stakeholders keep reaping the fruits of this industrialized criminal justice system, as a 'major business opportunity' of the twentieth and twenty-first centuries – by means of not only buildings, facilities and security technologies but also thousands of goods manufactured *for* prison interiors and *by* prisoner labour (Swan 2013). Meanwhile,

material effects[xix] of these extremely disciplined, controlled, segregated and isolated places are much heavier for queer, trans* and gender-nonconforming bodies – doubled if they do not belong to 'upper' racial and ethnic strata. Although architects and designers of these spaces do not take accountability for reifying the violence and claim their task-oriented impartiality, their contribution remains paramount (Swan 2013; Canlı 2017). Moreover, in the last decades, there has been a tendency to build 'less cruel' and 'more humane' prisons, along with new surveillance technologies for public space to allegedly prevent crimes, heralded by big firms with their affirmative designs. These seemingly good-willed intentions, however, continue to justify and consolidate the existence of spatial punitive justice. I thereby propound that 'queering [prison] architecture' is an oxymoron as long as these buildings serve as cages and as long as they are reformed instead of abolished.

[xviii] This is not to compare the physical and psychological effects of different types of confinement, but to draw attention to bodies under different spatial conditions.

[xix] In most countries and states, a trans* woman who has not undergone sex reassignment surgery or obtained a 'valid' ID authenticating her gender is confined in all-male prisons, based on her biological sex. On the other hand, a gay male inmate, whose sex and gender match, gets exposed to homophobic violence when he is put in an all-male prison. Solitary confinement is also a common practice where incarcerated gender and sexual minorities are put in total isolation, being stripped of human contact, social activity, medical assistance and access to basic goods, which marks permanent physical and physiological scars on these bodies (Spade 2012; Shay and Strader 2012). Moreover, they are more exposed to rape, sexual abuse and hostility both by other inmates and by law enforcement officers. Such maltreatments are mostly justified with the notion that they have been placed in the 'wrong prison' – like being in the 'wrong bathroom'[9] (Spade 2012; Shay and Strader 2012). These experiences, amplified by clothing politics and limited access to sanitary and grooming products, are not merely a concern of law and politics but also design practices.

[17] The concept of 'transparency', and thereby visibility, has been the hallmark of twentieth-century gay liberation in the West, for which coming out of the closet, expressing one's sexual identity and engaging in activism were deemed virtues. However, for 'othered' queers, including ethnic minorities, immigrant youth and 'overtly' trans* bodies, visibility has also been a trap due to issues around cultural affirmation, ethnic targeting and genderphobia (Haritaworn 2015; Mack 2017). This is one of the reasons why clubs, cabarets and raves have been sacred havens for uncloseted safety-seeking queers. On the other hand, even though today more sexual minorities manifest their identities openly, especially in 'the

urban centres of a handful of global cities' (Pilkey, Scicluna and Gorman-Murray 2015: 130), the number of queer-friendly spaces has been in decline (Anderson and Knee 2020). This is the consequence not only of unrelenting gentrification processes that effaced alternative venues and of increasing social acceptance of sexual minorities but also of emerging location-based online applications which have proliferated insomuch as they replace physical networks of connection, leisure and socializing activities with the 'virtual ethos of care' (Anderson and Knee 2020). These virtual spaces are alternatives to forced transparency of certain spatial structures that oftentimes 'contribute to controlling sexualities and relations' not only on individual but also 'on a transnational scale' (Vallerand 2018: 148). That the internet provides the fabrication of an online 'persona that may not be admissible outside the door to one's room' helps generate 'protective walls'[6] which 'also have doors that open on to large spaces where the clandestinity [. . .] is safely abandoned' if needed (Mack 2017: 26). Access to these multi-layered spaces of negotiation between public and private is a reminder 'to claim the right to opacity' (Hartman 2019: 227) and to demand translucency over transparency in diverse spatial contexts.

5

Crescent moon, descending sun, on a loop. Everything I write is already crumpled[18] under the brain-drilling sound of the elevator engine, as my reason that links every single word, space and memory is cut[19] wide open. My fifteen-year-younger and designer-to-be self draws a line on this cut and another and many other, until there are enough lines, walls,[6] chambers and things[11] to fill this space. She doesn't see that the cut is vast. She has a deadline to elude and capture, just like the sky and the future.[20] Mercury is in retrograde again and things are about to collapse. This time for good.

[18] Lucas Crawford (2020) suggests that the act of crumpling can be both a metaphor and a method for transness and queerness in architecture. Similar to Halberstam's (2020) attention to the very moment of the collapse[viii] rather than the outcome of the collapse itself, for Crawford, the process of crumpling is also a crucial moment of surrendering, a moment of changing mind, 'choosing otherwise', modifying what is not right. When an object or a body is crumpled, it means they are 'affected', taking on new dimensions and scraping by.

[19] *Cut* is another important conceptual and methodological tool to unravel not only the contiguity between the bodies and matters[xx] but also practices that effectuate them; those that are both material[xxi] and textual.[xxii] Moreover, as Eve Kosofsky Sedgwick (1993) indicated long

ago, queer shares etymological roots with Indo-European *twerkw* which means 'cross' and the German *quer* which means 'transverse', and together indicate 'a transversal movement; a "cut" across' through not only identities but also ideologies (Angelopoulou 2017: 28). In this sense, queer has strong relations with 'cutting', especially considering the surgical practices of trans* bodies whose 'flesh torn apart and sewn together again in a shape other than that in which it was born' (Stryker 238: 4); thus, its corporeal and material implications are worth examining.

[xx] Karen Barad (2003) argues that humans and nonhumans come into being only through their entangled enactments that demarcate and solidify their boundaries, which she calls 'boundary-drawing practices' or *agential cuts*. A cut, then, delineates 'surfaces' between a human, object, space, institution and technology at the moments of their *intra-actions* (Barad 2003). Thinking cuts as both moments of entanglement and separation corroborate the idea that the bodies and spaces are both relational and interdependent.

[xxi] Analysing the anarchitectural works of American artist Gordon Matta-Clark, Halberstam (2018) comments that Matta-Clark's cuts that split the buildings and walls apart exposed 'the shadow side of architecture, the brutal and exploitative qualities of the built environment', which can also be understood as echoes of 'a new landscape of trans* aesthetics whose primary feature is to be constantly "under construction"'. In contrast to the heteronormative cultural domain that professes their houses and buildings as 'lacking nothing', anarchitectural performative cuts lay bare 'what is not there, what has been removed, what is lacking – what has been destroyed, erased or blacked out in order for what remains present to look permanent' (Halberstam 2018). Moreover, for Halberstam, what is transgressive and transformative is not only the cut but also the very act of splitting which turns buildings 'into a form of living being and, as such, an active participant in their transformational process' (Angelopoulou 2017: 30). In such literal or metaphorical cuts lie also the unpredictability (i.e., how the cut or its respondent will behave after splitting) as opposed to computability and accuracy of today's architectonic practices, which proves itself a queer method employable by contemporary spatial practices.

[xxii] Literary techniques such as *Cut-up*, like the way it was idiosyncratically used by British novelist Kathy Acker in the late twentieth century's queer cyberpunk scene, not only challenged androcentric and heteronormative literary canons but also distorted the spatial, temporal and historical continuity of normative narratives by use of piracy, pastiche and montage (Canlı 2017). These 'cuts', which are also partially employed in this text, are material-discursive[ii] methods to rethink textual spaces queerly.

[20] Looking at the sky to imagine the future is not a merely reflexive, somatic or metaphoric gesture, considering the heated discussions around 'colonizing' Mars as the new promised land, which suggests an upward verticality in onward temporality[4]. Although the pretext underpinning such galactic expansion of spatial horizons stems mostly from the concerns about environmental disasters and depleted resources threatening human life on Earth, it also reveals the misconception that socio-spatial inequalities on this planet caused by coloniality are outdated. However, technocracy's desire for outreaching the limits of aerospace remains rather blinkered as its dream 'new worlds' is the evil twin of the world itself, spoiled by the to-be-exported social stratifications, identity categories and technophilia. In the meantime, women, queer folk, outsiders and misfits have long broadened their horizons through not only living in but also envisioning other worlds that are ambisexual, agamic, nonmonetary, intergalactic and chimeric.[xxiii] Such visions do not rely on a colonial futurism to bring about 'new spaces' but posit that new spaces – architectural or corporeal – can only arise through the reparations of the collective ruins of the past and by unsettling the biases of the present.

[xxiii] It is a 'desire for another way of being in both the world and time' (Muñoz 2009: 96).

Note

* This work is financed by national funds through FCT – Fundação para a Ciência e a Tecnologia, I.P., under the project UIDB/00736/2020 (base funding) and UIDP/00736/2020 (programmatic funding).

References

Ahmed, S. (2004), *The Cultural Politics of Emotion*, New York: Routledge.
Ahmed, S. (2006), *Queer Phenomenology: Orientations, Objects, Others*, Durham and London: Duke University Press.
Ahmed, S. (2017), *Living a Feminist Life*, Durham and London: Duke University Press.
Anderson, A. R. and E. Knee (2020), 'Queer Isolation or Queering Isolation? Reflecting upon the Ramifications of COVID-19 on the Future of Queer Leisure Spaces', *Leisure Sciences*, DOI: 10.1080/01490400.2020.1773992 (accessed December 28, 2020).
Angelopoulou, A. (2017), 'A Surgery Issue: Cutting through the Architectural Fabric', *Footprint*, 11 (2): 25–49.
Anzaldúa, G. (1987), *Borderlands/La Frontera: The New Mestiza*, San Francisco: Aunt Lute Books.

Anzaldúa, G. (2002), 'Preface (Un)Natural Bridges, (Un)Safe Spaces', in G. Anzaldúa and A. Keating (eds.), *This Bridge We Call Home*, 1–5, New York: Routledge.

Barad, K. (2003), 'Posthumanist Performativity: Toward an Understanding of How Matter Comes to Matter', *Signs: Journal of Women in Culture and Society*, 28 (3): 801–31.

Bender-Baird, K. (2015), 'Peeing Under Surveillance: Bathrooms, Gender Policing and Hate Violence', *Gender, Place & Culture*, 23 (7): 983–8.

Bryant, J. (2015), 'The Meaning of Queer Home', *Home Cultures*, 12 (3): 261–89, DOI: 10.1080/17406315.2015.1084754.

Butler, J. (2014[1992]), 'The Body You Want: In Conversation with Liz Kotz', in A. Jones (ed.), *SEXUALITY*, 185–90, Cambridge, MA: The MIT Press.

Canlı, E. (2017), 'Queerying Design: Material Re-Configurations of Body Politics', PhD diss., University of Porto.

Cavanagh, S. L. (2010), *Queering Bathrooms: Gender, Sexuality and the Hygienic Imagination*, Toronto, Buffalo and London: University of Toronto Press.

Crawford, L. (2015), *Transgender Architectonics: The Shape of Change in Modernist Space*, New York: Routledge.

Crawford, L. (2020), 'The Crumple and the Scrape', *Places Journal*, March 2020, DOI: 10.22269/200305 (accessed December 28, 2020).

Freeman, E. (2010), *Time Binds: Queer Temporalities, Queer Histories*, Durham, NC: Duke University Press.

Frichot, H. (2010), 'Following Hélène Cixous' Steps Towards a Writing Architecture', *Architectural Theory Review*, 15 (3): 312–23, DOI: 10.1080/13264826.2010.524310.

Gabrielsson, C., et al. (2019), 'Reading(s) and Writing(s)', *Writingplace*, l (3): 4–9, DOI: 10.7480/writingplace.3.4342.

Gorny, R. A. and D. van den Heuvel. (2017), 'New Figurations in Architecture Theory: From Queer Performance to Becoming Trans', *Footprint*, 11 (2): 1–9.

Halberstam, J. (2005), *In a Queer Time and Place: Transgender Bodies, Subcultural Lives, Sexual Cultures*, New York: New York University Press.

Halberstam, J. (2018), 'Unbuilding Gender', *Places Journal*, October 2018, DOI: 10.22269/181003 (accessed 10 December 2020).

Halberstam, J. (2020), 'Coming Undone', Queer Query Online event by SCI-Arc, Available online: https://livestream.com/sciarc/events/9285998/videos/214447853 (accessed December 5, 2020).

Haritaworn, J. (2015), *Queer Lovers and Hateful Others*, London: Pluto Press.

Hartman, S. (2019), *Wayward Lives, Beautiful Experiments*, London: Serpent's Tail.

herising, F. (2005), 'Interrupting Positions: Critical Thresholds and Queer Pro/Positions', in L. Brown and S. Strega (eds.), *Research as Resistance: Critical, Indigenous & Anti-oppressive Approaches*, 127–51, Toronto: Canadian Scholars' Press.

hooks, b. (2000), 'Choosing the Margin as a Space of Radical Openness', in J. Rendell, B Penner and I. Borden (eds), *Gender Space Architecture*, 203–9, London and New York: Routledge.

Kokoula, X. (2017), 'Opening up Bodyspace: Perspectives from Posthuman and Feminist Theory', *Footprint*, 11 (2): 11–24.

Lorde, A. (2007 [1984]), 'The Master's Tools Will Never Dismantle the Master's House', *Sister Outsider: Essays and Speeches*, 110–14, Berkeley, CA: Crossing Press.

Mack, M. A. (2017), 'Out of the Closet into the Courtyard', *The Funambulist*, 13: 22–7.

Morton, T. (2013), *Hyperobjects: Philosophy and Ecology After the End of the World*, Minneapolis: University of Minnesota Press.

Muñoz, J. E. (2009), *Cruising Utopia: The Then and There of Queer Futurity*, New York and London: New York University Press.

Pavka, E. (2020), 'What Do We Mean By Queer Space?', *Azure Magazine*, 29 June. Available online: https://www.azuremagazine.com/article/what-do-we-mean-by -queer-space/ (accessed 12 December 2020).

Penner, B. (2013), *Bathroom*, London: Reaktion Books.

Pilkey, B., R. M. Scicluna and A. Gorman-Murray. (2015), 'Alternative Domesticities', *Home Cultures*, 12 (2): 127–38, DOI: 10.1080/17406315.2015.1046294.

Preciado, B. (2012), 'Architecture as a Practice of Biopolitical Disobedience', *Log*, 25: 121–34.

Preciado, P. (2017), 'Trashgender: Urinate/Defecate, Masculine/Feminine', *The Funambulist*, 13: 15–17.

Reed, C. (1996), 'Imminent Domain: Queer Space in the Built Environment', *Art Journal*, 55 (4): 64–70.

Schalk, M. and K. Reisinger. (2017), 'Styles of Queer Feminist Practices and Objects in Architecture', *Architecture and Culture*, 5 (3): 343–52, DOI: 10.1080/20507828.2017.1386942.

Sedgwick, E. K. (1993), *Tendencies*, Durham: Duke University Press.

Shay, G. and J. K. Strader. (2012), 'Queer (In)Justice: Mapping New Gay (Scholarly) Agendas', *Journal of Criminal Law and Criminology*, 102 (1): 171–93.

Spade, D. (2012), 'The Only Way to End Racialized Gender Violence in Prisons is to End Prisons: A Response to Russell Robinson's "Masculinity as Prison"', *The Circuit*, 3: 184–95.

Stafford, L. and K. Volz (2016), 'Diverse Bodies-Space Politics: Towards a Critique of Social (In)justice of Built Environments', *TEXT Special Issue*, 34: 1–11.

Stryker, S. (1994), 'My Words to Victor Frankenstein Above the Village of Chamounix: Performing Transgender Rage', *GLQ*, 1 (3): 237–54.

Swan, R. (2013), 'Punishment by Design: The Power of Architecture Over the Human Mind', *SF Weekly*, August 21. Available online: http:// www.sfweekly. com/news/punishment-by-design-the-power-of-architecture-over-the-human-mind/ (accessed June 6, 2017).

Tuck, E. and K. W. Yang (2012), 'Decolonization is Not a Metaphor', *Decolonization: Indigeneity, Education & Society*, 1 (1): 1–40.

Vallerand, O. (2018), 'Learning From. . .(Or 'The Need for Queer Pedagogies of Space')', *Interiors*, 9 (2): 140–56, DOI: 10.1080/20419112.2019.1565175.

II

Practices

5

El Site

Queer approximations on fragments and writing

Regner Ramos

Each fragment of this chapter moves the reader through different essays that relate to – and some that directly come from – 'El Site', my self-publishing, research website. El Site is discussed in this chapter as a research method that informs my explorations on the relationship between queerness, the internet and the built environment in Puerto Rico, through performative writing. Via interruptions and open-ended essays, the chapter points to the work of scholars like Javier E. Laureano, Lawrence La Fountain-Stokes, Gisela Ramos-Rosario, Jane Rendell and Samuel R. Delany, while also using ethnographic and visual material such as an interview that lives in the depths of one of my Dropbox folders – part of a series of thirty-seven interviews I conducted during 2018 with queer people in the island – and drawings I made of my domestic space during quarantine. Through a critical reading of El Site's interface and design as a case study, my aim for this chapter is to situate how the fragment – as a methodological maneuver in architectural production – is evocative and responsive to the spatiality of queerness in the Caribbean.

'Files'
(Fragment 1)
Cosmo.m4a
Apple MPEG-4 audio – 72.5MB

Created 10/25/18, 5:47PM
Modified 10/25/18, 5:47PM
Last opened 1/7/19
Duration 2:30:40
Audio channels Mono
Sample rate 44.1 kHz

Me: In that moment I just wanted to flirt and technology allowed it. I couldn't do it in person.

Cosmo: We had the chance – a kid from Aguas Buenas that has no way of leaving those woods – we had the need to relate to other men and and there was no way to do it back then apart from Myspace or MSN Messenger. They were complete strangers that you'd never met in person. For older generations, this sounds so weird, but that's the only way for me! We completely extrapolate that. We still keep that way of relating to others. And it works for us. For other people and generations – heterosexuals – it might be a bit weird that the majority of our relationships started through social media, but that was a product of a historic necessity.

[. . .]

Me: And there's the matter of *rural* relationships in Puerto Rico, also. My mom met my dad because he played basketball with my uncles and was friends with them. That, for us, doesn't happen.

Cosmo: For us, that happens in movies.

Me: It wasn't like in your neighbourhood or in your street you had a bunch of people you could go out or flirt with. And even if there was, you couldn't say you were gay, nobody could find out you were gay. We couldn't do this in front of our families, if they were to come visit us either.

Cosmo: Not even in school.

Me: These were clandestine practices that the internet perfectly allowed.

Cosmo: That's the word. They were clandestine. This is what allowed you to be you. I think we wear this on our bodies. There's something about this that still helps us, people our age, even though we can now go out and meet people anywhere.

[. . .]

Cosmo: It's strange because we had these digital tools that empowered us and those tools have helped these topics to become visible. They've also helped our *bodies* become visible. There are people in Puerto Rico that live hidden lives because they live near forty heterosexual men who are all misogynists and violent and they have to go find other men who aren't from here, through the internet, looking for acceptance.

[. . .]

Me: One thing I hadn't initially contemplated in my research and I
remember talking to you about it, was Myspace.

Cosmo: During those days, Facebook was just starting and it was
one of the most universal things. It was very formal, Myspace and
there was something interesting in that you could personalize it
to such a degree that the page reflected the person you wanted to
be. With Myspace I think we started asking, how do I construct
myself, what do I put on social media? You had the ability to edit
with HTML, put whatever song you wanted, select which friends
you wanted to show off as your inner circle. . . . Myspace was the
precursor to everything that came after. Well, first we had MSN
Messenger; that came before Myspace. That was how I started
relating to people.

Me: How did you add them? Was it only the people you knew?

Cosmo: So what usually happened was, if you liked a boy, you'd find
out his email to add him on MSN Messenger – to see *if* he had
Messenger! If you added him with an email and he showed up on
your screen, it meant he was officially registered in Messenger. It was
curious, sometimes you'd get requests from people you didn't know.
You'd think, 'Someone added me, I wonder who it is . . .'

Me: Yes and without a photo or anything! It was so fucked up.

Cosmo: Without a photo or anything. That was around 2003.

    [. . .]

Me: You mentioned we could customize profiles on Myspace and there
was something nice about the relationship between profile, code and
the construction of identity. In ICQ, we could customize the chat
box only through your display name – like in MSN Messenger. So
you could use the '@' instead of the 'a' and we came up with really
elaborate names. The 'r' was '®'. Another way was by changing the
colour of the chat box. I would change the font, the font colour
and the background colour of the chat box, so that when I sent
a message, you'd read it exactly like I had designed it and you
automatically knew it was me. And sometimes, if your letters were
difficult to read or the colours were too bright, you'd get a 'I can't
read that, change it'.

Cosmo: That's fucking amazing.

    [We laugh]

Cosmo: It was crazy because suddenly in 2006, everyone was a coder!
Everyone knew HTML and I even knew how to hack through
HTML, certain things guys hid on their profiles. I found out how to
write the URL addresses that would take me directly to those hidden
parts of their profiles and that's how I'd see who their friends were,
what comments were hidden . . . I'd sidestep the things they wanted
to be invisible.

Note: This interview has been translated from Spanish to English.
'About'
(Fragment 2)

A space of doubles, my research website, El Site, is fluid and structured; spatial and digital; readable and coded; playful and systematic; camp and simple. Contrary to other experimental – and truly interesting – websites that deal with architecture and gender, such as *The FX Beauties* or *Alien Sex Club*, where graphic elements, gradients and animations help orient visitors on the page, those who land on www.elsite.xyz via a computer arrive to a page where the white background's empty space balances out the amount of bold, chunky text that appears when the page loads (Figure 5.1). The top left corner, due to its hierarchy in size, eventually grabs users' attention and the website announces itself: *EL SITE*. Directly below it is the menu, indicated solely by plain Times text written across a single baseline. There are no icons, no shapes, no overlaid graphic effects that communicate that this is the navigational part of the website: 'Notes', 'Messages', 'Photos', 'Calendar', 'Files', 'About'. The different sections of the website are named after standard iOS apps.

On El Site, words are both content and ornament. The sans-serif typeface is called 'El Site' too – a bespoke typeface created by the designers, Regular Practice, to give the website an assertive tone. The bold type is softened through the use of bright colours that adorn the screen, which is organized

FIGURE 5.1 *Homepage on El Site, showing double scrolling columns with the website's articles, as well as the menu bar. El Site went live in 2018.*

in two vertical columns. If a visitor refreshes the page, El Site reloads with a different colour combination – composed of seven preselected colours that appear at random. When scrolling, visitors are pulled in opposite directions: half of the page's content floats up, the other half comes down. The different post titles appear from within the edges of the screen, filled in black, but as the smooth scrolling floats them to the centre, the interface fills them with colours. Question marks, exclamation points and colons all appear in a different colour than the text they accompany; punctuation is used not only for grammatical purposes but also as decoration. In addition, photographs and images scroll past each other with only a few pixels of separation, as if they are nearly sliding against themselves, indicating that there is a nuanced spatiality to El Site, through the way that distances and proximities are both enacted via words and images, borders, movements and margins.

Finally, in the bottom left corner is a barely perceptible grey button. In the mobile version of El Site, the button is entirely absent. By clicking on the grey button, enormous red letters appear on across the screen: 'AFTER CLICKING COMMENT, PLACE YOUR MESSAGE ANYWHERE'. The instructions disappear and visitors are then able to write something which they can then place/stick somewhere on the page (Figure 5.2). The plain white background with the double columns of text becomes disrupted by stickers and gifs, selected at random by the interface, from a series of custom-

FIGURE 5.2 *Homepage on El Site, showing the prompt for visitors to leave behind a secret comment. Overlaid on the page are stickers with messages by different visitors.*

FIGURE 5.3 *Image of a secret message left behind by visitor 'ezra' over a photograph on El Site.*

drawn catalogue of drawings and animations. Each of these indicates that a secret message has been left behind by a visitor. Hovering over the stickers shows messages like: 'So COOL!', 'Hi!', 'groetjes uit Rotterdam', 'going out, anyone want anything?', 'This is like a playground' (Figure 5.3). Each section of *El Site* – and each post – gives visitors the ability to leave their comments behind and to read what others have written, inserting new, divergent voices that interrupt the researcher's primary voice and causing randomness and messiness, in an otherwise structured and constrained design.

'Notes'
(Fragment 3)

This fragment, originally written in April 2020 and published on El Site, is composed of four fragments. In italics is a travel article I wrote for *Glass* magazine, where I review Celestino Boutique Hotel, located in Medellin, Colombia: the site where I fell in love with my ex-boyfriend. I wrote the article very shortly after our breakup. In small text reminiscent of captions are a series of iMessages – written in Spanglish and inclusive of typos – between myself and four friends who were checking up on me during the breakup. Text messages and the occasional video chat were the only contact we had, given the state of lockdown. Depicted visually are AutoCAD drawings of spaces in my apartment – a project I called 'Spaces I've Cried In' – where I spent the entirety of the breakup period in isolation. Lastly, based on Jenny Holzer's 'Inflammatory Essays', in bold quotes are a series of thoughts I had, during the breakup/lockdown/break

NO ONE IS CURRENTLY WINNING. THE SUN REMINDS ME OF YOU AND THAT IS A PROBLEM. MAYBE GOD IS AN ALGORITHM. I AM NOT HERE. YOU ARE GOING TO STAY WITH ME AS A WRINKLE ON MY FACE.

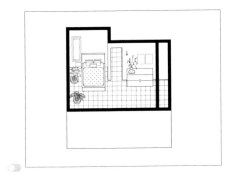

FIGURE 5.4 *'I Am Not Here' as displayed on El Site on desktop browser. Written, drawn and laid out by Regner Ramos, 2020.*

EL SITE   Notes Messages Photos Calendar Files About

I STILL FEEL THE EARTH TREMBLING, BUT I AM WRONG BECAUSE NO ONE IS POSTING ABOUT IT ON FACEBOOK. LOVE TAKES ME BACK TO LOVE. THIS APARTMENT IS A PRESSURE COOKER. IF I SCREAM AT YOU, YOU STILL WOULD NOT HEAR ME.

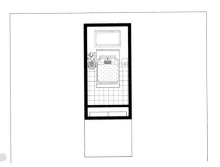

FIGURE 5.5 *'I Am Not Here' as displayed on El Site on desktop browser. Written, drawn and laid out by Regner Ramos, 2020.*

"Although location is one of its perks, the inside is just as important (and special). The boutique hotel—or 'Hotel Botánico' (botanic hotel), as its main facade announces with metallic letters imposed on a gorgeous Art Deco lattice—has got undeniable flair. Having only 22 rooms allows Celestino's service to be impeccable, with staff greeting guests on a first-name basis, always ready to help. Breakfast at Azul Salvaje offers a wonderful selection of healthy dishes to recharge you for the day, while the rooftop jacuzzi gives guests access to city views."

OF COURSE I DO. SILENCE CAN ALSO BE A FORM OF TORTURE. THANK THE HEAVENS I AM A CAPRICORN. NOT ANSWERING QUESTIONS IS FOR POLITICIANS AND COWARDS.

5/30/20, 12:19 PM
Yo: Yo voy a try to keep it together pero yo llevo crying nonstop for the last hour and a half.
Shellac: ok baby, yo no vi ni un análisis bueno pero voy a estar calm. Lo que no puedas. I got you.

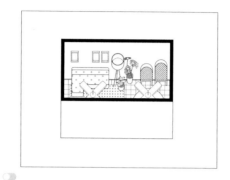

FIGURE 5.6 Spaces I've Cried In 3.

"Celestino is like a terrarium encapsulating the life and vibrancy of Zona Rosa, with deep greens, plant life, wood furniture and details, rich textures in textiles, and the shine of metallic surfaces in warm tones that remind me of the sunlight that kisses me from my balcony every afternoon. An unforgettable place to stay in Medellín, Celestino Boutique Hotel is a true reflection of its location: a small jewel where a bit of Great Gatsby meets the City of Eternal Spring."

I HAVE FORGOTTEN YOUR FATHER'S NAME AND WHAT YOU SMELL LIKE. HELLO TO WHOEVER IS STEPPING ON ME. I WAS ONCE WILLING TO SHARE ALL MY TOYS. YOU WILL NEVER UNDERSTAND THIS.

31/30/20, 12:39 AM
Alejandra: Si quieres estar con al y otros que he's the one, ve te rodeas
Yo: Na, yo llevo tiempo. I need to let this go, hey llevo TODA la tarde

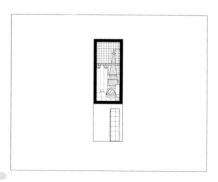

FIGURE 5.7 'I Am Not Here' as displayed on El Site on desktop browser. Written, drawn and laid out by Regner Ramos, 2020.

down, that I wished to express to my former partner, but was unable to. I directly borrow this fragmented mode of writing from Jane Rendell's *site writing* (Rendell 2010). The fragments explore the lived experience of love and loss through three different sites: the hotel, my apartment and my body (Figures 5.4–5.7).

'Messages'
(Fragment 4)

I never intended El Site to be a finalized and polished output, but rather a dynamic and fragmented playground that I could actively use to think about my research on queer spaces in Puerto Rico and how internet technologies inform queer culture in the island. When I commissioned the website's graphic design and coding, I made sure the designers understood and incorporated this, along with a long wish list of features I wanted El Site to have. At the time, I had just won the FIPI Award 2017–2019 for my research proposal, 'Sites Queer: Technologies, Spaces and Otherness' and along with a series of site drawings and architectural models (Figure 5.8), as well as one-on-one, intimate interviews with queer Puerto Ricans, El Site was a way for me to introduce performative, fragmented writing as part of my research.

FIGURE 5.8 *Models of the 'Los Sites' series and exhibition, each depicting the location of queer spaces in San Juan, Puerto Rico. Photography by Stephanie Segarra, 2021.*

A common theme in El Site is a recurrent emphasis on *my* identity. The use of 'I' – of speculating in the first person – marks an intimate position of subjectivity: the X, Y, Z of a *particular* body and the addresses and locations that body navigates *through* and performs *in*. As both queer and Latinx, writing from my own subjectivity in fragments accounts for a form of resistance. It is also a way of making my own otherness manifest. El Site's URL – using the .xyz domain – hints at this, subtly. The idea behind El Site and the site models, then, was not to have the writing passively describe the models or vice versa. Instead, writing and publishing on El Site was intended as an active research method that allowed each design and textual component to feed into, shape, contest, explain and challenge the other. It allowed me to think about the writing through the models and to think about the models through writing, thus informing my design and theoretical decisions within a piece of research strengthened by unpredictable pairings, unlikely situations and bizarre aesthetics that manifested in both writing and design (Figure 5.9).

Regular Practice designed El Site's backend to be simple and straightforward. At the same time, though, their design allows me to experiment with a set of layout configurations, hierarchies of text, placement of texts throughout different columns, hyperlinks, images, size of images, as well as secret messages visitors can leave me and that I can leave for visitors

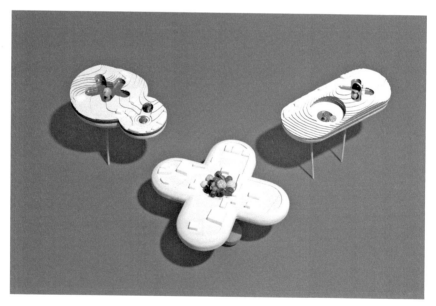

FIGURE 5.9 *Models of the 'Los Sites' series and exhibition, each depicting the location of moments of becoming queer in Aguada, Puerto Rico. Photography by Stephanie Segarra, 2021.*

too. As a site where I play with the conventions of architectural publishing, in terms of tone, graphics and format, El Site helps me queer my mode of writing about spaces by *fragmenting* my writing – by breaking it apart, performing ruptures, allowing multiple voices to speak, creating rhythms and rethreading stories. First, this practice resonates with the space of the Caribbean in general. Second, it responds to Puerto Rican queer culture particularly.

Antonio Benítez-Rojo argues that some of the many obstacles in studying the Caribbean are its fragmentation, its instability, its cultural heterogeneity, its lack of historical and historiographic continuity, among other things (Benítez-Rojo 1986: 116). The very nature of the Caribbean region is a mosaic of land formations, which Benítez-Rojo describes as a bridge between North and South America – given the indigenous cultures that migrated to and fro across/throughout the Caribbean archipelago. He writes that '[t]his geographic accident confers to the area, including its continental foci, an archipelagic character, which is to say, a discontinuous set (of what?): empty spaces, frayed voices, connections, sutures, journeys of signification' (Benítez-Rojo 1986: 116, translated from Spanish to English). Benítez-Rojo's masterful text focuses on the processes of colonization imposed onto the Caribbean islands – which he proposes are actually *one island which repeats itself* over and over, though one could argue against this, as does Jonathan Pugh in 'Island Movements: Thinking with the Archipelago' – but I see overlaps between Benítez-Rojo's description of the Caribbean and its formation of identity and processes of *queering* and *becoming* queer: taking norms apart, reconfiguring them and re-signifying them through political acts of self-assertion.

For Benítez-Rojo, the Caribbean can be summarized in two words, *performance* and *rhythm*: our culture is a constant flow of improvisations and *interrupted rhythms*, which we use as tools to reconstruct, reproduce or reinterpret (Benítez-Rojo 1986: 125). These rereadings of Benítez-Rojo's arguments have recently begun taking an important point of reference in my work on queerness in Puerto Rico's built environment and the methods I employ while researching it. At its core, his is a text exploring fragments; their scale is the Antilles. His arguments open up possibilities within my own design and performative writing work, in that the Caribbean archipelago 'represents a culture of directions, not routes; of approximations, not exact results; of fluidity and curves, not of straight lines and angles; and an eternal return, a purposeless detour that always leads you back to itself' (Benítez-Rojo 1986: 121). And due to this, Benítez-Rojo proposes that the Caribbean has long resisted the methods designed for researching it. I find this resistance to be quite a queer strategy as well. My reluctance to construct seamless, clean and clear narratives of LGBTQ+ people also responds to this: queerness in

Puerto Rico (and the spaces where it unfolds) is never seamless, clean, definitive or clear – if anything, queerness here is disruptive, vibrant, unexpected, ever-changing and is more useful as an act of un-defining than one of defining. And so the methods I use begin to increasingly reflect this, through each of my projects.

For instance, during the first episode of my *Cüirtopia Live* radio show (2021), Puerto Rican LGBTQ+ historian Javier E. Laureano proposed that studying, understanding and approaching Puerto Rican queer culture today is impossible via traditional methods. Joining Laureano in that particular episode, titled 'Caribe Cüir', were also Lawrence La Fountain-Stokes, the gender and American culture theorist, as well as filmmaker and artist Gisela Rosario-Ramos – a powerhouse trio of Puerto Rican scholars/ activists who have propelled LGBTQ+ discourse in the island through their different projects and disciplinary fields. Their valuable contribution to a production of *spatialized* knowledge on queerness in the Caribbean exists in the informality of this radio show conversation recorded via Zoom during the Covid-19 pandemic, not yet in a book or research paper, which no doubt also speaks about where and how queer scholarship and queer spatial discourse is currently being produced in Puerto Rico – and perhaps the Caribbean.

The idea of the Caribbean as a fragmented space not just geographically but also in relation to the construction of queer culture was a central part of our conversation; La Fountain-Stokes maintained that even though the Caribbean has over fifty years of queer activism, we need to have better understandings of what the neighbouring islands are doing today. Apart from the stereotypes of homophobia and aggression in islands like Jamaica, there is little that we know about what is happening in Haiti's queer culture or in the Dominican Republic, for instance. Laureano attributes this in part to the Caribbean being a place of 'uncomfortable identities, in tension, in struggle' and to the fact that the Caribbean islands lack communication among each other. Laureano claims that the Spanish-speaking Caribbean communicates very rarely with the English and French-speaking Caribbean and 'it's a difficult thing to look within ourselves' and to exchange queer discourses within the Caribbean. For Laureano, 'Colonialism has been a factor in the rupture within this fragmented Caribbean'. This fragmentation goes, of course, hand in hand with issues of different historical contexts, languages, sovereignty, as well as migration, particularly to the United States, in the case of many Puerto Ricans. The diaspora and their back-and-forth movement of scholars, activists and artists – such as Laureano, La Fountain-Stokes and Rosario-Ramos themselves – helped move queer culture to and fro, *bringing* new references, *exporting* others and *building* references on top of that.

Macha Colón – Rosario-Ramos's artistic persona – is a good example of this because she is a product of her experiences as a Puerto Rican, Black, queer, female migrant in New York in the 1980s. For her, the experience of feeling like an immigrant played a part in *recognizing* herself as Afro-descendant and Afro-Caribbean, it redefined what tropicality meant to her and still informs her artistic practice today. Similarly, currently living in Michigan, La Fountain-Stokes's drag persona, Lola Von Miramar, is a vehicle for him to negotiate between Spanish and English, between the United States and Puerto Rico, between what is considered kitsch and what is considered high culture. According to La Fountain-Stokes, Lola is from Miramar – an upper-class neighbourhoodneighbourhood in San Juan – but she also loves to eat and cook Puerto Rican fritters in high heels. La Fountain-Stokes thus maintained that idiosyncrasy and humour are important elements that help define Puerto Rican queerness.

Though the Caribbean scholars I've mentioned – Benítez-Rojo, Laureano, La Fountain-Stokes and Rosario-Ramos – offer a very focused insight into the spatial politics of Caribbean fragmentation – in terms of geography as well as queer culture – my methodological attempts to actively *write* in fragments points to two texts by two theorists that have shaped my own: architectural and feminist theorist Jane Rendell's *Site Writing: The Architecture of Art Criticism* (2006) and literary critic and novelist Samuel R. Delany's *Times Square Red, Times Square Blue* (1999). I've previously written about how Rendell's mode of fragmented writing informs my work (Ramos 2021: 14–32), in that '[t]he use of analogy – the desire to invent a writing that is somehow 'like' the artwork – allows a certain creativity to intervene in the critical act as the critic comes to understand and interpret the work by remaking it on his/her own terms' (Rendell 2010: 7). The way I've structured this chapter, for instance, is *like* the object of study, El Site, with each fragment being titled after a particular section where they would be found – and in some cases, the sections where they're *actually* located.

Through site writing, Rendell doesn't write *about* the object of study. Instead, she plays with prepositions that allow for new configurations in the relationship between herself and the object: Rendell writes *through, besides, under, below* any piece of art or building she's studying. In this way, she writes through multiple positions in relation to an object or building and the material repercussions of this reflect on the textual qualities themselves: often fragmented essays composed of archival material, visuals and voices that tell the building's stories through multiple formats that elicit open-ended interpretations and readings of her text, not a clear and definitive reading of it. It's in this process of Rendell's *undoing* and *dismantling* that I find her work to resonate with acts of queering.

Delany has a similar approach in *Times Square Red, Times Square Blue*. Where Rendell's site writing approach is deployed mostly for essays, catalogues, posters and other forms of concise intellectual production, Delany fragments his entire book. Divided into two primary parts – originally written as two distinct essays about Times Square – Delany begins the book's first section while writing in an autoethnographic tone, narrating and describing his experiences in New York City's red light, queer circuit and the network of spaces relevant to these – such as pornographic movie theatres, video stores and clubs. Delany is undoubtedly *storytelling* – which may or may not be entirely 'factual' – bringing us along to meet different characters as he remembers them and the queer and at times illicit spaces and practices that made up his experiences of the red light district. The second part, however, is written in a more 'academic' tone; Delany here is historically critical, not anecdotal in the way he discusses the spatial politics of Times Square's regeneration scheme, which he argues ultimately wiped out these aforementioned queer spatial networks in order to help 'clean up' the city's image and attract multimillion-dollar investors to capitalize on the regeneration plans.

Although the book is perhaps best known for Delany's categorization of social relationships – 'networking' and 'contact' – what I have personally found intriguing and stimulating is Delany's mode of *writing* and *structuring* his book. *Times Square Red, Times Square Blue* is part literature, part urban theory; part performative, part archival. And Delany is very clever in that the reader gets to experience and understand this duality even in the materiality of the text itself. In the second part of the book, Delany carves out marginal spaces within the paragraphs themselves, interrupting the main text's flow and in those spaces, he adds a *third* text in bold letters. These are almost like footnotes on the *side* of the pages, musing on space, art, urbanism and more. The book is disruptive in that you read multiple texts at once because they converge in the materiality of the book and its pages and through their clashing, explanation and contestation, they bring out each other's particular, critical qualities.

Following these ideas, Rendell and Delany's work has enabled me to write through multiple tones on El Site – which in turn has granted me the confidence to deploy this mode of writing in other forums of architectural publishing outside of my editorial control, such as this book chapter, as well as in my other research projects, which I briefly discuss towards the end of this text. But it also allows me to express these tones in the actual identity/design/layout of the website itself: how text appears on the screen, where it is placed, what point size it assumes and what images I use and where. Writing and publishing on El Site is most evocative of my first attempts at writing *overall*: the days of Live Journal, Myspace and even the message board of the Trading Spaces website, in the late 1990s and early 2000s.

Media theorist Vincent Miller states that '[b]logging as a popular phenomenon peaked around 2004/2005, when personal journal blogging was adopted wholeheartedly by youth culture in the developed world. Blogs in particular have been lauded for greatly expanding the accessibility for the "average" person to publish on the internet, resulting in an explosion of online content' (Miller 2011: 169). From my small, coastal town on the northwest coast of Puerto Rico, as a seventeen-year-old hiding his identity from family, friends, the school administration and everyone else, the possibility of writing on the internet opened up spaces of dislocated connections with other people. And for the first time, I was no longer alone nor bound to the spatial politics and limitations of the physical places I inhabited. Blogging sites, personal home pages and instant messaging platforms granted me and many others on the island, the ability to have a voice that could say many things and sound in many tones and fluctuations.

From interviews I've conducted with queer people in Puerto Rico as part of my research, I've found that *what* and *how* we speak online isn't necessarily about having multiple identities, but about the possibility of editing, constructing and fragmenting the self according to where the performance of self takes place. Although some, like Master Top (fifty-two years old at the time of interview), mentioned that they presented a different persona in digital spaces such as Grindr, many of my interviewees spoke about how they tempered what they posted on Facebook, for instance, because the audience included conservative family and family friends, whereas Twitter was used more liberally. One of them, Yamil (eighteen years old at the time of the interview), mentioned the way Tumblr allowed him to post anything he wanted in regards to his sexuality because it functions primarily as a reblogging platform, where users don't need to add any information about themselves, not even a profile picture. According to him, Tumblr allowed him to be who he really was, without worrying that his conservative family might find his profile and see what he was posting.

For others like Cosmo (twenty-eight years old at the time of the interview) – whose partial story is told in the first fragment of this chapter – the space of the internet helped actively shape his queer identity into what it is today. Those of us who came of age while the internet arrived in mainstream homes in Puerto Rico (1998–2000), the mere fact of having an empty profile page – on ICQ, for instance – prompted us to find a language to describe ourselves on the web for the very first time. And because we could always go back and change it with ease, who we were and how we wrote was an endless process (as evidenced even today, with my continuous writing and re-writing of my Instagram bio). Miller writes:

> [Home pages] suggested that everyday life is fragmented and multiple in terms of the demands that it makes upon people in different contexts and that subjects actually work from within to create some sense of a coherent self and identity among a number of different roles, interests and preferences. [. . .] Rather than portraying a decentred, fragmented, disembodied self, personal home pages are actually attempts at identity integration by demonstrating to others what is important to the individual. (Miller 2011: 166)

The internet, for a Puerto Rican queer group of millennials, helped construct our identities. It's no wonder then that the way I use El Site – which went live in 2018 – is not that different to the way I used websites of the 2000s, because the construction of a spatialized, queer identity in Puerto Rico often points back to earlier experiences, spaces, aesthetics and desires that shaped us.

In *Cüirtopia Live*, Laureano reminded us of the intermittent, fragmentary relationship between what is visible and what is invisible when it comes to how we appropriate/queer spaces in Puerto Rico. Although I've written about the ephemerality – the flickering on-and-off – of these spaces and the difficulties in maintaining a register of them due to their precariousness (Ramos 2021: 14–32), in our conversation, Laureano referenced Laboratoria Boricua de Vogue (commonly known as *laborivogue*), a group of queer people who organize online, show up to a baseball field, a basketball court or an alley, to create a vogue ball that doesn't try to imitate balls in the Global North. Instead, they look to celebrate our past as island-dwellers, as *Afro-Caribeños* hailing from the island of *Borikén*. Laureano rightly mentioned, for instance, how these groups of queer people organize differently as well as organize themselves in non-traditional ways; they're not taking minutes and organizing in committees, but rather going viral on the internet, rallying online, they appear in public, protest and then they disappear. Laureano mentions:

> [t]he visible gone invisible is really important in Puerto Rico's queer movement. It's impossible to approach it from a traditional lens. It's born out of need, it's chameleonic, it's fascinating and I'm only starting to articulate it here. It's not the future, it's our present, it's how queerness is developing in the island. (*Cüirtopia Live*, 2021)

In Puerto Rico, the fragmented state of queer spaces and architectures calls for alternative, geographically and culturally specific methods of documenting, writing, theorizing, preserving and/or protecting them. By writing in fragments, I'm practising interruptions and incompletions as active modes of production within queer spatial theory in Puerto Rico and it's something that has informed and mutated into my two new research projects, 'Coloso' (funded by the Graham Foundation 2021–3) and 'Cüirtopia' (funded by the FIPI Grant 2020–2) and worth briefly contextualizing here.

Named after one of Puerto Rico's largest sugary refineries dating back 200 years ago (1820–2003), 'Coloso' will be a web-based, virtual 'factory' for users to produce digital monuments that commemorate LGBTQ+ spaces in Puerto Rico. The project, which is co-led by me and my partner Kleanthis Kyriakou, aims to destabilize monuments as static representations of patriarchal, colonial ideals. Instead of immobile statues and architectural elements, 'Coloso' reimagines monuments as distributable digital icons and data. Taking the form of 3D digital models, drawings and animations, 'Coloso's' monuments will exist freely on the internet, where they can be generated, accessed and shared by individuals, groups and organizations. The monuments will be generated from a pre-designed kit-of-parts and users will be able to screen-shoot, print, laser-cut and 3D print them as objects to be folded, stacked and assembled. Thus, through this project, the act of creating *queer digital monuments* both appropriates and rejects colonial ideals of memorialization; contests who and what is commemorated; democratizes who gets to decide and commission; and reimagines the very materiality of monuments. 'Coloso' critically reflects on the loss of LGBTQ+ spaces. But rather than simply looking back on them nostalgically, it gives them agency, distributing and immortalizing them through the internet for generations. Thus, the project aims to contribute to contemporary architectural discourse through the creation of a performative website that celebrates, commemorates and registers LGBTQ+ architectures. By using the architectural typology of the monument as a tool to contest the displacement and ephemerality that defines Puerto Rican queer spaces, 'Coloso' is a subversive tool advocating for permanence, claim and ownership and the right to the built environment.

'Cüirtopia', on the other hand, is an interactive, web-based *map* of LGBTQ+ spaces in Puerto Rico. It is the first architectural and urban register of LGBTQ+ spaces in Puerto Rico from the 1960s until today. By recognizing spaces of *queerness* within contemporary cartographic practices, Cüirtopia inserts the buildings and spaces that are significant to the LGBTQ+ community into the island's architectural history, cultural infrastructure, urban memory and political future. The map is *both*: an archival artefact and a speculative research method, testing innovative approaches between urban field research and socially oriented GIS technologies, as well as allowing autoethnographic accounts of these spaces, as written and uploaded by visitors. More than a historically accurate, factually verifiable account of LGBTQ+ spaces, I'm interested in the partiality of these spatialized stories, their informality, their subjectivity, the hearsay and the gossip-like qualities that characterize how Puerto Rican LGBTQ+ spaces are recounted and remembered today (Ramos 2021: 27).

Part of my research method for the Cüirtopia project has been through fictional storytelling as well as a series of satellite projects that surround it – a radio show, drawings, paintings, Instagram filters, Instagram reels and so on. In fact, Cüirtopia's initial story is told through Instagram posts and captions, as a fictional account of a group of exiled migrants who set sail across open waters to reach a fabled island where LGBTQ+ people live freely. The fictional story – inspired by the Caribbean's history – builds up to the project launch, when Cüirtopia's website goes live in March 2022 via a solo exhibition at the Museo de Arte Contemporáneo de Puerto Rico (MAC).

The MAC is conceived, not as merely the *setting* for the exhibition but as a vital *agent* in the Cüirtopia project itself: a co-conspirator whose very materiality is activated, challenged and queered by and through performances, making and events. The MAC's position in relation to a queer, urban circuit in its Santurce neighbourhood offers the building as safe space for queer modes of spatial appropriation, cultural production and artistic imagination. This is why the MAC is written directly into the Cüirtopia story itself: it is not only the *launch* site of the project, it is very importantly reimagined as the *actual landing* site of the group of migrants who have, after years of travelling, arrived at the island of Cüirtopia. The Cüirtopia story exists through multiple, fragmented sites, each of them embodying specific narratives that only exist through the site conditions and physicality (or lack of it) of those spaces.

Playing with the possibilities of the fragment on El Site – responding to the work of scholars like Benítez-Rojo, Laureano, Rendell and Delaney – led me to deploy this mode of writing in other forums of architectural production, such as this book chapter, as well as in my other research projects. Confronting violent processes of colonization, the intentional fragmentation in my research looks to archipelagic thinking, architectural modes of making, performative writing and cartographic representations to carve out a space for queer futures in the Caribbean. Incompletion and interruption are precisely what's powerful about the fragment: evoking the possibility of reconstruction and re-assemblage in response to our Caribbean context – a queer one at that.

References

Benítez-Rojo, A. (1986), 'La isla que se repite: para una reinterpretación de la cultura caribeña', *Cuadernos Hispanoamericanos* 429: 115–32.

Cüirtopia Live (2021), 'Caribe Cüir', Episode, season 1, no. 1. San Juan: Radio Universidad de Puerto Rico.

Delany, S. R. (1999), Times Square Red, New York and London: New York University Press.

Miller, V. (2011), *Understanding Digital Culture*, Los Angeles, London, New Delhi, Singapore, Washington, DC: Sage.

Pugh, J. (2013), 'Island Movements: Thinking with the Archipelago', *Island Studies*, 8 (1): 9–24.

Ramos, R. and S. Mowlabocus (eds.) (2021), *Queer Sites in Global Contexts: Technologies, Spaces and Otherness*, Oxford and New York: Routledge.

Rendell, J. (2010), *Site-Writing: The Architecture of Art Criticism*, London and New York: I.B. Tauris.

6

After the party with the lights on

A case study of queering architecture

Timothy Moore and
Adam Nathaniel Furman

Scarlett So Hung Son entered a buzzing Melbourne café. On cue, the lights dimmed; the techie pulled and twiddled some knobs and the breath of antipodean pop princess Kylie Minogue mellifluously flowed from the speakers. Also out of So Hung Son's mouth. 'I should be so lucky', she lip-synched to a burlesque remix of the spangly 1980s hit. She hitched up her cheongsam and ascended the stairs of a yellow circular cake-tiered podium. The stage – painted with bodily motifs that reminded some patrons of boobs, bums and balls – may have dominated the space, but So Hung Son dominated the stage. She undid her cheongsam and flung it towards the podium's voluptuous central column. She remained in sheer red negligee, lingerie, garters and heels. It seemed like a lot of garments to wear, but she was really wearing almost nothing. Patrons looked on from cabaret seating surrounding the stage, divided by self-supporting screens into twos, threes and larger clusters of onlookers. These screens had peepholes that framed views to other patrons, including those that loitered against the walls, which had been transformed into a vivid pattern of bent coloured stripes and mirror. 'I should be so lucky', the crowd sang along to the Aussie chanson.

Boudoir Babylon, the café that Scarlett So Hung Son headlined over a dozen times that summer, was an installation for the exhibition *Triennial 2020* at the National Gallery of Victoria (NGV), located in Melbourne on Wurundjeri Woiwurrung Country. This brightly coloured and patterned interior brought together a range of architectural devices – including screens, baffles, oculi and a podium – to play with the settings that influence how people gather and socialize. The installation had a playfulness which celebrated the right to joy and pleasure and the right to be different and particularly, to be queer. As its designers, we developed strategies to achieve this through the study of three historically queer spaces – the salon, the nightclub and the boudoir. From this study, a new space emerged.

Queering the café

Our invitation to participate in the Triennial 2020 exhibition from 19 December 2020, until 18 April 2021, came from Ewan McEoin, the Hugh D.T. Williamson senior curator of contemporary art, design and architecture at the NGV, who was one of the commissioners of architecture and design projects within the exhibition. The NGV is Australia's most-visited gallery and the second iteration of its triennial comprised eighty-six new works from over 100 artists, architects and designers from over thirty countries (Butler 2021). The show was significant not only in national terms but also for connecting Australian audiences to international artists and designers. McEoin's brief for us was to create a project that explored 'queering the café', namely in the NGV café space known as Gallery Kitchen. The design commission agreement extrapolated on the brief further, stating that 'The design should explore a queer expression through an aesthetic style different from the norm. In parallel, it is also important to acknowledge the experiences of the LGBTQ+ community seeking spaces of difference that are safe and symbolic'. McEoin matched us to this brief due to our previous writing and discussions on queer expressions in architecture (e.g. see Furman 2019, 2022; Kalms 2018; Moore 2021).

Our brief was broad in terms of how 'queering a café' could be materialized. This breadth is also reflected in the discipline of architecture in terms of how to 'queer' a space – a debate which has played out in writing and spoken word, more than it has in completed built work.[1] Spaces put to queer use, rather than spaces designed with queer theory at the fore, have been prevalent in architectural discourse over the past decades. In the essay 'Home Is the Place We All Share: Building Queer Collective Utopias', Olivier Vallerand outlines various interpretations of how queer spaces have been considered historically by the discipline of architecture (Vallerand 2013). Spaces put to queer uses may be spaces where LGBTIQA+ communities congregate and with which they self-identify. These spaces could be nightclubs, bathhouses, cafés and bars. They can also be spaces where typical uses are challenged, such as through sex acts at public parks and toilets. The appropriation of normative spaces echoes the recent understanding of queering as a process, which 'demonstrates a capacity or agency of performance and acting out with the aim to pervert and undermine power constructs to unleash suppressed and marginalized desires' (Gorny and Heuvel 2017: 2). It also highlights a marked shift from spaces of self-identification to prioritizing spaces that challenge disciplinary and societal privilege and power.

The throuple: boudoir, salon, nightclub

Investigating precedents of spaces put to queer use underpinned our design process for the NGV brief, as we sought to extract various approaches and apply them in a contemporary setting. Three spaces were investigated – the boudoir, salon and the nightclub – due to their each being significant historical interiors that challenged normative understandings of gender and sexuality at the time of their emergence. Understanding their spatial conditions, including their architectural props that script behaviour, was integral in the design of Boudoir Babylon, to reflect on what design strategies could contribute to queering a space: to make it both symbolic to the LGBTIQA+ community and also to challenge dominant approaches to designing space.

The first space analysed was the boudoir: which emerged as a place of retreat for women between the dining room and the bedroom in the mid-eighteenth-century France. As defined by Charles-Francois Roland Le Virloys in his 1770 architecture dictionary *Dictionnaire d'architecture civile, militaire et naval, antique, ancienne et moderne*, a boudoir is a place where 'a woman may retire to think, or read, or work or, in a word, be alone' (Reynolds 2004: 107). Elements we located in our analysis of boudoirs were props, which included paired seating, modesty screens, mirrors, chaise lounges, curtains and veils; they created intimate seating arrangements for singles and couples. Some of these props were to remerge in Boudoir Babylon.

One specific source of inspiration was Eileen Grey's Boudoir de Monte Carlo presented at XIV Salon des Artistes Décorateurs in Paris, 1923, which modernized the boudoir from a space to retreat, to a multidimensional space for rest, parties and pleasure, with a daybed at its centre (Bonnevier 2007). Katarina Bonnevier observed that Grey's interpretation of the boudoir 'was the most public space of the apartment, as well as the most intimate. There is no spatial opposition between these two categories. Visitors are greeted and entertained in this space, but one can also settle in. No simple norm decides what kind of space this is' (Bonnevier 2007: 40). This supports the notion of the boudoir as a place of empowerment for women, but simultaneously a space that can be decoupled from a strictly feminine reading. It also influenced the design of Boudoir Babylon, which looked to overlay strategies observed in different historical precedents across the whole space rather than in discrete segmented areas.

The salon was the second space of investigation to inform Boudoir Babylon. Historically, the salon was a theatre of conversation and exchange – particularly for women and for those with non-normative religious and ideological beliefs. The private interiors of French salons, such as that of Suzanne Curchod, hosted the loosening of social hierarchy as 'nobles and non-nobles were brought together on a footing of equality' (Goodman 1989: 333). This is reflected in the spatial arrangement of furniture with chairs, sofas and tables arranged in an ad hoc manner to reflect the gathering of people in different constellations of groups. The variegated approach to seating arrangements was integral to the spatial planning of seating for Boudoir Babylon.

The third space of exploration was the nightclub, which became prominent in the 1960s in Western Europe as a multi-functional space for entertainment. As 1960s Radical Design collective Gruppo 9999 claimed, discos should be 'a home for everything, from rock music, to theatre, to visual arts' (Bucknell 2018). They were also spaces that broke 'with traditional couples dancing as the basis of social dance' (Lawrence 2011), which could liberate the dancer from heterosexist and patriarchal relationships in the club. This contributed to clubs as being 'safe spaces for populations whose lives were marginalized in the daylight' (Chua 2019). The analysis of the nightclub revealed reoccurring spatial devices, including platforms, podiums and stages. This can be seen across many examples, such as the moveable black-and-white platforms at Piper in Rome (Rossi 2014), the cylindrical volumes for dancing at the Maddox Club in Platja d'Aro (Esteves 2018) or the stages at multiple clubs like Melbourne's Metro or Manchester's the Hacienda. The podium was a prop that was extracted from this observation study for the Boudoir Babylon commission at NGV.

The throuple at play

Boudoir Babylon was located at a significant juncture of the NGV building, after the visitor had entered through the main entrance off St Kilda Road and passing through its institutional fripperies (including a foyer, the information booth and cloakroom). Turning left, the visitor found the Gallery Kitchen, a threshold between several spaces: a shop, lobby, escalator and Jeff Koons's Venus 2016–20. A tiered circular stage dominated the space, an object for people to mount, in a manner similar to the podiums, stages and catwalks of nightclubs. It provided a place to sit, stand, eat, drink, sing and dance, including for drag performances, including Scarlett So Hung Son.[2] The podium rested between an aedicule and stereobate (created from vinyl) that further framed vignettes of café life on the podium.

While the podium provided a space for extroverts, there were also places for the introvert and voyeur facilitated by curved modesty screens, suggestive of the boudoir and allowing for different seating arrangements by acting as dividers. These screens were placed strategically to enclose a series of two-seater tables to form small groups suggestive of a salon. The screens provided opportunities for concealment, but they did not divide people. They encouraged curiosity and the game of seeing (and being seen) calibrated as a gradient of disclosure within an otherwise open social setting. These screens also allowed for different angles of bodies and identities to be viewed through oculi that punctuated the modesty screens. This is noted by gender studies academic Hannah McCann in the *Triennial 2020* catalogue who wrote, 'We remain [in Boudoir Babylon] at once physically safe but visually together, connected as we peer through these openings, allowing new and unexpected connections to arise as the space is arranged and rearranged' (McCann 2020: 152). You could look through a bum and see someone else's body part; or take a photo of yourself through the hole.

Bodily motifs dominated Boudoir Babylon with circles, curves, arcs and bends that suggest the intimacy of undressing in the boudoir. They appeared as graphics along the podium risers in green and white and as the headstone shape of the screens. Bodily motifs reached their crescendo above the podium where a central 'column' was created from overblown classical column capital elements, which reflects our 'strong appreciation of classicism as an infinitely flexible architectural language' (Brooks 2020) and this case, flexible enough to suggest complex corporeality. The ambiguous forms embedded in the design referenced body parts: a penis, vagina, earlobe, buttock, breast, cheek, testicle or anus. However, they were pushed together and refashioned centrifugally, which rendered their exact meaning impossible.

The podium and dividers provided spaces for a spectrum of users, which was a strategy for making the space welcoming for different patrons. Orientation was also integral to making people feel safe. This was made difficult by several entry points from the café – to a shop, galleries, forecourt, bathrooms – alongside an escalator that zooms patrons from the galleries on the level above, directly into the café. While the condition of having many exits allows people to feel safe, there was also a need to locate these exits. The design attempted this through creating walls with bent coloured stripes interchanged with mirror, which provided direction for egress. The new wall surface made it no longer (just) a wall, because it reflected the space. Reflective surfaces are also important for people to see themselves; however, it's not always a narcissistic or selfie moment. People see themselves and others in a reflection as part of something larger than themselves.

Surface treatment went to the crux of Boudoir Babylon, which extended from the walls and columns, to the podium and to above and below with the aedicule and stereobate vinyls. The use of colour and pattern was not only used for wayfinding or to bring joy. This is an outcome of an aesthetic choice (alongside an efficient budget). The semiotic performativity here was to challenge the taste of bourgeois sophistication that we think dominates architectural and design practices, which can result in a restrained use of colour.[3] The determination of the project as one of the major architectural commissions of *Triennial 2020* – alongside Liam Young and Kengo Kuma – gives a platform for our position, witnessed by over 520,000 visitors (Booker 2021). We are attention-seeking for the queer cause by using a rainbow of colours. This is conferred by McCann: 'Queerness here takes centre stage: no longer relegated to the sidelines, no longer only found in nightlife but also in daily life; and no longer only in the privacy of one's home, boudoir or closet' (McCann 2020: 152).

Bodily motifs alongside colour contributed to symbolism in the space for the LGBTQIA+ community. In particular, the curvaceous elements in Boudoir Babylon suggested sexuality and gender. We were aware that not every queer person would necessarily recognize themselves in this space, but we hoped they would acknowledge the installation's queerness through the corporeal references. This is supported by architectural theorist Claude Dutson who remarked, 'Even if I do not recognize my own queerness in BB, I am sympathetic to it. I get that it is doing something on behalf of me, even if it is not speaking directly to me' (Runting et al. 2021: 113). We were also aware that not everyone would recognize the inherent symbolism but they

FIGURE 6.1 *The podium and dividers provided spaces for a spectrum of users, which was a strategy for making the space welcoming for different patrons.*

FIGURE 6.2 *A central 'column' was created from overblown classical column capital elements, which also referenced body parts: a penis, vagina, earlobe, buttock, breast, cheek, testicle or anus.*

FIGURE 6.3 *Surface treatment is integral to the installation, which extended from the walls and columns, to the podium and to above and below with the aedicule and stereobate vinyls.*

FIGURE 6.4 *A tiered circular stage was painted with bodily motifs that reminded some patrons of boobs, bums and balls.*

would still be engaged in our queer agenda by entering the mis-en-scene. This was recognized by McCann, who wrote: 'As the wider public moves through and inhabits the space, they are participants in this queer world rather than simply spectators' (McCann 2020: 151).

Spatial elements derived from the boudoir, club and salon returned in Boudoir Babylon: modesty screens connected and divided, patterned walls reflected passers-by, decoration was celebrated and seating options were multiple and flexible – for singles, couples, throuples, throngs and more. They created a spectrum of relationships between bodies and identities that were not fixed or not wholly seen. This goes to the significance of the work in its endeavour to queer the café: it created a space that was safe through clear egress and sightlines; symbolic through bodily motifs, colour and pattern; and social through providing different constellations of seating, including celebrating a throng of people on the central podium surrounded by boobs, bums and balls. These strategies deriving from the study of queer spaces allowed each person that visited Boudoir Babylon to find a way to occupy this space and if they somehow did not, there was no way they could not have acknowledged the somewhat queered café as they sauntered, darted or paraded past that summer (Figures 6.1–6.4).

Notes

1   The exploration and translation of queer theory in the architecture discipline has been limited over previous decades, with a focus on events, university design studios, talks, writing and paper architecture rather than built works.

2   Helen Runting, in her review in Inflection, remarked on this feature: 'I was a little revolted by the sheer number of bodies that completely covered the thing: cranky old couples with overpriced sandwiches, the design crowd with glasses of wine, hanging out and staring at each other and children running around, everywhere. . . . It is irresistibly popular' (Runting et al. 2021: 110).

3   One of the authors of this chapter, Adam Nathaniel Furman, would argue that their queer aesthetics can be considered a method to critique and disrupt normative architectural conventions. This doesn't necessarily hold up in Melbourne, which has several large-scale practices (including ARM, Lyons Architecture and MCR) that purvey bright colours, popular symbolism and other postmodern techniques.

References

Bonnevier, K. (2007). *Behind Straight Curtains: Towards a Queer Feminist Theory of Architecture*. Stockholm: Axl Books.

Booker, C. and Webb, C. (2021). 'Buzz Is Coming Back to Melbourne: Weekend Foot Traffic Nears Pre-pandemic Level'. *The Age*, Melbourne.

Brooks, E. (2020). 'Adam Nathaniel Furman Q&A'. Retrieved from https://designanthologyuk.com/article/adam-nathaniel-furman-qa/

Bucknell, A. (2018). 'Do It, Do It Disco'. *Metropolis*, 37(9), 152–7.

Butler, A. (2021). 'A Risk-Averse Triennial at the NGV Struggles with Its Own Mission'. Frieze. Retrieved from https://www.frieze.com/article/ngv-triennial -2021-review.

Chua, L. (2019). 'Night Fever: Designing Club Culture, 1960 – Today'. *The Journal of Architecture*, 24(1), 130–8.

Esteves, P. (2018). 'Total Space'. In M. Kries, J. Eisenbrand and C. Rossi (Eds.), *Night Fever: Designing Club Culture, 1960-Today* (pp. 130–47). Weil am Rhein: Vitra.

Furman, A. N. (2019). 'Outrage'. *Architectural Review*, 245(1459), 55.

Furman, A. N. and Mardell, J., eds. (2022). *Queer Spaces: An Atlas of LGBTQIA+ Places and Stories*. London: RIBA Publishing.

Goodman, D. (1989). 'Enlightenment Salons: The Convergence of Female and Philosophic Ambitions'. *Eighteenth-Century Studies*, 22(3), 329–50.

Gorny, R. and Heuvel, D. (2017). 'New Figurations in Architecture Theory: From Queer Performance to Becoming Trans'. *Footprint*, 21, 1–10.

Kalms, N., Spooner, M., Ball, T., Stead, N., Moore, T., Dyring, S., Perkovic, J. (2018). *Queering Architecture and Design*. Melbourne: MPavilion.

Lawrence, T. (2011). 'Disco and the Queering of the Dance Floor'. *Cultural Studies*, 25(2), 230–43.

McCann, H. (2020). 'Queer I: Seeing Queerly'. In Maidment, S. et. al. (Eds.), In *NGV Triennial 2020 Catalogue* (pp. 138–53). Melbourne: National Gallery of Victoria.

Moore, T. and Castricum, S. (2021). *Queering Architecture: Simona Castricum and Timothy Moore in Conversation. Contentious Cities: Design and the Gendered Production of Space*. Ed. J. Berry, T. Moore, N. Kalms and G. Bawden. Oxon, UK: Routledge, 182–93.

Reynolds, N. (2004). 'Boudoir Stories: A Novel History of a Room and Its Occupants'. *Literature Interpretation Theory*, *15*, 103–30.

Rossi, C. (2014). 'Architecture Goes Disco'. *AA Files*, *69*, 138–45.

Runting, H. R., Dutson, C. and Ozmin, J. (2021). 'Oh BB BB! A Collective Review of Sibling Architecture and Adam Nathaniel Furman's Boudoir Babylon'. *Inflection*, *8*, 110–15.

Vallerand, O. (2013). Home Is the Place We All Share: Building Queer Collective Utopias. *Journal of Architectural Education*, *67*(1), 64–75.

7

Fabulous façades

Ben Campkin and Lo Marshall

Planning delirium

We are sitting side-by-side in our office in the newly refurbished home of The Bartlett School of Architecture in central London. We're running on empty. Or, rather, we're full to the brim, with an excess of content: too much caffeine, certainly, but more importantly, data, having spent many months wading through the murky labyrinths of London councils' planning databases, tracing the contours of large-scale redevelopment schemes, attempting to unpick complex planning disputes, counting LGBTQ+ venues, recording their coordinates and categorizing their distinguishing features. Our journey has involved numerous hours of scanning dense information. We've downloaded thousands of pages of plans and appendices into a small city of subfolders and spreadsheets, which reflect the numerous detours, cul-de-sacs and broken links of our sources. Fans whirring, our laptops complain in white noise. Scratching our heads, rubbing our dry eyes, our sense of scale and proportion have been skewed by the laborious processing of miles of text, from the weighty to the frivolous and everything in between. Our past fun encounters with the palaces of queer culture have been long forgotten, faint memories submerged under layers of bureaucracy.

Calling queer fun

In this chapter we reflect on Fabulous Façades, a performance that we created and staged with a group of educators, artists and researchers, in three cultural venues in London, between 2017 and 2019. These were the Royal Vauxhall Tavern, an established queer cabaret pub known fondly as the RVT; the Museum of London, as part of a Queer Salon that we curated in an exhibition and events season called *City Now, City Future*; and at the Whitechapel Gallery, for the press opening of the exhibition *Queer Spaces: London, 1980s–Today*, which presented case studies from our research alongside sculptural and visual artworks engaging with queer space.[1] As we performed and reperformed Fabulous Façades, we continually evaluated our efforts, adapting its form and content to respond to each institutional environment. These performances connected to, but somewhat detoured from, the main thrust of our research at the time, on the heritage of London's queer venues (Campkin and Marshall 2017a, 2018). Broadly, we defined these as venues operated by and/or for LGBTQ+ populations. Our research was prompted by and set out to understand, campaigns to protect these premises in contexts where they were threatened due to rapid redevelopment. The work we did through Fabulous Façades offered an opportunity for us to encounter and present the archives and architectures we were investigating in new ways. As a troupe of six, the preparation and performances enabled us to digest and communicate the affective terrain of the planning cases we were working with, in modes that travelled beyond the more conventional and linear outputs and methods of our research and dissemination and that connected with the histories of the venues and the cultural practices they are associated with in queer ways. In the following, we reflect mainly on the first incarnation of Fabulous Façades at the RVT. We do so drawing architecture, architectural history and urban studies into what sociology and queer studies researchers Amin Ghaziani and Matt Brim describe as the current moment of a 'renaissance of queer methods' (2019: 3).

The initial prompt for Fabulous Façades was a call by the arts collective Duckie to participate in Queer Fun, pitched as 'an ivory-tower vaudeville', programmed by critic and researcher Ben Walters, aka Dr Duckie (Walters 2017). The event was framed as a chance to explore how 'queer fun builds muscles' and to reflect on the kinds of fun that might be deemed specifically 'queer' (Ibid). Artists, researchers, performers and others were invited to present an eight-minute turn, which would be located somewhere within or around the RVT – a venue Duckie had used since 1995. As an iconic cabaret pub, one subject to the threat of closure and redevelopment and the focus of a high-profile campaign to secure its future, the RVT had been one of the case studies of our research (RVT Future 2022; Campkin forthcoming). Although Queer Fun welcomed academic contributions, we were feeling burnt out by the experience of giving multiple conventional academic presentations about the research and by arduous trawling through technical planning cases. We relished the chance to engage through modes more suited to the venues that we were working with, including the RVT, which had an association with sexual and gender experimentation, including drag shows, since at least the 1940s (Campkin 2022: 127; Walters 2015).

Our research practice prior to Queer Fun had already deployed multiple methods. As well as workshops, interviews and archival analyses, it included exercises in mapping and counter-mapping (Campkin and Marshall 2017a, 2018). Our data on venue numbers had been adopted by City Hall and published in digital maps alongside datasets on other forms of social and cultural infrastructure in London (GLA 2019); but we worked against the grain of quantitative data collection by drawing attention to cartography's reductive tendencies, interlacing maps with an array of other qualitative evidence. Our research had been produced collaboratively with activists and communities of interest in the orbit of LGBTQ+ venues. The survey and dataset we had produced were co-designed with Queer Spaces Network and RAZE Collective – two entities that emerged from a crisis of venue closures and ongoing threats to some of the longest-standing spaces in the mid-2010s (Campkin forthcoming). Alongside the reports we had presented to the Mayor of London's Culture Team, we had produced collages (Figure 7.1), unorthodox charts (Figure 7.2) and an open access issue of a print and digital publication, *Urban Pamphleteer*, which contested hierarchies in the production of knowledge, bringing out multiple perspectives on the history and politics of LGBTQ+ night-spaces in London (Campkin and Marshall 2018; Campkin, Marshall and Ross 2018).

Planning has a strong association with technocratic documents and procedures, but as a political battleground it also frequently features high emotional intensity. This was clear in the debates about the value or redundance, of LGBTQ+ venues we had been studying. We read the archives around planning cases attuned to their affective content, particularly where

FIGURE 7.1 *LGBTQ+ nightlife collage, published in* Urban Pamphleteer #7.

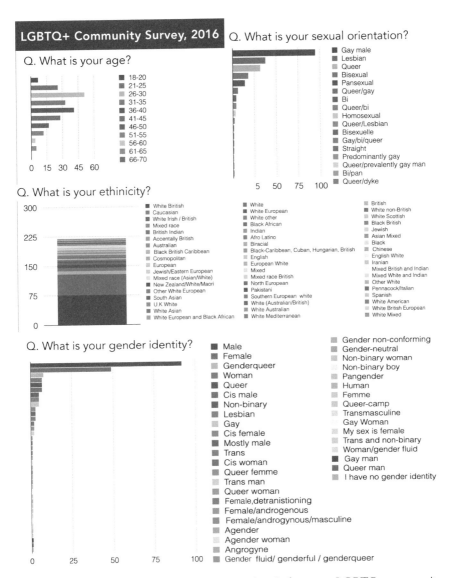

FIGURE 7.2 *Demographic data from UCL Urban Laboratory LGBTQ+ community survey.*

they took the form of public consultation responses and especially where similar planning schemes had been submitted repeatedly, magnifying responders' frustrations. Our research had also taken us down unexpected side paths: into public exchanges on TripAdvisor, for example. In one sour case, managers, regulars and visitors to 'London's oldest gay pub' vented accusations over conflicts that had occurred. The statements gave witness to the sense of freedom and joy that venues can provide, as well as the everyday management of somewhat messy night-time spaces. Our desire was to both work with and against the dry technocratic details of the planning sources we were examining. We wanted to voice the many moments within these ostensibly bureaucratic, procedural systems when they cracked open to reveal raw emotional content or where personal histories and collective memories embedded in contested queer venues were evoked or where there were openings out to other idiosyncratic archives.

Coordinates: architecture in drag

Discussing this in our workplace – a design school, famed for aesthetic and technological sophistication, and for fostering professional competitiveness – we were keen to step outside of the academy on to an esteemed cabaret stage in a mode of collaborative DIY amateurism to take another perspective. But making this step and performing the tales contained in our planning sources in public, necessitated a stretch of our imaginations and a level of discomfort. To help get over our stage fright and the anxiety of mixing serious professional work with the social world and queer fun that the RVT stood for, we pondered potential precedents within the built environment disciplines and professions.

Where, we asked, with bleary eyes and tired minds, did architecture and planning already do drag? Where were its moments of joy and incongruity? Where were the glitches that exposed the artifice of professional formalities?

Delirious in London, we turned to *Delirious New York* and Rem Koolhaas's (1994 [1978]) contemplation of the twelfth Beaux-Arts costume ball. Staged during the Depression, *Fête Moderne: A Fantasie in Flame and Silver* was based on the annual costume ball of the École Nationale Supérieure des Beaux-Arts in Paris. Koolhaas reports a press release from the *New York Herald Tribune* which promised that the *Fête* would be 'modernistic, futuristic, cubistic, altruistic, mystic, architistic and femininstic' (ibid: 191). On the night of 23 January 1931, 3,000 guests, primed for a programme of 'eventful events and delightful delights', arrived at Hotel Astor on Broadway. This oblique, theatre-lined conduit through Manhattan's urban grid offered an apt location for the drama of architectural drag. This was a famously off-kilter moment in architectural history and practice from which we felt we could riff.

The Beaux-Arts architects and artists had been invited to participate in the search for the 'Spirit of the Age' (ibid). On the night, headlining the *Fête Moderne*, forty-four male architects donned elaborate costumes, mostly personifying the exteriors of their New York buildings in a 'Skyline of New York' ballet (ibid: 193). In this peculiar line-up, as anyone can watch on YouTube, the smiles, waves and prideful comportment of some juxtaposes the embarrassed expressions and awkward postures of others who seemingly feel out of place in this dalliance with the theatrical. This collective public display of silliness may have sat uneasily with the less explicitly embodied and more behind-the-scenes and serious business of architecture and enculturation into the professional status of 'the architect'. A lone woman, Edna Cowan, stood in costume as the Basin Girl, described by Koolhaas as:

> An apparition straight from the men's subconscious, she stands there on the stage to symbolize the entrails of architecture or more precisely: she stands for the continuing embarrassment caused by the biological functions of the human body that have proved resistant to lofty aspirations and technological sublimation. (ibid. 198)

It is unknown what kind of negotiations and conversations occurred behind the scenes or how Edna herself felt. Did anyone care to ask? The line-up celebrated the architect's mastery over materiality and form, and dominant role in producing public urban modernity. Following Koolhaas and generations of feminists' analyses of the gendered production of the urban socio-spatial order, we might interpret Edna Cowan's Basin Girl as representing both opposition and obstacle. Her costume confines her – and by implication women generally – to a domestic, interior, private realm; she embodies the inconvenient and often disobedient, leaky plumbing of bodies and buildings, veiled behind the grandeur of façades, servicing buildings masterminded by men (Bondi 1998; Burns 2012; Cavanaugh 2010; Kristeva 1982; Penner 2010; Shonfield 2000). Despite the futuristic and fantastical framing, in practice, the skyline ballet personified the age-old elitist, patriarchal and gendered capitalist building blocks that formed the Manhattan urban grid.

In *Delirious New York*, Koolhaas described the Fête Moderne as 'research, disguised as a costume ball' (Koolhaas 1994[1978]: 191). Delirious in London, we wondered if *research, disguised as drag* might offer a mode of re-imagining planning queerly. Using the New York skyline ballet as a springboard for our contribution to Queer Fun, we wished to refuse the Western canon it represented. Instead of landmark modern buildings and noted architects, our skyline would comprise a queer and trans collective, personifying closed and threatened LGBTQ+ venues, those that had emerged in the interstices and infrastructural remnants of the modern city, sometimes with ornamental, DIY, kitsch, fresh or industrial postmodern aesthetics which countered its regularity and purity. The costumes our troupe made and wore were fashioned from the façades that conceal and cocoon queer fun, which have sustained queer safety and survival in the late-twentieth and early-twentieth-century city and have been increasingly under threat from rapid redevelopment.

Our research focused on venues with direct links to gay and lesbian social movements, queer culture and visibility politics in the UK and the United States, so our nod to the New York skyline was appropriate. The research had been triggered by renewed calls to make London's queer spaces visible in the urban terrain, in order to protect them from closure due to the rapacious momentum of infrastructure-led renewal in the 2000s. Campaigners' claims to the value of these venues required them to narrate what was specific about the form, aesthetics and other qualities of buildings and interiors, as well as their uses. For us, discussions of queer space and of gay or queer aesthetics in architecture and urbanism, therefore provided another context.

Writing on the relations between urban memory sites and gay identities, literature scholars Christopher Castiglia and Christopher Reed remind us of architecture critic Charles Jencks's 1970s account of the origins of stylistic postmodernism as 'gay eclectic' (Castiglia and Reed 2012: 91). This was a reference to playful, camp exteriors, associated with the residences of gay men, but it also spoke to the interiors and aesthetics of some of the 1980s venues we were investigating. Castiglia and Reed observe that Jencks's phrase quickly disappeared from later versions of *Postmodern Architecture* (1977), as it rapidly entered the Western architectural canon (ibid). Signposting a wide literature on gays and gentrification, they note that early accounts of the geography of gay space, including sociologist Manuel Castells's 1980s commentary on gay migration to the Castro in San Francisco in the 1960s and 1970s, associated certain aesthetic markers with the presence of gay populations, such as in the renovation and painting of Victorian façades (ibid: 98). Despite the articulation of gay aesthetics in these early discussions of gay space, Castiglia and Reed surmise that queer space theories of the 1990s, which were a strong feature of the newly emerging wave of 'queer theory', featured an 'insistence on the architectural invisibility of queer life', focusing instead on the low imageability of venues (ibid). Their arguments about a certain historical amnesia regarding the memory sites of gay liberation and the neglect of visual codes of queer place-making in the built environment, seemed pertinent. In London we were witnessing a marked attempt to map and raise the profile of queer venues, many of which were incidental monuments to an earlier politics of visibility within the lesbian and gay movement.

Category is: DIY town planning

Our proposal for Queer Fun was to substitute the modernist architects of the Fête Moderne with our queer troupe – six researchers, artists and educators – who would personify notable venues, attired in outfits made from the planning documents and ephemera, associated with them. The collective would read extracts from the planning processes, revealing affective qualities embedded in even the most ostensibly dry bureaucratic statements, as well as voicing moments of obvious emotion, as in public

FIGURE 7.3 *Tom Kendall as The Black Cap in Fabulous Façades, photo by Rafael Pereira do Rego.*

consultation responses, when statements expressed passion, frustration and frayed tempers (Figure 7.3).

We sought to repurpose and re-contextualize the policy, legal and other documents that described and determined 'the kinds of queer fun these spaces have accommodated behind their fabulous nineteenth-century façades – whether decorative, discrete, transparent, shuttered or tinted' (Campkin and Marshall 2017b). In the venues we had encountered in our research, the façades (and other elevations) were telling – a kind of architectural drag themselves. Fronting buildings often repurposed from other uses, they revealed changing dynamics in queer life, of visibility and invisibility, of the desire to remain hidden or to be seen. In the recent controversies over the closure, sale and redevelopment of these premises, the exterior features took on new meanings. As much-loved cabaret venues closed, to be replaced by bland chain cafés, these once reticent and mundane elevations became settings for colourful protests, battle lines in a war against homogenizing gentrification aesthetics.

Our research had been considering how queer populations had, to borrow Cuban American theorist José Esteban Muñoz's words, imagined hopeful 'urban landscapes of astonishment' under 'the cover of a protective darkness', inhabiting quotidian spaces and subverting neoliberal zoning and licensing regulations (Muñoz 2009: 52). The performance we devised channelled the DIY spirit of queer activist and performance cultures Muñoz engages. This is an ethos that celebrates resourcefulness and creativity and embraces tensions without attempting resolution: the silly and serious, joy and pain, love and loss and, in our case, hedonism and planning, queer fun and dry details.

Our Fabulous Façades came to life through carefully and collectively crafted outfits, with canonical drag flourishes: high heels and big boots, paper and plastic, lipstick and lashes, glitter and gaffer, crowned with cardboard millinery and bonded by tenderness and an appreciation of absurdity. The ephemera we wore changed each time, strings of words and images pulled and collaged from otherwise unapproachable archives. We made these fragments visible and vocal. Intimacy and vulnerability were integral to our endeavour. Finding high heels for big feet, learning costume-making and make-up skills, selecting, editing texts and posing with unwieldy headpieces and clipboards, presented different challenges to each of us, requiring us to share knowledge, craft, time and the contents of our drag bags.

Queer Fun's producers located performances all around the RVT, siting ours outside and behind the venue, in the Vauxhall Pleasure Gardens, a public park with a distinctly queer history of hedonism, performance and experimentation with sexuality and gender. We had not anticipated that we would be outside. Once our troupe had posed for a photo call on the RVT stage (Figure 7.4) we formed a ramshackle procession to our positions for an impromptu dress rehearsal. The location had a particular resonance since Duckie had long drawn links between their work, the RVT and the Pleasure Gardens. These associations had featured strongly in the successful grassroots campaigns to designate the RVT as an 'Asset of Community Value' in planning parlance and later as a Grade II listed building (Historic England 2015). Using our bodies, performative readings from glittered clipboards and the cardboard models we had made to wear as headsets, the pop-up network of venues we created felt appropriate to the transitory architectures and legacies of pleasure implanted within the historical gardens, which had been dismantled and dispersed in the 1850s, as well as to the RVT's herstories of drag and alt cabaret (Walters 2021). Assembled along the rear wall of the RVT, we were located immediately behind the stage (Figures 7.5 and 7.6), which has a cult status in queer performance.

When we came to rehearse the readings, we experimented with repetition, pacing and layering, reciting excerpts in turn, then moving incrementally into multi-vocal layers of shorter snippets, which crescendoed into a cacophony (Figure 7.7). This way of expressing the documents was intended to articulate interconnectivities across them, while reproducing the complex layering and intertextuality of documents submitted and mobilized as evidence in planning cases. These demand time and technical skill to negotiate and often involve the repeated submission of only subtly amended proposals, requiring a pedant's eye. Consequently, queer space campaigners have been required to gain new knowledge and carve out the time to navigate frustrating and overwhelming digital repositories of planning documents, containing competing voices, which we sought to echo. In selecting the texts, we had in mind how evidence is considered 'material' in planning, the term which designates whether it is substantive or not, against tests of policy and

FIGURE 7.4 *Top: London Skyline: Fabulous Façades on the RVT stage, photo by Rafael Pereira do Rego. Bottom: New York Skyline: Architecture on the Beaux Arts ball stage.*

the law. These documents had not been written with the intention of being read aloud. Doing so, in situ, in the urban environment, gave them new and different substance and heightened the sense of their ephemerality as traces (Figure 7.8).

Queer as folk

In planning and performing Fabulous Façades we were participating in modes of queer scholar-activism that have an extended history in London, just as in many other cities. In the 1970s, for example, there were strong lines between empirical and theoretical sociological, geographical and historical work, practices of archiving and the direct-action campaigns of lesbian and gay social movements. These movements, of which the Gay Liberation

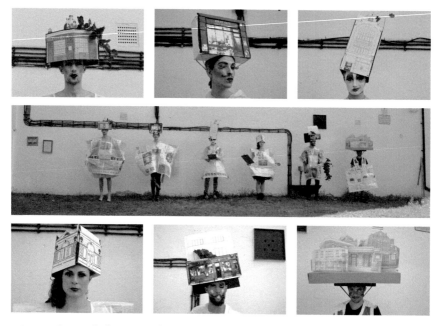

FIGURE 7.5 *Fabulous Façades at the RVT – a queer skyline comprised of City of Quebec, First Out, The Black Cap, The Glass Bar, The Joiners' Arms and Women's Anarchist Nuisance Café, photo by Rafael Pereira do Rego.*

FIGURE 7.6 *Still image depicting multiple layers from digital scan of the RVT, showing the location of the stage, behind our performance location, now occupied by a tent. UCL Urban Laboratory, 2021.*

[Joiners Arms] It's very heterosexual, white and boring.
[First Out] Oh no! I've been coming since 1994! End of an era.
[London Lesbian and Gay Centre (LLGC)] My honourable friend is correct: it is a disgraceful waste of money.
[The Black Cap] Please do not allow more blandness in the borough! No, no, no!
[Glass Bar] If you identified as a woman, that's it, you could come in.
[Women's Anarchist Nuisance Café (WANC)] semi-legal space, semi-legal vibe.

[Joiners Arms] The space that brought us together allowed more than just dancing, or whatever.
[First Out] Coming out was pretty scary back in 1997.
[LLGC] You know, we don't always think we deserve these places, but we do.
[The Black Cap] This is the 5th application, 4 times refused. Get the message!
[Glass Bar] They gave me 4 days to pack up everything and go.
[WANC] It was really well organised and quite plush

[Joiners Arms] For so many people I know it defined a period in their lives.
[First Out] And they also said they walked up and down, up and down, up and down before they could take the plunge to go in.
[LLGC] There was a triumph of hope over reality…it was crushed by the weight of expectations.
[The Black Cap] A back window had been left open, so they took their chance and climbed in.
[Glass Bar] Brought to a grinding halt. 29th of December 2008, the final pint was pulled.
[WANC] The offence will come into force on 1 September 2012.

[Joiners Arms] It seems like it's a sort of victory, but the fight isn't over.
First Out We went out with quite a bang.
[LLGC] We exceeded and succeeded…. in all kinds of ways - way beyond what we were financed to do.
[The Black Cap] North London's 21st Century, Premier LGBTQ+ Cabaret & Entertainment Venue.
[Glass Bar] Difficult to find (and hard to forget) you knock on the door and become a member to enter.
WANCI The person knows or ought to know that they are a trespasser.

[Joiners Arms] I wish to formally object.

FIGURE 7.7 *Fabulous Façades, cacophony script.*

FIGURE 7.8 *Lo Marshall as The Glass Bar at the RVT, photo by Rafael Pereira do Rego.*

Front was one manifestation, unfolded between the settings of the street and park, the university and through engaging with what we might now call queer venues, in their existing and imagined forms (Campkin forthcoming; Feather 2014; Power 1995; Walter 1980).

Queer urban history and theory do not exist in a separate realm but are rather part of everyday praxis, of the making of queer lifeworlds and strategies of survival. This was evident in the framing of Duckie's 'Queer Fun', an artistic-academic collaboration. It was also evident more generally in the crisis over venues that had prompted our work – mapping them and collating evidence to understand their value. These campaigns were intentionally linked to other forms of activism around the commemoration of queer histories and exclusionary impacts of gentrification (Broomfield 2017; Glass 2020; de la Motte and Cheetah 2020; Segalov 2017;). Initiatives such as Queer Tours of London had been using performative, place-based storytelling, such as guided walks, to narrate the queer past in a dialogic mode, within and beyond LGBTQ+communities and across generations (Queer Tours of London 2022). As we patched up the outfits ready to parade as Fabulous Façades for the third time at the Whitechapel Gallery, in 2019, we watched YouTube clips of queer theatre troupe Bloolips. We took inspiration from their low-budget looks and confrontation with the elitism of theatre in the 1970s, a decade when they took 'gender fuck' drag to the streets, squats and cabaret stages of London and New York (Burns 2019).

Ghaziani and Brim (2019) discuss the current renaissance of queer studies through an interest in method and empiricism. We would note, in this context, that in the built environment disciplines, the connections between conceptualization and material productions of knowledge were strong in the past, whether in the mapping of urban phenomena by geographers of the 1970s, or in the architectural criticism and installation work around the Storefront exhibition *Queer Space* (1994) in the 1990s. More recently, however, philosopher Paul B. Preciado, who trained in architecture, has criticized the discipline's old-fashioned feminisms and lack of attention to the insights of queer, transgender and disability studies. Beyond outing canonical (white, cis, male) architects as gay, he argues for the necessity to 'invent a practice of epistemic architectural disobedience' and expects this shift to come from 'activism, art and performance' (Preciado 2012: 134). Preciado's moving speech at the École de la Cause Freudienne's annual conference in Paris (2020) gives a sense of what this may mean in practice. Published as *Can the Monster Speak?*, this lecture contains a richly layered, urban, architectural, ecological and archaeological description of trans embodiment and subjectivity, as a counter to the expertise claimed within the pathologizing institutions of psychoanalysis:

My living body, I will not say my unconscious or consciousness, but my living body, which encompasses all its constant mutation and its multiple evolutions, is like a Greek city in which, at varying levels of energy, contemporary trans buildings, postmodern lesbian architecture and beautiful Art Deco houses coexist with ancient rustic buildings beneath whose foundations lie classical ruins both animal and vegetal, mineral and chemical substrates that tend to be invisible [. . .] here I'm not speaking of the living body as an anatomical object, but as what I call 'somatheque', a living political archive. (2020: 34–5)

At the micro-scale, Fabulous Façades performed a 'somatheque' of LGBTQ venues, creating a 'living political archive' in overt, literal ways. At a more macro-scale, Preciado's call for a practice of epistemic architectural disobedience provides a touchpoint for our investigations of planning categories and expertise and the ways these have been unsettled by grassroots movements for spatial justice within and extending beyond, queer populations.

The framing of Queer Fun as an 'ivory-tower vaudeville' provided an opportunity to poke fun at the 'proper' professional research practices of architectural and urban scholars, including ours. In these disciplines, etiquette and a certain performative awkwardness convey seriousness and scholarly authority, commanding respect within hierarchical systems of expertise. Such gestures and repetitions are of course a way to mitigate feelings of vulnerability, conveying a reassuring sense of security, even for introverts and imposters like us. The event's location at the RVT, a venue with queer performance at its heart, gave us permission to draw attention to conventional modes of academic performance and to experiment by stretching and parodying them.

Was drag ours to use as academics? If it was, could we overcome our anxieties about our own amateurism?

Questions of permission and imposition featured in discussions about whether we could or *should* perform drag. We revere drag as a practice of incredible skill, through which queer cultures transmit and we are fans and frequenters of London's alt drag nights.

For Muñoz (1999: 32), queer performance and activism, often located in cabaret venues, 'push against reified understandings of theory'. He continues:

The cultural workers whom I focus on can be seen as making theoretical points and contributions to the issues explored in ways that are just as relevant and useful as the phalanx of institutionally sanctioned theorists that I promiscuously invoke throughout these pages. (ibid.)

He clarifies that this is not an 'anti-theory' position. This understanding of queer performers as knowledge producers and 'theory-makers' connects with

Antonio Gramsci's theory of 'organic intellectuals' (ibid: 33). Our vision for Fabulous Façades echoed the hopeful subversion that Muñoz imagined.

Fabulous Façades also resonated with the 'theory-making' of artist Scottee concerning lip-syncing as a queer folk practice. Scottee's thinking had stuck with Lo and they brought them into early conversations where we were navigating our performance anxieties. When asked in an interview, 'lip-syncing is a queer art form: discuss', Scottee (2016) responds:

> I think many a queen's awakening has been in front of the mirror, lip-synching to one of the gay gods. I think it's more than just an art form, I think it's something that we do that is our awakening, is our respite when we can't tell the world what we are. It's the thing that gives us hope, femmeness and it's something that we do to perform to each other. Essentially, I'd say it's more than a queer art form it's essentially queer Folk, it's the way that we've shared stories in social spaces.

Within queer performance cultures there is a close relationship between lip-syncing and drag as queer folk practices that hold the potential to enable explorations of identity through performance, to find respite, to process trauma, to empathize and tell stories. Lip-syncing was not a feature of Fabulous Façades, in which the performers narrated fragment stories of queer venues that have been buried in planning archives, but this concept of drag as a queer folk practice resonated. Being schooled on queer theories emanating from Ivory Towers may mean that we struggle with the notion of queer folk as being an essential *thing* that 'properly' belongs to a specific social group. Nonetheless, there is a value in the democractizing impulse underlying Scottee's thinking. He locates practices like drag as inherited and reproduced through queer performance cultures and modes, which require neither permission, professional credentials, nor a cabaret stage. Drag is not and has never been reducible to the emblematic polished queen, with a razor wit – fabulous and hilarious as they may be – who dominates popular imaginaries, especially following the mainstream success of *RuPaul's Drag Race*. Scottee's thinking directs us to this wider constellation of possibilities for queer folk practices performed by anyone across the spectrum, amateur, professional and everything in between, in spaces ranging from the bedroom to the stage or a Pleasure Garden behind the RVT.

The qualities of amateurism, DIY approaches and queer folk practices are deeply embedded in the creation and operation of queer venues, which our wider research has demonstrated (Campkin and Marshall 2017a, 2018). This is something that Dr. Duckie, as a researcher, member of the Duckie collective and producer of Queer Fun, has brought out extensively in his work (Walters 2020a, 2021). In doctoral research forged between Duckie and Queen Mary, University of London, he has analysed amateurism as a mode of queer futurity in Duckie's work, including Slaughterhouse Club, a drop-in arts project for people experiencing homelessness. This research was conducted in parallel with playing a prominent role in activism and media discussions to raise awareness of threats to queer night-time venues; and writing the successful application for the architectural heritage listing of the RVT (Historic England 2015). Walters contests derogatory associations of amateurism with the novitiate or with incompetence, delusion and/or failure to achieve professional standing and instead highlights 'the kinds of creativity and relationality enabled when professionals put themselves at the service of amateurs' (Walters 2020b: 97). This framing reflects the French etymological roots of 'amateur', as a lover who pursues pleasure (Clarke 2010). Amateurism embraces the disruptive and utopian potential of refusing or intervening in normative professional expectations, ambitions and systems of value and validation.

For us, these ideas resonate strongly with Fabulous Façades. The process of making this work disrupted the hierarchies and orthodoxies that condition professional scholarly practice and embraced the uncertainty, vulnerability and naivety of amateurism. The performances shaped intimate forms of relationality between performer and audience that are uncommon to academic practice. Aesthetically, refusing the polish of mainstream drag or the precise costumes of the Beaux Arts ball architects, we embraced the crafted construction of our paper outfits which comprised a bricolage of fragments, visibly grafted with glue and gaffer, transforming us into walking documents of lost and threatened venues. As embodied archives and through awkward choreography, we objectified ourselves as human automatons performing the mechanics of urban planning. We refused eye contact or to acknowledge those around us, since we were not intending to didactically address an audience or classroom. Our movements knowingly cited and accentuated the (presumably) unintentionally awkward and robotic mannerisms exhibited by the Beaux Arts architects, as serious professionals turned amateur performers in the '"Skyline of New York" ballet' (Koolhaas 1994[1978]: 198) (Figure 7.9).

With the naivety of amateurs, uncertain how our audience would respond – or how we want them to respond – we begin our performance as a skyline against the RVT's rear wall. Backs turned to the RVT's hallowed stage, feet planted on turf and facing out towards the Pleasure Gardens, we occupy the same horizontal plane as our expectant audience. They are probably more used to being loomed over by towering drag queens from the RVT's elevated stage. Nonetheless, our spectators assemble in anticipation, keeping their distance: a gap proper to rules of public proximity and to the separation of performer and audience.

Breaking our line, we walk forward, stilettos sinking in sodden grass, forming a staggered constellation. We begin reciting our narratives, one by one and eventually all at once: a messy cacophony. Variations in the volume, pitch and timbre of our voices reflect our relative shyness or confidence with projection. We have to rise above the buzz of nearby traffic and the bluster of the breeze. Gripping our hats, our shifts in formation, the practicalities of hearing our voices and the evident silliness of our dead-pan expressions juxtaposed with

FIGURE 7.9 *Performance in progress at the RVT, photo by Rafael Pereira do Rego.*

outlandish DIY drag give our audience permission to weave between us. They stop and lean closely into our readings and embodied archives.

Coda

Learning from the experience at the RVT, we played on these dynamics in subsequent performances. To give a brief example, curating the Queer Salon at the Museum of London in 2018 offered our amateur performance the professional skills of technicians and a museum space in which to stage ourselves, with reference to New York skyline counterparts, in a display which included polished imagery of global London landmarks. Here we accentuated our objectification, so that we became, in contrast to the version we performed at the RVT, more like animated statues, temporarily interrupting the exhibition. After a procession into the space, each performer took up a post, spot lit on low platforms staggered around the gallery, with archival footage from the 1931 Ball projected onto the back wall (Figure 7.10). The staging invited audience members to move between us, directed by the arrangement of our readings, which diverted the audience's bodies and attention back and forth across the room, rather than in a tidy circuit. Audience members variously drifted between and clustered around us, again leaning in close to read our archival bricolage. As our voices constructed a cacophony of repetitious dialogue, the exhibition visitors, now familiar

FIGURE 7.10 *Enda Cowan cross-fades with Beaux Arts architects in projection as part of Fabulous Façades performance at the Museum of London, photo by Ivan Denia.*

with our words, began to speak, at first in hushed tones then more loudly, recounting memories of the venues we personified. Their murmurs added to the embodied archive and intensified the cacophony, which aptly came to resemble the soundscape of a busy bar: myriad conversations bouncing around the room, ricocheting off hard surfaces. What might be considered by some professional performance standards as a failure to command attention might also be interpreted as our amateurism serving to enable an improvised and ephemeral collective archive. As Dr. Duckie notes, moving away from a simple correlation between amateurism and failure can wield queer power, through embracing alternative value systems beyond professional norms and expectations (Walters 2020b: 99).

As an intervention that we had not imagined when we began to research the heritage and architecture of queer venues, Fabulous Façades consolidated, extended and enabled us to articulate various themes. We had found ourselves with both an excess of data and an exhaustion from processing it. In contrast with the isolation of archival work or the structure and privacy of interviews, this iterative performance intervention required us to embrace a collaborative ethos, unpredictable and transient outcomes and to work within constraints set out by external parties – the curators, producers and institutions that we worked with. Developing the performance collaboratively and relationally with other queer space researchers and activists was energizing and enabled us to give voice and material presence to the eclectic range of archives associated with the venues in ways that we had not anticipated. As a field of discourse, the discussions over venues and threats to them featured a variety of commercial, activist, scholarly and professional discourses, cross-cutting different institutions and informal networks. Fabulous Façades both enabled and required a dynamic transversing of these multiple forms of knowledge and evidence and enabled us to engage across our own multiple positionalities as researchers, scholar-activists, who had direct experience of queer venues and commun members. As a queer method of engaging with and sharing knowledge, it operated within the paradoxes highlighted by Ghaziani and Brim (2019) between the slipperiness of queer and the orderliness of methods, with an awkward embrace of tensions between professionalism and amateurism, ephemerality and longevity, the elusive and tangible, the orderly and improvised, the institutional and grassroots, the serious and irreverent.

In *Queer Method and Methodologies*, Kath Browne and Catherine J. Nash (2016: 12) highlight the potential for 'queer research' – a term that intentionally remains nebulous, plural and contestable – to constitute and destabilize the onto-epistemology of conventional research practices. Through this chapter we have aimed to bring architecture and urbanism into the current wave of discussions of queer methods. If these disciplines and their professions are to rise to the challenge set out by Preciado (2012), then they will need to embrace the multiplicity of ways of knowing cities and the built environment and to actively challenge established hierarchies in the politics of expertise. Fabulous Façades proceeded organically, alongside our other research endeavours. Retrospectively, it suggests to us the possibilities of irreverence in combining different methods, layering sources in unexpected ways and engaging idiosyncratic archives alongside more established ones. Through adopting these approaches and locating a queer moment in architectural history, we were able to engage the often-overlooked emotional terrain of planning and its handling of dense layers of text and information. We were also able to draw from queer scholar-activist traditions to traverse the built and embodied archives associated with a network of venues, which have come to the foreground and receded, at different moments in the history of LGBTQ+ struggle and creativity.

Note

1   The Fabulous Façades were: Sebastian Buser (Wanc Café), Ben Campkin (City of Quebec/London Lesbian and Gay Centre), Thomas Kendall (The Black Cap), Gabrielle Basso Ricci (First Out), Lo Marshall (The Glass Bar), Sé Tunnacliffe (First Out) and Zia Álmos Joshua X (Joiners' Arms). The performances took place at 'Queer Fun', Royal Vauxhall Tavern, programmed by Ben Walters and Duckie, 10 June 2017; 'The London Salon: Queer Night Scenes', *City Now City Future* programme, *Museum* of London, 13 February 2018; *Queer Spaces: 1980s–Today*, Whitechapel Gallery, 2 April to 26 August 2019.

References

Bondi, L. (1998), 'Gender, Class and Urban Space: Public and Private Space in Contemporary Urban Landscapes', *Urban Geography*, 19 (2), 160–85.

Broomfield, M. (2017), 'We Watched Activists Ad-hack London to Commemorate LGBT History: Sexual Avengers', Huck Magazine, 22 February 2017, Available online: https://www.huckmag.com/perspectives/activism-2/sexual-avengers-blue -plaques/

Browne, K. and Nash, C. J. (2016), 'An Introduction', in K. Browne and C. J. Nash (eds.) *Queer Methods and Methodologies: Intersecting Queer Theories and Social Science Research*, Abingdon: Routledge.

Burns, K. (2012), 'A Girl's Own Adventure', *Journal of Architectural Education*, 65 (2), 125–34.

Burns, S. (2019), 'In Pictures: Bloolips and the Empowering Joy of Dressing Up', Frieze, 15 July 2019, Available online: https://www.frieze.com/article/pictures-bloolips-and-empowering-joy-dressing (accessed 8 December 2021).

Castiglia, C. and Reed, C. (2012), *If Memory Serves: Gay Men, AIDS and the Promise of the Queer Past*, Minneapolis and London: University of Minnesota Press.

Cavanaugh, S. (2010), *Queering Bathrooms: Gender, Sexuality and the Hygienic Imagination*, Buffalo: University of Toronto.

Campkin, B. (forthcoming), *Queer Premises: LGBTQ+ Venues in London Since the 1980s*, London: Bloomsbury.

Campkin, B. (2022), 'The Royal Vauxhall Tavern, London, England', in A. N. Furman and J. Mardell (eds.), *Queer Spaces: An Atlas of LGBTQIA+ Places and Stories*. London: RIBA Publishing, 126–7.

Campkin, B. and Marshall, L. (2017a), *LGBTQ+ Cultural Infrastructure in London: Night Venues*, 2006-Present, London: UCL Urban Laboratory.

Campkin, B. and Marshall, L. (2017b), *Fabulous Façades Proposal*, unpublished.

Campkin, B. and Marshall, L (2018), 'London's Nocturnal Queer Geographies', *Soundings*, 70: 82–96.

Campkin, B., Marshall, L. and Ross, R. (2018), 'LGBTQ+ Night-time Spaces: Past, Present and Future', Urban Pamphleteer #7, London: UCL Urban Laboratory.

Clarke, M. (2010), *Amateur, The Concise Oxford Dictionary of Art Terms* (2nd ed.), Oxford: Oxford University Press, Available online: https://www.oxfordreference.com/view/10.1093/oi/authority.20110803095406990 (accessed: 5 May 2022).

Feather, S. (2015), *Blowing the Lid: Gay Liberation, Sexual Revolution and Radical Queens*, Winchester: Zero Books.

Ghaziani, A. and Brim, M. (2019), *Imagining Queer Methods*, New York: New York University Press.

Glass, D. (2020), *United Queerdom: From the Legends of the Gay Liberation Front to the Queers of Tomorrow*, London: Zed Books.

Greater London Authority (2019), *Cultural Infrastructure Plan*, London: GLA.

Jencks, C. (1977), *The Language of Post-Modern Architecture*, London: Academy Editions.

Historic England (2015), *Pride of Place, Historic England*, Available online: https://historicengland.org.uk/whats-new/news/royal-vauxhall-tavern-listed/ (accessed 31 January 2022).

Koolhaas, R. (1994), *Delirious New York: A Retroactive Manifesto for Manhattan*, New York: Monacelli Press.

Kristeva, J. (1982), *Powers of Horror: An Essay on Abjection*, New York: Columbia University Press.

de la Motte, D. and Cheetah, L. A. (2020), *GLF at 50: the Art of Protest*, London: Platform Southwark.

Muñoz, J. E. (1999), *Disidentification: Queers of Color and the Performance of Politics*, Minneapolis and London: University of Minnesota Press, 33.

Muñoz, J. E. (2009), *Cruising Utopia: The Then and There of Queer Futurity*, New York; London: New York University Press.

Penner, B. (2010), 'Entangled with a user: inside bathrooms with Alexander Kira and Peter Greenaway,' in L. Norén and H. Luskin Molotch (eds.), *Toilet: Public Restrooms and the Politics of Sharing*, New York: University Press, 233–4.

Power, L. (1995), *No Bath But Plenty of Bubbles: Stories from the London Gay Liberation Front, 1970–73*, London: Continuum International Publishing Group Ltd.

Preciado, P. B. (2012), 'Architecture as a Practice of Biopolitical Disobedience', *Log*, 25, 121–34.

Preciado, P. B. (2020), *Can the Monster Speak?*, London: Fitzcarraldo Editions, 34–5.

Queer Tours of London (2022), *Queer Tours of London*, Available online: https://queertoursoflondon.com/ (accessed 3 December 2021).

RVT Future (2022), *RVT Future*, Available online: http://www.rvt.community (accessed 31 January 2022).

Scottee (2016), *Scottee, Loverboy*, Available online: https://www.loverboymagazine.com/scottee/ (accessed: 12 June 2022).

Segalov, M. (2017), 'Cockroaches, Cops and Cow Shit at the British Property Awards', Huck Magazine, 5 April 2017, Available online: https://www.huckmag.com/perspectives/activism-2/cockroaches-cops-cow-shit-british-property-awards/ (accessed 19 May 2022).

Shonfield, K. (2000), *Walls Have Feelings: Architecture, Film and the City*, London: Routledge.

Walter, A. (1980), *Come Together: The Years of the Gay Liberation 1970–73*, London: Gay Men's Press.

Walters, B. (2015), 'Supporting Statement for an Application to Have the Royal Vauxhall Tavern Added to the National Heritage List for England', January 2015, Available online: http://www.rvt.community/wp-content/uploads/2015/09/Initial-RVT-listing-application-January-2015.pdf (accessed 25 November 2018).

Walters, B. (2017), 'Queer Fun, Duckie', Available online: https://www.duckie.co.uk/events/queer-fun (accessed 31 January 2022).

Walters, B. (2020a), 'Homemade Mutant Hope Machines, Duckie', Available online: https://duckie.co.uk/media/documents/PhD%20ebook%20Dr%20Duckie.pdf (accessed 9 February 2022).

Walters, B. (2020b), 'Being Among Bluebells', *Performance Research*, 25 (1), 96–103, 97, 99.

Walters, B. (2021), 'Once Upon a Time, There Was a Tavern': Metadrag and Other Uses of the Past at the Royal Vauxhall Tavern', in M. Edward and S. Farrier (eds.), *Drag Histories, Herstories and Hairstories: Drag in a Changing Scene*, Vol. 2, London: Bloomsbury Publishing, 2–27.

8

From *STUD* to Stalled!

Embodied identity through a queer lens, 1996–2021

Joel Sanders

This chapter was originally written as a new preface to a re-print of STUD *to mark the work's silver anniversary, documenting the development of my thinking over the course of twenty-five years from the book's original publication in 1996 to the later practices of my inclusive design think-tank and consultancy MIXdesign in 2021. This expanded version of the chapter situates* STUD *not only in my personal life and career but also as a historical artefact capturing a turning point in the study of queer architecture in the wake of the AIDS epidemic. The chapter also examines* STUD*'s shortcomings in light of my own subsequent exposure to trans and disability studies through Stalled!, an ongoing project of MIXdesign.*

In 1996, while I was an assistant professor at Princeton University and just opening my architectural practice, I edited *STUD, Architectures of Masculinity.* The book compiles essays and projects by academics, architects and artists, many especially commissioned for the book, that consider how the design of an everyday space – homes, offices, bathrooms, gyms and 'outings' (city streets and parks) – makes possible the 'performance' of male identity. *STUD* begins with an introduction intended as a strident manifesto, articulating the methodological framework for the book whose agenda was to interrogate architecture's role in the 'construction' of masculinity seen through the lens of a gay architect who was embarking on a new field of architectural inquiry – queer space. My conception of the book came not from the viewpoint of a dispassionate scholar but from an angry young practitioner attempting to respond to the spatial inequities confronted by the American gay community during an urgent health crisis – the AIDS epidemic – at a time when municipal, state and federal governments were indifferent to or actively hostile to the plight of the LGBTQ+ community.

I am now writing this chapter twenty-five years later to mark the occasion of *STUD*'s silver anniversary. Needless to say, times have changed. I am a professor at Yale School of Architecture, subsequent generations of architects and scholars are producing work from a queer perspective and significant progress has been made in securing the rights of the LGBTQ+ community in the United States and around the world. Milestones include the Supreme Court's legalization of gay marriage in 2017 and the court's upholding the Civil Rights Act barring worker discrimination on the basis of sex in 2020. In 2016 the UN Human Rights Council adopted a resolution that called on member nations to protect against violence and discrimination based on sexual orientation and gender identity. However, today I am writing this against the backdrop of two interrelated current events reminiscent of the mid-1990s when *STUD* was originally conceived, that threaten to erode the slow but steady progress we have made: first, the resurgence of discrimination against queers and other minorities due to the rise of right-wing governments, grassroots extremist groups and terrorist organizations and second the ravages of another global health crisis – the coronavirus pandemic. Like AIDS, Covid-19, in the United States and around the world, has disproportionately impacted vulnerable communities that fall out of the cultural mainstream – including people with low incomes, people of colour, people who are homeless and people with disabilities.[1]

In contrast with *STUD* this chapter does not take the form of a manifesto written in the third person, but rather a memoir meant to recast the earlier book within its human and historical context. It begins with the genesis of *STUD*, showing how it was the product of the convergence of personal, professional and political circumstances – my coming out as a gay man, while an assistant professor in a school of architecture, during the AIDs crisis in the early 1990s. I am hoping that this account might be of interest to a younger generation of architectural historians who are mapping the emergence of what was then a new field of inquiry, 'queer space'. In the rest of the chapter, I reappraise *STUD* from a contemporary vantage point: tracing how my thinking about the principles and methods that informed the book has evolved. I am hoping that this retrospective narrative will be relevant to twenty-first-century readers as a barometer that registers how the relationship between gender studies, embodied identity and architecture has grown over the past twenty-five years, based on the premise that my own intellectual development mirrors trends in the design community at large.

Genesis

STUD was indebted to my exposure to two vibrant and interrelated tendencies associated with 'identity politics' – namely queer theory and queer activist art – which were gaining traction in the Anglo-American academic and art world during the early to mid-1990s, the period when *STUD* was hatched. Both were responses to urgent social justice challenges confronting what was just beginning to be referred to as the 'LGBT', as opposed to the 'gay' community. I was drawn to this work for both personal and professional reasons. I had recently come out as a gay man. One of my best friends, John Pozzi, to whom *STUD* is dedicated, had been diagnosed with AIDS a few years earlier, a time before the development of effective anti-viral drugs when HIV was considered a 'death sentence'. As a member of John's chosen family, I was one of his inner circle of caregivers. We, like many gay men of this era, were consumed by a combination of grief and rage directed against the Reagan administration that had turned a blind eye to the epidemic. In 1994, the year of John's death and one year before *STUD*'s publication, AIDS was the leading cause of death for American adults twenty-five to forty-four years old. By 1995, 300,000 Americans had died of AIDS-related causes.[2] By 1996, nearly 30 million people were living with AIDS and 11.7 million had died worldwide.[3]

Wanting to make a contribution to queer activism through the discipline that I knew best – architecture – I looked to the work of my peers. The influence of 'Deconstructivist' architecture, the movement showcased in MoMA's 1988 exhibition of the same name, was dominant but left me cold. Although formally inventive, it seemed out of touch with the social and political realities of the time. More inspiring was the work being produced by young scholars, including those collected in two then-recently published books: *Sexuality and Space* (1992), edited by Beatriz Colomina and 'House Rules', the catalogue of an exhibition at the Wexner Centre curated by Mark Robbins, in which I was a participant, which was featured in a special issue of *Assemblage* (issue 24) in 1994. However, as was typical of explorations of gender and architecture at that time, both collections were shaped by a largely feminist perspective that looked at architecture's complicity in reproducing patriarchal structures and processes but did not address queer issues head-on.

Instead, I found the queer inspiration that I was looking for by looking outside the discipline of architecture. I tapped into two overlapping worlds inhabited by queer artists and queer theorists, whom I came to know largely through two friends – John Lindell and Diana Fuss. Both of them had recently become mentors, helping me to immerse myself in queer intellectual and artistic culture by introducing me to books, exhibitions, films and, most important, networks of people who became friends and eventually contributors to the book.

John Lindell, whom I met through John Pozzi, was trained as an architect and was gaining a reputation for his site-specific wall drawings, one which is included in *STUD*. A few years earlier, I had commissioned John to create one such drawing for the lobby of Princeton's School of Architecture. It used abstract symbols representing male body parts – mouth, anus, penis and cum – to map queer sexual encounters.

Lindell introduced me to members of Gran Fury, an activist art collective affiliated with ACT UP, 'a band of individuals united in anger and dedicated to exploiting the power of art to end the AIDS crisis' who at that time were making headlines for their provocative AIDS infographics, like the famous 'Silence = Death' poster (Meyer 2002). As a book, *STUD* was designed by Bureau, a firm known for their activist 'typographics', which had been founded by two members of Gran Fury, Marlene McCarty and Donald Moffett. Together we came up with the book's vertical proportions meant to recall the dimensions of a wooden 'stud', namely a milled lumber member used in building construction. But it was Marlene and Donald who came up with the concept for the book's cover image. During a memorable meeting, they blindsided me with an unnerving proposition: to swap out the discrete faux wood grain cover that I favoured with the image of an architect baring his chiselled chest. It was intended to illustrate a central theme of the book – 'that authors of buildings, like the structures they design, embody the very essence of manhood' (1996: 11) – by making a tongue-in-cheek reference to the 'hunks' often depicted on the covers of Harlequin Romance novels. I resisted, fearing the undercurrent of homophobia rampant in the architectural community. Sunil Bald, then an employee of the architectural firm Keenan/Riley that shared office space with Bureau and now a close friend and colleague, was brought in to settle the dispute. He reassured me that even 'straight' architects like himself would purchase the book.

Marlene and Donald then insisted that the cover's creation should accurately follow the cover illustration process of the Harlequin paperbacks that *STUD*'s cover referenced; they were illustrations based on photographs. Bureau enlisted the services of another Gran Fury collaborator, Loring McAlpin, who recruited his friend, a former Marlboro Man Jeffrey Cayle, to pose for the photograph. It depicted him holding two elements of the architect's wardrobe, black-framed eyes glasses and a phallic roll of blueprints. The late Michael Pearlman, whose work is also included in *STUD*, then translated this photo into the final cover illustration (Figure 8.1).

If Lindell was *STUD*'s unofficial art director, Diana Fuss was the book's behind-the-scenes editor. When we met, Fuss, a professor in the English Department at Princeton, was known for her ground-breaking books *Essentially Speaking: Feminism, Nature and Difference* and *Inside/Out*, a widely read collection of seminal essays by queer theorists that established her at the forefront of gender and queer studies. We bonded as fellow riders of Metro North commuting between New York City where we lived and Princeton, New Jersey. In addition to collaborating with me on the essay 'Inside Freud's Office' published in *STUD*, Diana recommended that I

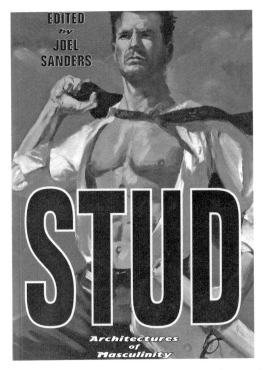

FIGURE 8.1 STUD *cover design by Bureau (Loring McAlpin and Michael Pearlman).*

commission essays from three of her friends and colleagues – Lee Edelman, D. A. Miller and Marcia Ian – who, like her, were initially reluctant to apply their thinking to architecture, for them an unfamiliar field.

STUD was indebted to the help of a network of queer and queer-friendly artists, architects and academics. However, some of my Princeton colleagues were less supportive. The book was originally conceived as part of a book series, 'The Pathologies of Architecture', each volume to be edited by a Princeton junior faculty member: Beatriz Colomina, Elizabeth Diller, Thomas Leeser, Alexandra Ponte and Mark Wigley. I was the only one who pursued the project and the series as a whole never came to fruition.

One afternoon when the completed galleys for *STUD* were waiting for final approval at the printer, I received a call from the dean of the School of Architecture, the late Ralph Lerner, informing me that he had decided that the book's content and some of its illustrations – referring to images of cocks in Mark Robbins's 'Fashion Plate' – risked offending the architecture school's community. Rather than pull the plug altogether, Lerner would authorize the book's publication based on two stipulations. The first was that, although the book was funded by the School of Architecture, which also owned its copyright, it would no longer be published (as originally intended) under the department's imprint 'Princeton Papers on Architecture'. Second, my expression of thanks to members of the dean's administrative staff who helped me with the book would be deleted from the Acknowledgements. To my knowledge, students and faculty were aware of the dean's decision. But as far as I know, no one contested the outcome. Nor did I have the confidence or courage to fight back: at that time, there were fewer protections for LBGTQ+ faculty and fewer examples of anti-discrimination suits filed by gay faculty that I could learn from. Now over two decades later, I am setting the record 'straight', not to cast blame, but as a reminder, especially to a younger generation of readers, of how the LBGTQ+ issues that we take for granted today were not that long ago deemed threatening, even at progressive schools of architecture.

Methodology

Performing identity: dismantling boundaries between architecture, interiors and landscape

Perhaps Diana Fuss's most significant contribution to *STUD* was that she helped me formulate *STUD*'s intellectual foundation and methodology, an approach that shares affinities with, but ultimately differs from, the work of my gay contemporaries who were also thinking about queer space at that time. Aaron Betsky's book *Queer Space: Architecture and Same-Sex Desire* (1997) examined the work and sensibility of gay designers while Mark Robbins was creating projects that took as their point of departure spaces occupied by gay men. Except for *STUD*'s final chapter 'Outings', which treats gay-specific sites that facilitate cruising like peep shows, sex clubs and parks, *STUD* does not focus so much on spaces occupied by gay men. Instead, it borrows the analytical framework pioneered by queer theorists, like Judith Butler and Eve Kosofsky Sedgwick, who use a queer perspective to unpack the way mainstream discourses like literature and film reproduce heteronormative ideologies that reinforce problematic male/female, gay/straight binaries. Following in their footsteps, *STUD* employs a 'queer' lens filtered through the perspective of its roster of male and female contributors, most but not all of whom identified as gay men or lesbians, who employ theoretical concepts derived from gender, cultural and media studies to interrogate and expose the role that the designed environment plays in the 'performance' of human and male identity in the spaces of our everyday lives.[4] *STUD* borrowed the notion of gender as performance from Butler who, in her influential book *Gender Trouble* (1990), argues that masculinity and femininity are culturally constructed, learned modes of behaviour.

Two insights derived from queer studies inspired me to question my own architectural training in a way that would ultimately shape *STUD*'s methodological framework. As was typical of architectural education and professional practice at that time, my education as a graduate student at Columbia and a young professional had encouraged me to pay attention to the formal properties of buildings, conceived of and represented in drawings and images as 'pure' photogenic objects, generally devoid of any traces of human occupation, like furniture, objects and *people*. In contrast, queer theory encouraged me to consider the dynamic interplay between two terms that were both cultural 'constructions' – the body and the built environment. It encouraged me to shift my attention from the building as an object, to *space* conceived of as a medium in which human interaction takes place. Influenced by Butler, I came to embrace a conception of the built environment as a 'stage' that enables people, like actors, to perform various roles. Second, Butler's analysis of the way drag performers rely on costume to perform identity, led me to discover the affinities between clothing and cladding – the ephemeral elements like wall finishes, paint, fabrics, curtains, upholstery and furniture – that interior designers use to dress the interiors designed by architects: both are culturally coded applied surfaces used to fashion human identity.[5]

Discovering the crucial yet overlooked relationship between the dressing of bodies and buildings allowed me to embrace an expanded definition of 'architecture', one that encompassed sister fields like fashion, interiors, landscape and product design which were and often still are considered subsidiary to and outside the purview of architecture. This curatorial perspective shaped the selections included in the book. Rather than discuss buildings in isolation, *STUD*'s contributors collectively adopt a holistic perspective that cuts across design disciplines and scales. They consider the built environment as composed of an ensemble of elements – objects, furniture, finishes and landscape – that facilitate the performance of identity. This includes domestic appliances (the hi-fi equipment and electric carving knives found in the bachelor pads and dining rooms discussed by Steven Cohan and Ellen Lupton), furnishings (the beds, carpets, wall coverings and housewares found in the homes and offices interpreted by Renee Green andrea Zittell, George Stoll and Diana Fuss + Joel Sanders), fixtures (the sinks, urinals and partitions considered by Robert Gober [Figure 8.2], Kennedy and Violich and Lee Edelman), equipment (the uniforms, rifles, weights and barbells found in the gyms and military academies investigated by Marcia Ian, Matthew Barney, Matthew Bannister and John Lindell) and landscape elements (the trees, plants and streetlights that enable cruising in parks and city streets considered by Tom Burr and George Chauncey).

Formulating *STUD*'s queer editorial approach that collapsed traditional distinctions between design disciplines did not come easy. It forced me not only to challenge the values that shaped my architectural education but also to resist following the accepted academic career path prescribed for young architects at the time, which entailed winning design awards or writing scholarly papers about research topics that tended to marry architectural

FIGURE 8.2   *Robert Gober,* Untitled *(1991–3).*

theory with exemplary buildings designed by canonic, generally white male architects.

Moreover, *STUD* forced me to re-assess my own upbringing. Long before I understood the meaning of the term 'gay', as a boy and later as an adolescent and young adult, I struggled to come to terms with my own sense of male inadequacy. Growing up, I was ashamed of the interests that I was drawn to – like art, interiors and set design – because I intuitively perceived them as 'feminine' activities inappropriate for 'normal' boys growing up in the 1960s. For example, as a child, I would accompany my mother on shopping expeditions to Lord and Taylor, housed in a streamlined post-war building that I later learned was designed by Raymond Lowey in 1945. For me, the experience lived up to the name of the suburban retail corridor where the department store was located – the Miracle Mile. I was in heaven, trailing my mom through the glamorous retail interiors or waiting outside her dressing room as she tried on outfits. Later, during middle-school holidays spent in Miami Beach with my grandma Sonia, I would look forward to accompanying her on strolls down Collins Avenue that involved stepping into glamorous Art Deco and mid-century hotel lobbies, including the Fontainebleau and Eden Roc designed by an architect I would later befriend, Morris Lapidus. I felt a combination of rapture and anxiety gazing at their Brooklyn Baroque interiors which combined boomerang curves, suspended staircases, crystal chandeliers and faux Louis 14th furniture in a way that exemplified the title of Lapidus's memoir *Too Much Is Never Enough*. In that book, Lapidus bitterly recounts how he was excluded from architecture's post-war elite by powerful architects like Philip Johnson for designing hotels that were vilified as bastardized vulgar examples of modern design.

Queer theory allowed me to attribute the source of my childhood shame to my internalization of problematic masculine ideals that had the power to transform these exhilarating early experiences into scenes of guilt that would later haunt me as a graduate student and young professor charting my career trajectory. It equipped me with the critical tools to analyse these experiences from a socio-historical perspective, confirming that my sense that architecture was manly as opposed to interiors which were for 'sissies' was not self-imposed but rooted in problematic gendered conceptions about the nature of the design disciplines and the people who practised them – a theme that would become central to my subsequent work.

Debunking the false opposition between architecture and interiors, which queer theory helped me to realize stemmed from gender prejudices, would become one of *STUD*'s central themes. The book includes such austere 'manly' projects as Playboy's Penthouse Apartment, the US Airforce Academy in Palm Springs, Matthew Bannister's Badlands Gym and Tom Burr's Platzpitz Park installation. All of them expose one of the contradictions underlying modernism's famed vilification of ornament for its association with female masquerade: these seemingly naked buildings are meticulously dressed in applied materials – metal, leather and wood veneer – with masculine connotations.

Two years after publishing *STUD* I would expand upon the theme of the false opposition between two allied fields, architecture and interior design, from a cultural and historical perspective. In 'Curtain Wars: Architects, Decorators and the 20th Century Interior', I argued that problematic assumptions about gender and class shaped both design approaches and professional identities in these fields. Ever since the emergence of the interior decorator as a design professional in the mid-nineteenth century, interior decoration has been dismissed as a superficial pastime associated with the wealthy upper and middle classes. By the twentieth century, interiors had become tainted by their association with femininity and homosexuality. It was thought that architects, typically men, worked conceptually, organizing space by manipulating durable materials and elements (structure and walls), while decorators, typically women and gay men, worked intuitively, adorning rooms with ephemeral materials (fabrics and upholstery) linked with fashion and domesticity. In contrast to architects who (in this conception) think in abstract terms to solve practical programmatic and technical problems, interior designers create spaces that cater to corporeal needs, the material body considered a female principle, as opposed to immaterial male intellect.

Ten years after completing 'Curtain Wars', I began teaching and collaborating with Yale colleague and landscape designer the late Diana Balmori, which led me to consider the obstacles keeping another of architecture's allied disciplines at a distance, namely landscape architecture. In my introductory chapter to *Groundwork: Between Landscape and Architecture*, co-edited with Diana (Figure 8.3), I drew parallels between the troubled relationship linking architecture and interiors and architecture

FIGURE 8.3   *Cover of* Groundwork, *Diana Balmori and Joel Sanders, 2011.*

and landscape – each rooted in problematic gender stereotypes (Sanders 2011). Like interiors, landscape architecture was a discipline discredited by its association with women and the domestic realm. In the mid-nineteenth century, gardening had become a pastime reserved for upper-class women and by the mid-twentieth century a hobby for middle-class housewives, publicized in popular magazines like *House and Garden*, whose title and content made explicit the affinities between interiors and landscape. And while landscape architecture, like interior design, was embraced by the mainstream media, it too was largely overlooked by the academy. At that time, there was a conspicuous absence of serious scholarly books and exhibitions devoted to landscape design as compared to architecture, a phenomenon that both reflects and reinforces landscape's secondary status.

Moreover, landscape design methodologies, like interiors, have been shaped by misleading assumptions about the gendered body and the human senses. The landscape/architecture divide mirrors the long-standing split between the spirit and the flesh, the Western binary that opposes immaterial intellect, considered a male prerogative, with the material corporeal body, deemed a female principle that since antiquity has been linked with Mother Earth. In addition, landscape, like the other design disciplines, adheres to a long-standing Western bias espoused by philosophers and art critics, including Aristotle, St. Augustine, Goethe and Clement Greenberg, among others, who categorize the human senses in a hierarchy, differentiating between the immaterial higher senses – sight and sound, linked with male intellect – and the lower senses – touch, taste and smell, associated with the sensuous female body. Modern architects like Le Corbusier famously validated this ocular-centric perspective. They privileged the visual rather than the multi-sensory dimension of architecture in contrast to interiors and landscape, two professions that work with soft ephemeral elements – fabrics and vegetation – to create indoor and outdoor spaces that engage not only sight but the 'lower' senses, touch and smell.[6]

Since the publication of STUD, the hard and fast boundaries between design disciplines have blurred. Starchitects like Rem Koolhaas, Zaha Hadid and David Adjaye have designed furniture and retail interiors while high-profile landscape architects like Field Operations, West 8 and Hood Associates collaborate with architectural firms on sustainable parks and urban plans. In a similar vein, my own thinking about gender has evolved as well. I credit this to my exposure to transgender studies, which has encouraged me to think about gender in a more nuanced and complex way. I have come to realize that earlier writings like *STUD*, 'Curtain Wars' and *Groundwork* were all shaped by a reductive binary conception of gender predicated on what trans theorists call cis-embodiment, in which the category of sex (male/female) remains a stable referent against which a queer deviation of gender signification (hetero/homo) plays out. Trans theory, on the other hand, argues that both sex and gender are malleable, demonstrating that there are multiple ways of living one's gender independent from biological sex and sexual orientation. To use a mathematical analogy, if queerness is a one-variable equation, then transness is a two-variable equation that includes those who do not identify exclusively as male or female, gay or straight – like nonbinary, intersex, genderqueer, pangender and agender individuals, who refuse stable gender categories altogether. My recent teaching, writing and professional practice attempts to transcend binary thinking by registering the complex and fluid nature of all human embodied identities rather than risk reinforcing the false gender oppositions foundational to the design disciplines that I still believe need to be dismantled.[7]

Queer design appropriation

The organizational logic of *STUD* – divided into five sections each devoted to a different quotidian space – mirrors the book's objective: to expose the entrenched ideologies transmitted through the conventions of architecture through the interrogation of everyday building 'types'. This approach is based on a premise I still subscribe to today: the performance of human identity takes place within formulaic architectural 'types' associated with specific activities that distribute bodies within spatial configurations, which in turn shape the way humans interact with each other and the world around them. Typologies tend to perpetuate the status quo, but architects and users can decide to contest these norms and their attending ideologies through appropriation and revision.

For example, in 'Men's Room', Lee Edelman analyses the privacy partitions installed between urinals to prohibit 'wandering eyes', which can elicit fears of inadequacy and same-sex desire between men and that these architectural elements were designed to ward off. Essays by Marcia Ian and George Chauncey as well as projects by Mark Robbins and Stephan Barker demonstrate how gay men have mined the homoerotic potential of such normative spaces as bathrooms, gyms, bars and parks by appropriating typical design elements and using them in subversive ways. For example, gay male cruising in public restrooms depends on mirrors as well as the gaps, cracks and holes found in urinal and toilet stall partitions.

Shortly after completing *STUD*, my newly launched architectural studio JSA received a series of commissions for bachelor pads like the 'Lee Loft' and 'House for a Bachelor' that afforded the opportunity for me and my staff to transpose tactics derived from *STUD*'s analysis of men's rooms and gyms to residential design. For example, the 'Vitale Loft' (1999), a loft renovation for a gay male client, dissolves the boundary between two adjacent 'wet' spaces – bathroom and kitchen – that are traditionally divided from one another due to prevailing standards of domestic privacy and propriety (Figure 8.4). Our scheme celebrates rather than conceals the spatial proximity of these two zones that share a common plumbing riser by consolidating both functions in a concrete 'plumbing island'. A translucent glass panel bisects the island, screening the kitchen from the master bathroom, now treated as a stepped platform that opens directly onto the master bedroom. The glass partition is intersected by a continuous waterproof concrete surface that connects these normally isolated wet functions, allowing them to freely overlap. Inspired by Lee Edelman's essay in *STUD*, the Vitale Loft attempts to destabilize the active/passive, subject/object, male/female binaries that inform conventional domestic spectatorship, by dissolving traditional boundaries between bedroom, bathroom and kitchen, treating them as intercommunicating spaces dedicated to embodied pleasure. Keep in mind that in 1999, translucent bathroom walls, as well as media images of male nudity, were not as commonplace as they are today.

When the 'Vitale Loft' was published in mainstream publications like *Interior Design Magazine* in 2000 and *New York Times Magazine* in 2001, we received sceptical and sometime hostile feedback from readers who argued that its design would appeal only to a niche market of clients who led 'alternative lifestyles'. However, beginning in the early 2000s two developments – the greater acceptance of more fluid standards of masculinity embodied by celebrity 'Metrosexuals' like David Beckham, coupled with the need to make small spaces appear larger due to skyrocketing residential

FIGURE 8.4 *Vitale Loft, New York, NY JSA, 1999.*

real estate prices in cities like New York – led to a shift in my practice. Beginning in 2000, JSA began to receive commissions that gave us the chance to reinterpret gay-specific design strategies, many of them inspired by *STUD*'s contributors, for the design of domestic spaces for clients beyond the gay community. The Millennium Apartment (2002) and 25 Columbus Circle (2012), both designed for heterosexual parents with grown children, incorporate signature design elements like sliding bedrooms walls and switch light bathrooms glass, first featured in JSA's early bachelor pad projects. In less than a decade the subversive tactics illustrated in *STUD* had become mainstream. Today they are a commonplace feature not only of JSA's work but of high-end residential and hotel design around the world.

Ironically, as design tactics derived from queer subcultural spaces have been absorbed into the mainstream, a new generation of queer historians, architects and artists are looking back at these gay cruising grounds that are becoming a thing of the past. Two exhibitions exemplify this newfound interest. The 'Cruising Pavilion: Architecture, Gay Sex and Cruising Culture' by curators Pierre-Alexandre Mateos et al., mounted at the Venice Architecture Biennale in 2018 and reprised at ArkDes in Stockholm in 2019,[8] featured works by artist and designers dealing with the changing spaces of queer cruising, both virtual and actual. 'Queer Spaces: London, 1980s – Today', curated by Vassilios Doupas et al. and mounted at the

Whitechapel Gallery in 2019, was an archival exhibition that documented London's disappearing nightlife spots.⁹ Today, when sexual encounters are more often initiated over social media than through face-to-face encounters, many queers have become fascinated not only with bathrooms but also with nightspots like bars, sex clubs and cabarets which are threatened to be orhave been, closed due to real estate development and the rise of the internet. It is still too early to tell what drives this burgeoning interest: the rise of queer historiography, a backlash against disembodied social media ornostalgia for an idealized chapter of queer cultural life that is vanishing.

Intersectionality

One of *STUD's* guiding principles – the conviction that a rigorous analysis of familiar building types seen through a non-normative perspective can lead to innovative design ideas that can be applied to a broader audience – continues to inform my design approach today. However, seven years ago, the convergence of my academic, theoretical and professional interests led me to reconsider this notion in a new light, this time sparked by another global crisis impacting the queer community: national debates and moral panic surrounding the question of transgender access to public restrooms.

In 2015, JSA was invited to design the NYC headquarters for GLSEN (the gay, lesbian, straight, education network), a non-profit dedicated to making schools safe and nurturing environments for K–12 students. Building codes coupled with an uncooperative landlord prevented us from implementing the client's request for (what was at that time referred to as) 'gender-neutral' bathrooms. These project-specific challenges coincided with current events: I became fascinated by mainstream media coverage of national debates triggered by the perceived threat, for some, of transgender people using public restrooms. Bathroom politics led me to delve into transgender studies and rekindle a dialogue with Susan Stryker, a leading transgender historian, theorist and activist, about the design implications of this urgent social justice issue. Together we co-authored an essay published in the *South Atlantic Quarterly*, that grew into Stalled!, a cross-disciplinary design/research initiative dedicated to coming up with design recommendations and prototypes for inclusive public restrooms.

In 2015, Susan assumed a role similar to that which Diana Fuss had two decades earlier: expanding my intellectual horizons by encouraging me to look outside the field of architecture. Susan encouraged me to delve into two overlapping fields – transgender and disability studies – that led me to see the conceptual and methodological limitations of my earlier work. If, as I mentioned earlier, trans theory encouraged me to jettison a binary conception of gender, delving into another unfamiliar field, namely disability studies, led me to call into question the narrow conception of embodied identity that had informed my work until that time.

I came to realize that I had unconsciously absorbed problematic preconceptions about the human beings who inhabit the buildings Western architects have designed since antiquity. From Vitruvius to Le Corbusier architects have designed buildings based on studying and measuring the characteristics of an 'ideal' body or, beginning in the eighteenth century, a 'typical' body, one that was presumed to be white, able-bodied, cisgender, heterosexual and male. This ergonomic data has been the basis of design standards encoded not only in building typologies but also through architectural guidelines and regulatory codes still in use to this day. With the rise of medicine and anthropometrics in the nineteenth century, this ostensibly objective data was used to sort humans into two categories – 'normal' versus 'abnormal' bodies – that were enlisted to support 'scientific racism', central to the ideologies of European and American movements like Eugenics and Nazism. In the name of science, anthropometric studies have been used at different moments in history, including our own, to justify discriminatory policies determining who has access to and who is excluded from public space – including women, people of colour, immigrants and the disabled – based on the assumption that they possess innate physical, mental and moral deficiencies rendering them unfit to enter the public realm.

In the United States, these prejudicial categories have had design consequences, past and present. They were manifest in legislation like Jim Crow laws that mandated racial segregation in public restrooms, trains and restaurants from 1865 to 1965; as well as the Immigration Act of 1924, put in place 'to preserve the ideal of U.S. homogeneity' that until 1952 denied Asians, Italians, Jews and Eastern Europeans from setting foot on American soil. However, more often, they were expressed in less explicit ways: the disabling design conventions implemented by architects and designers that exclude 'undesirables' from using everyday building types and public spaces – implementations that we have inherited and employ to this day. Consider the steps leading to the entrances of public buildings elevated on podiums that make the transition between sidewalks and streets difficult to traverse for the elderly and people with mobility and sensory disabilities; sex-segregated facilities like restrooms, locker rooms and military barracks that discourage trans and nonbinary people from using them; border walls that prevent Mexican immigration orsub-standard housing projects that work in conjunction with red-lining to perpetuate structural racism and feed the prison industrial complex that disproportionately incarcerates Black men.

During a memorable phone conversation early in our Stalled! collaboration, Susan suggested that we leverage trans visibility in the media, a trend exemplified by Caitlyn Jenner having been featured on the cover of *Vanity Fair* in 2015 and use Stalled! as a platform to cast a wider net and advocate for the marginalized communities historically denied participation in the public realm due to exclusionary environments designed by architects. We came to refer to them 'non-compliant bodies', people including the elderly, trans and nonbinary folk, Black and Brown people, Muslims and people on the Autism spectrum, to name a few of those whose needs fall outside of the federal and municipal regulations governing the building codes that architects and owners must comply with in the United States.

This shift from focusing on gender to the overlapping needs of a spectrum of diverse humans became central not only to Stalled! but to subsequent initiatives conducted by MIXdesign, the inclusive design think-tank and consultancy that I established as a branch of my architectural studio in 2017. MIXdesign works with progressive clients to develop toolkits, guidelines and prototypes for making everyday building types – like restrooms, campuses, museums and residential spaces – safe and accessible for a wide spectrum of people with different identities and embodiments. Our work is guided by an intersectional approach based on the conviction that human experience and embodied identities are constituted by a variety of interconnected factors, including age, gender, race, religion and ability. Our approach differs from most accessibility guidelines in the United States, for example the ADA that focus on physical disabilities (people in wheelchairs, the blind and those with low vision) and subscribe to an 'equal but separate' mentality that equips buildings with architectural interventions like accessible ramps or entrances. Although a step in the right direction, this approach isolates and as a consequence stigmatizes people with 'special needs'. In contrast, MIXdesign's objective is to design public spaces that promote sharing among individuals, friends, families and caregivers while recognizing that there are no universal solutions. Hence our name: MIXdesign.[10]

An example of this is how Stalled! advocates for an alternative to the generally accepted code-compliant solution for all-gender bathrooms, namely the single-user restroom that supplements traditional sex-segregated facilities by adding a single-occupancy room, often with wheelchair access, with signage designating it as gender neutral. Although a step in the right direction, this conventional approach stigmatizes non-normative bodies, not only trans people but also disabled people, isolating them in a separate room and preventing them from mixing with others in public space. Instead, we favour the multi-user type that treats the restroom as a single open space with communal areas for washing and grooming and toilet stalls with floor-to-ceiling partitions that afford privacy.[11]

Stalled!'s version of this type eliminates two crucial boundaries – the wall between the men's and women's rooms and the corridor wall – and allows us to treat the restroom as a semi-open precinct now activated by a lounge. This solution has two advantages: by consolidating a greater number of people in one rather than two rooms, restroom users can visually monitor one another, reducing the risk of violence and it ensures that gender-nonconforming people aren't stuck between two options that don't align with their identities. However, in addition to accommodating trans and nonbinary folk, the multi-user type also meets the needs of a wide range of non-normative users usually neglected in public restrooms – of which we became aware by forming a research collaboration with Yale Public

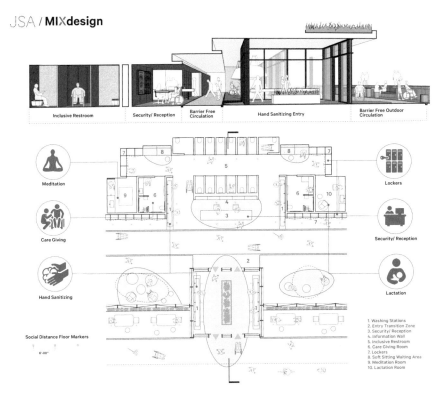

FIGURE 8.5 *University Wellness Hub Prototype, JSA/MIXdesign, 2020.*

Health in 2017. Our Stalled! prototypes include dry counters for people who administer insulin injections, foot showers for Muslims who perform ablutions and product dispensers for people (including trans men) who menstruate (Figure 8.5).

MIXdesign's intersectional approach poses a host of contradictory challenges. Our objective is to foster the mixing of intersecting communities without siloing people into reductive categories. This mentality, which characterized STUD, is also one of the pitfalls of accessible design. Both lead to the creation of user-specific solutions that isolate people in spaces tailored to their different functional needs. It can be attributed to the enduring legacy of identity-based politics that often employed the category of identity as an instrumental tool to combat inequality through political action that promotes agency and belonging by highlighting differences rather than commonalities between groups. Instead, MIXdesign draws inspiration from the many political and intellectual alliances formed between Black, feminist, queer and disability rights movements from the 1960s to the present day, by looking for shared design solutions that meet the overlapping needs of diverse users.

One of the challenges of this approach is how to accomplish such goals without subscribing to a questionable principle of Universal Design, namely that it is possible to create 'environments that can be accessed, understood and used to the greatest extent possible by all people regardless of their age, size, ability or disability'. Although well intentioned, this approach can lead to all-purpose solutions that do not account for the many varieties of embodied differences that sometimes require unique spatial accommodations. MIXdesign is working to reconcile the design implications of this apparent contradiction between sameness and difference that is central to the future of inclusive design. Our objective is to promote sharing while respecting differences by providing choice. For each project, our aim is to allow the maximum number of people with different identities and embodiments to share common facilities while providing options for those users with specific functional or privacy needs. For example, our Stalled! bathroom multi-user prototype includes at least one larger stall equipped with mirror, sink and toilet for people who require visual and acoustical privacy like caregivers, Muslims, Orthodox Jews and people who suffer from shy bladder syndrome.

MIXdesign's intersectional design methodology stems, at least in part, from my own self-critical attempt to compensate for the queer-centrism of my earlier work, including *STUD*. Nevertheless, a consistent thread connects them. In the same way that JSA's residential projects from 1996 to 2015 recontextualized queer-specific spatial tactics for spaces used by non-queer users, today MIXdesign's schemes for inclusive public restrooms, museums and university campuses incorporate lessons learned from studying the intersecting behavioural needs of non-compliant bodies. Then and now, my work is based on the conviction that looking at the world through the lens of marginalized humans can be a catalyst for creativity, a process that encourages designers to generate unforeseen design innovations that can enhance the experience of the general public.

Critical retrospection

I hope this chapter that treats the silver anniversary of *STUD* as an opportunity to reflect on the book's genesis and the evolution of my thinking about the relationship between human embodied identity and the built environment has not been self-indulgent, but touched instead on issues that resonate with twenty-first-century readers.

Hindsight is 20/20. *STUD* is a time capsule that was shaped by and in many ways was limited by attitudes which, by today's standards, seem narrow or out of date. *STUD* suffers from a reductive conception of gender and human embodied identity that narrowly focused on the experience of white able-bodied cisgender men and women, a mentality that was prevalent in both gender studies and queer activism in the mid-1990s. Another drawback is the book's American and Western-centric perspective.

Except for Renee Green, a Black artist, all of *STUD's* contributors are white, able-bodied, cisgender Americans or Europeans. In addition, the book's conceptual framework also took for granted a Western viewpoint. Each section of the book invited contributors to critique the way a generic spatial type constructs masculinity without taking into consideration that both the typologies and conceptions of masculinity under scrutiny were late-twentieth-century Western constructions that manifest themselves differently in different part of the globe. A similar critique can be levied against the Stalled! initiative today. Despite its intersectional purview, we have developed bathroom guidelines and prototypes that can be implemented in America and Europe. Acknowledging this limitation, MIXdesign is in the process of expanding our geographical reach. For example, we formed a team with Matilda Cassini, Ignacio Galán and Iván L. Munera to design a research station 'Your Bathroom Is a Battleground' at the 2021 Venice Architecture Biennale. Our installation uses dioramas linked with podcasts to illustrate eight international case study sites in Bogata, Columbia; Canterbury, UK; Port-au-Prince, Haiti; Philadelphia, Pennsylvania; and Gloucester, Virginia; and Khayelitsha, South Africa, that allow viewers to compare the social justice and environmental issues posed by bathroom controversies being waged around the world.

Nevertheless, despite *STUD's* drawbacks, there are aspects of the book that I still stand by. The principles that shaped its methodology – the notion of performativity and the imperative to analyse and dismantle the architectural conventions encoded in everyday building typologies remain central to my own work and I believe they are still relevant today. Moreover, the process of writing this memoir has made me aware of what I consider to be *STUD's* most relevant insight: that design progress requires critical reflection through a historical lens.

Editing *STUD* during a transitional period in my own life proved to be a cathartic experience that allowed me to look back, confront and exorcize my own inner demons that took the form of internalized cultural conceptions of Western masculinity with which I had wrestled since childhood. Reflection, informed by insights learned from queer studies, gave me the confidence to establish my own professional identity as a queer architect and academic. At the same time, the liberating process of looking back at my own personal history led me to formulate what I consider to be *STUD's* most relevant premise and one that that shares affinities with a notion central to social justice movements like Black Lives Matter that are gaining momentum today: reckoning.

STUD invited contributors to interrogate the design conventions that we take for granted, through a historical lens, using this analysis as a tool to hold the discipline of architecture accountable for contributing to the perpetuation of what today we refer to as 'toxic masculinity'. This issue was painfully foregrounded during the AIDS epidemic when gay men were portrayed as infectious deviants who threatened the health and well-being of the body politic. As I write this chapter quarantined in my apartment, current events have made us painfully aware of a related and no less pernicious phenomenon – the emergence of far-right political movements in the United States and around the world that target minority communities who have been disproportionally impacted by the Covid-19 pandemic. In response, members of the design community are stepping forward. They include anti-racist Black architects and academics like Mabel Wilson, Mario Gooden and Justin Moore (the founder of Dark Matters University), who are demanding that educators, curators, administrators and design professionals mine the histories of educational and cultural institutions to reveal how the pedagogies, canons and practices they disseminated were complicit in upholding structural racism, heteronormativity and ableism.[12]

What was true twenty-five years ago still holds true today. Moving forward means looking back. Design activism depends on self-reflection through a rear-view mirror: imagining alternative futures requires us to first interrogate and then transcend the engrained cultural assumptions about the human embodied difference that are encoded in the design standards and protocols of professional practice that we have inherited from the past.

Notes

1 In this chapter I follow the DCFPI Style Guide for Inclusive Language that recommends using 'People-first language that places personhood at the centre and considers all other descriptive social identities that one holds as secondary and non-essential'. DC Fiscal Policy Institute, December 2017.

2 Morbidity and Mortality Weekly Report, CDC. 24 November 1995.

3 Report on the Global HIV/AIDS Epidemic, UN Joint United Nations Programme on HIV/AIDS and World Health Organization, June 1998.

4 It was not until the publication of Jack Halberstams's important book 'Female Masculinity' in 1998 that I would become aware of the concept of 'female masculinity', historically practised by marginalized lesbian, nonbinary and trans women, that is a distinct alternative to mainstream or 'toxic' masculinity.

5 This notion builds on Gottried Semper's famous discussion of the origins of architecture in the Four Elements of Architecture. Semper describes how the first builders used fabric enclosures to protect the hearth from wind and wild animals that were made of textiles that eventually came to be decorated with colourful designs that would anticipate architectural ornament as a medium of social communication.

6 I elaborate on my own experience as an academic and practitioner trying to overcome the disciplinary and professional prejudices that separate architecture from landscape and interior design in my essay 'The Future of Cross-disciplinary Practice', *Shaping the American Interior: Structures, Contexts and Practices*; Routledge: pp. 195–204.

7　I describe the shift in my thinking about queerness and space prompted by my exposure to transgender studies in 'From Stud to Stalled! Architecture in Transition', *Log* (Issue 41) Anywhere Corporation, pp. 145–54.

8　More on the Cruising Pavilion can be found at https://arkdes.se/en/utstallning /cruising-pavilion-architecture-gay-sex-and-cruising-culture/. Credits: Pierre-Alexandre Mateos, Rasmus Myrup, Octave Perrault, Charles Teyssou; working with Curator at ArkDes: James Taylor-Foster.

9　Crusing Pavillion: Pierre-Alexandre Mateos, Rasmus Myrup, Octave Perrault and Charles Teyssou; curator at ArkDes: James Taylor-Foster. Queer Spaces: London, 1980's-today: curated by Nayia Yiakoumaki, curator: Archive Gallery and Vassilios Doupas, independent writer and curator, with Cameron Foote, assistant curator at the Whitechapel Gallery. Archive section presents case studies from research led by Professor Ben Campkin, The Bartlett School of Architecture and UCL Urban Laboratory.

10　I have elaborated on the mission, principles and methodology that inform MIXdesign in lectures, podcasts and publications that can be found on our website www.mixdesign.online.

11　More detailed discussions of the Stalled! initiative can be found on the open-source website Stalled! (www.stalled.online) that also includes a list of related essays, publications and interviews by different members of the Stalled! team including Susan Styker, Terry Kogan and Sebastian Choe.

12　There is a growing body of scholars, curators and architects addressing the disciplines of architecture's historical accountability for upholding structural racism. Many of them are included in 'Reconstructions: Architecture and Blackness in America', mounted at MoMA in 2021, curated by Mable Wilson and Sean Anderson as well as 'Race and Modern Architecture: A Critical History from the Enlightenment to the Present', edited by Irene Cheng, Charles L. Davis II and Mabel O. Wilson, University of Pittsburgh Press, 2020.

References

Cruising Pavilion: Pierre-Alexandre Mateos, Rasmus Myrup, Octave Perrault, Charles Teyssou; curator at ArkDes: James Taylor-Foster.

Halberstam, J. (1998), *Female Masculinity*, Durham: Duke University Press.

Interior Design Magazine, October 2000.

Meyer, R. (2002), *Outlaw Representation: Censorship & Homosexuality in Twentieth Century American Art*, Oxford: Oxford, pp. 225–37.

MIXdesign, www.mixdesign.online

Morbidity and Mortality Weekly Report, CDC. 24 November 1995.

New York Times Magazine, Men's Fashions of the Times, Part 2, Spring 2001.

Queer Spaces: London, 1980's-today, Curated by Nayia Yiakoumaki and Vassilios Doupas, with Cameron Foote.

Report on the Global HIV/AIDS Epidemic, UN Joint United Nations Programme on HIV/AIDS and World Health Organization, June 1998.

Sanders, Joel, ed. *Stud: Architectures of Masculinity*. New York: Princeton Architectural Press, 1996.

Sanders, J. (2011), 'Human/Nature: Wilderness and the Landscape/Architecture
    Divide', in J. Sanders and D. Balori (eds.), *Groundwork: Between Landscape
    and Architecture*, 12–33, Monacelli Press.
Sanders, J. (2017). 'From Stud to Stalled! Architecture in Transition', *Log* (Issue
    41), Anywhere Corporation, pp. 145–54.
Sanders, J. (2018), 'The Future of Cross-disciplinary Practice', in P. Lupkin, P.
    Sparke (eds.) *Shaping the American Interior: Structures, Contexts and Practices*,
    London and New York: Routledge, pp. 195–204.
Stalled! www.stalled.online.

III

Spaces

9

Architectures of darkness in Derek Jarman and Mark Bradford

Nicholas Gamso

In July 2017, on a visit to the Museum of Fine Arts in Boston, I became transfixed by two works, exhibited in counterpoint.[1] The first was Derek Jarman's 1993 film *Blue*, which shows a brilliant cobalt field for 79 minutes, accompanied by Jarman's voice. With a sonorous cadence, Jarman describes something altogether horrible: the debilitating effects of AIDS, which has reduced his weight, destroyed his immune system and made him blind (a result of cytomegalovirus). The film is an urgent conclusion to Jarman's cinematic and painterly oeuvres as well as an inquiry into the last, transitive chapter in his life. He would die within a year of its release.

The second work on view was Mark Bradford's 2015 installation *Spiderman*. In a cavernous gallery, lit with a single red spot, a loudspeaker plays a six-minute standup routine, delivered by a character called Spiderman. Bradford voices the character – a fictional Black, transgender comedian – and wrote the script, which is spelled out in white lettering and projected onto the gallery wall. The cheers and raucous laughter of an adoring crowd accompany Spiderman's bawdy stories, creating an immersive sonic environment that feels like an after-hours comedy club. The work, a parody of Eddie Murphy's controversial homophobic standup special *Delirious*, from 1983, boldly appropriates and reimagines Murphy's style in a fierce, queer idiom. Like Jarman's film, Bradford's installation is referential and reflexive, calling attention to its mediated format and challenging its audience to see and to sense differently.

The two works are formally alike and thematically adjacent. They convey related experiences of loss, injury and erotic longing, hedging what the curators describe as 'personal fears and public phobias'. This description is evocative

– mixing public and private is one of the key leitmotifs of queer politics and culture – but more needs to be said about the space of spectatorship within which these effects take shape. When I visited the museum, it was early in the day and I was the only viewer in the adjoined galleries. Alone, I could luxuriate in silent darkness, concentrating on the works, enjoying the whole duration of Bradford's six-minute piece without interruption before walking into *Blue* and imbibing the vivid, monochromatic wash that Jarman's film cast upon the room. Each work filled the surrounding gallery space with a single colour, effectively creating a new, suspended architecture. The rooms' edges disappeared into shadows – the walls were painted black and Bradford's room was strung with heavy velvet curtains. I was absorbed by the works' aura, manifest in the two irradiant colours, but also aware of myself as a body: I recall the air conditioning, I remember moving through the rooms, sitting down in one gallery and walking about the other. As I sat watching *Blue*, a young man in a black T-shirt and studded belt entered the room. We locked eyes for an instant, staging a tableau of recognition in the dissimulating blue light, before I stood up and walked out, leaving the two works behind, my body warming to the daylight that suffused the next gallery.

This brief encounter led me to reflect upon the range of aesthetic experiences, singular and shared, that may occur within a space of spectatorship. I considered how the make-up of an artwork's audience (differentiated by race, gender identity, sexuality and dis/ability) and the setting in which it is shown (gallery, movie theatre, seminar room) may induce certain kinds of interactions, not just between object and spectator but between the spectators themselves. The galleries were, in Giuliana Bruno's words, 'architectures of public intimacy' in which feeling and imagination are 'transiently lived in the presence of a community of strangers' (2019: 136). The effect is especially pronounced when the audience is framed – silhouetted – by the glimmers of cinematic projection. To enter such a space, as film theorist Jean Ma has observed, is to 'leave behind the lucid sunlit world', indeed to be 'cutoff from external reality' and 'conditioned to a different disposition of the body and senses' (2021: 59). Jarman's and Bradford's works clearly induce these sorts of dispositional changes. Their uses of monochromatic light and dense, at times disorderly soundtracks create atmospheric sensory environments for queer social and erotic interaction. Both artists have described personal aesthetic investments in cruising grounds and queer bars or clubs. But here the effect is more nebulous. The idea is not simply to imitate or replicate these spaces – it was not a winking allusion to *blue* movie houses and *red* light districts that defined the two works – but rather to instantiate certain moods, to impel attractions and identifications, even to provoke feelings of ambivalence and hesitation. In inviting audience members to share in the creation of an emergent and indeterminate social world, the two works exceed their statuses, per the curator's statement, as testaments to fear, debility and social death.

It is true that conditions of widespread homophobia and repressive anti-gay and racist law are of grave consequence to the artists. Jarman, who was diagnosed with AIDS in 1987, at age forty-five, became politically active in opposition to Section 28, Margaret Thatcher's law forbidding the 'intentional promotion' of homosexuality. Bradford experienced the moment under different but not unrelated circumstances: he was raised in Los Angeles in the 1980s, when Black men were perishing from AIDS at an alarming rate exacerbated by Reaganite cuts to public healthcare and social services. He describes *Spiderman* as a consideration of 'that moment of hysteria and fear and homophobia in the eighties and the black community's relationship to it' – though the final product does not represent the most traumatic and immediate aspects of the AIDS crisis, does not show death and dying and does not show protests against government inaction. In neither of the works is there a direct commentary on homophobia or political violence. Rather, the works' oblique references and ambient audio/visual components allude to 'atmospheres of violence', to borrow a phrase from geographer and trans theorist Eric Stanley (2021). The works imply a set of diffuse social conditions, lived across communities, that cannot be relayed through figurative representation or individual narrative testimony. In refusing these modes of exposition, the two works implicitly offer themselves as gathering points for new relations, new dynamics, producing what scholars Jill Stoner (2012) and John Paul Ricco (2002) refer to as 'minor architectures' of contingent social interaction.[2] Through abstracted sensory impressions and interactive plays of appearance and withdrawal, the works call attention to circumspect modes of queer world-making, which invariably arise in the wake of devastating losses.

I begin this chapter with a focus on the formal multi-modality of Jarman's *Blue* and Bradford's *Spiderman*, specifically their use of monochromatic light and atmospheric sounds, before speculating on how these dynamics can illuminate transformative social processes. In calling attention to the works' formal attributes, I am following Jack Halberstam's writing on queer and trans artists who 'spatializ[e] identities' through practical engagements with 'the abstract, the symptomatic and the architectural' – engagements that are consistent with shifts in the expression of sexual and especially gender difference from 'from binary to multiple' and 'from definitive to fractal' (2018). I want to show how the fragmented, disorderly and abstracted effects in *Blue* and *Spiderman* challenge the clinical ethos associated with representations of HIV/AIDS, sheltering the phantasmatic forces that give rise to community. Engaging these operations will mean defying the conventions of normative architectural criticism, thinking in and with the themes of darkness and abstraction – rather than definite or positivest understandings of built space – in order to cross the boundaries of genre, medium and disciplinary knowledge. Film, performance, writing, architecture – these forms become richly and inextricably entangled when they appear within the spaces of spectatorship and subjection that comprise the museum. We must consider their interplay if we are to make sense of minor architectural spaces and their astonishing transformational potentialities.

Darkness made visible

Jarman's film employs Yves Klein's ultramarine pigment, sometimes called International Klein Blue or IKB, as its principal visual component.[3] The colour fills the screen for the full duration of the film, effacing the logics of visual exposition typical of cinematic work.[4] Though the screen is effectively blank, its illuminated reflection does disclose an image of the work's social and architectural environment. The blue light saturates the gallery (or screening room or living room – the film was televised on BBC4 shortly after Jarman's death), tinting viewers' appearance, veiling their faces and movements. The film in this way seems to fulfill a wish that both Klein and Jarman shared: to create a formal 'ambience' that clouds any singular object of visual focus (Klein 2000: 51). In Jarman's words, 'The key to *Blue* was to do away with the images altogether' (quoted in Wollen 2000: 125). Writing on Jarman's film, John Paul Ricco has described such a negation in the language of space: 'a geography becoming imperceptible through colour, a spatiality that is nothing more or less than a chromatic surface, a superficiality that literally under-mines the facial, as well as landscape, bionarrative and every other figural mode of representation' (lxx). *Blue* calls attention to its own emptiness, 'forc[ing] us to reckon with the incapacity of visual representation to register this aporetography' – a field of non-existence. Unlike discreet art or architectural objects, these forces have no 'positive type', but rather act in and through the spaces where they are shown: they compromise a 'hollowing out of architecture', even a 'forgetting of architecture' (xxxi) – as if the containing walls of the screening room were washed out of sight.

This effect is enhanced by the film's soundtrack. The film's audio is dense with ambient music and street sounds, over which Jarman's monologue dispenses a jumble of fragmented ideas: diaristic reflections, descriptions of physical frailty (talk of itchy skin and fatigue) and dissociative references to Yves Klein. His words skirt on the film's surface, receding into traces with each new phrase. 'Blue Bottle buzzing / Lazy days / The sky blue butterfly / Sways on the cornflower / Lost in the warmth / Of the blue heat haze / Singing the blues Quiet and slowly'. As film critic Peter Wollen (2000: 127) has observed, Jarman's film moves between a desire to vanish into pure blue and a pull into the worldliness and avidity that Jarman so exemplified throughout his career. A tension between these effects mirrors a greater tension between the forms of dispossession that characterize queer life (particularly in the context of an HIV/AIDS moral panic) and the specific forms of mobility and social aptitude that queer people often have to assume

– a mix I have elsewhere (2020) referred to as 'queer worldliness' or a queer ethic of place characterized by lateral movement, social class crossing and profane (high/low) aesthetic sensibility.

The film's disordered soundscape and its reflective blue screen seem at once to absorb and to divert visual attention, provoking audience members' minds to wander about the ambient space the work creates. You are, as Ricco suggests, set into an aporetographic field where you have to discover, create or imagine for yourself – or in the company of others. In my encounter with a stranger, the experience of Jarman's work became charged with feelings of identification and affinity, as well as the frisson of physical attraction. But when I was alone, I felt an equally profound sense of communion. I communed with the work itself – disassociating, receiving Jarman's film as a sensing, feeling body rather than a disinterested spectator. Thus, while the film may strip away certain kinds of worldly, identifying features by offering a trance-like passage into aesthetic absorption, it can also heighten a sense of identification with past and future viewers of the film and even with the artist, who remains present through his voice but absent from the visual field. The play of presence and absence is redoubled since Jarman died soon after the film was released – his voice is a spectral trace.

Yet my experience may not be the same as yours. Any prospect of communion with an artwork is contingent upon who one is and where one is situated – an idea that was highlighted in the display of Bradford's and Jarman's works in counterpoint. Just as a museum can enable charged social encounters and sublime dissociative experiences, it may also be a restricted space that enforces certain regimes of visibility and performance among its spectators – often around questions of physical appearance, specifically race and dis/ability. Bradford's work alludes to these restrictions. In Spiderman, the gallery space is in some places a muted crimson (from a single red spotlight) and in others a field of absolute darkness, enabling audience members to recede, as if they were leaning into the shadows of a smoky barroom. *Spiderman* does not create the total chromatic environment of Jarman's *Blue*, but rather becomes a crumpled field of exposure and invisibility, with sound, smoke, light, shadow, text and audio obscuring any one point of focus. The disorienting effect is intensified by the recording of Bradford's performance as Spiderman and the uproarious laughter that accompanies and accentuates the character's monologue.

These medial aspects of the work give the space some formal dimension yet also tend to make the gallery feel cluttered and enclosing. Spiderman assaults the audience with ironic declarations: 'Get your beauty license', 'Bring back the jeri-curl', 'I'm paranoid as a mother fucker of MJ's ghost' – a satirical litany meant to vanquish calls for respectability through what Richard Powell has described as 'ritualistic public exhortations of obscenities and verbal abuses' (2020: 22). Spiderman's bawdy routine is, further, relayed through a garbling sound system and accompanied by 'bootleggy' electronic music. The cluttered and chaotic mix of referents risks overtaking the performance.[5] It is as if these sensory effects were papering over Bradford himself and, along with him, a host of other figures who are referenced obliquely in the piece. Bradford's works are in this sense akin to 'anti-portraits' that toy with received ideas of visibility and power.[6] He explains his intention:

> It's almost like existing in the shadows a little bit. I throw out these fragments and details of things I'm interested in. I notice it's a distancing from some kind of over-determined black body that is so media-driven and politically embattled. Sure, in *Spiderman*, I reference something that happened with a man who couldn't breathe in the subway [Eric Garner, who was killed by NYPD in 2014], but I had to find a way into it where the body wasn't there. When I'm grappling with things, I'm also trying to figure out how I feel about them. I'm always speaking from a subject position. Especially with recent history, I'm never even sure how I feel about what's going on around the African American man and the policing. To want to talk about current topics and find a freedom in them, I had to pull the body out. (quoted in Cohen 2015)

There is a politic to such withdrawals – a refusal to be flattened into the logic of visual commodification that prevails in liberal society, especially for Black men whose exposure, as Bradford attests, is 'media-driven and politically embattled'. (Withdrawal has become a hallmark of minoritarian aesthetic practice in recent years, often with reference to Edouard Glissant's discourse of *opacity*.)[7] Here the withdrawal of Spiderman, the work's central figure, is a deliberate move on the part of the artist to conceal a racialized body from the site of museological display. Bradford had planned to perform the work live but eventually chose to make and broadcast an audio recording. This decision also offers some protection to audience members, as the space itself becomes overtaken by the work's medial components: Spiderman's frenzied routine, the laugh track and canned music, become an escape route for the viewer, obstructing the scrutinizing looks of others or perhaps concealing an encounter or exchange with another viewer. As curator Connie Butler observes, Bradford 'likes to provoke his public with the idea of the potential violence of the gaze and the prurience of surveillance' – but here the audience is left to consider 'our own projection about what that body might mean' (2018: 114).

Gestures of withdrawal and opacity are avowed interests in Bradford's work, though they are often paired with bold, at times ironic displays of queer visibility. The most striking example in his oeuvre may be his performance in the 2005 video *Niagara*, featuring a neighbor, Melvin, swishing down the streets of Black Los Angeles in an act of embodied defiance; the work alluded to practices of everyday queer performance that open up minor architectures of seduction in the real space of city life (the gesture is adopted from a 1953 Marilyn Monroe film of the same name). The video is slowed so that we move with Melvin's sashaying hips. Yet his back is turned to us

– we never see his face. Bradford presents an act of emplaced performance distinctly related to his recreation of a club environment in *Spiderman*: both works acknowledge certain kinds of minor social arenas where transgressive acts of appearance (and withdrawal) can and do occur. But standup comedy venues, like dance halls and night clubs, are especially potent spaces of 'every-night' worlds, to paraphrase José Muñoz's writing on spaces of queer nightlife and performance culture (1999): they become stages on which queers not only exist beside social antagonists such as homophobic comics and closet cases but confront them and transform them. For Bradford, a repressed comedian's homophobic delirium offers an opening to spaces nominally defined by deviance and self-negation, where shadows darken all manner of creative invention.

Abstraction as an architecture of change

I have tried to show how Bradford's and Jarman's uses of ambient visuality and dense, atmospheric sound, as well as the themes of negation and withdrawal, can mark out grounds were the phenomenology of queer relation can take shape. I see the works' abstracted and abstracting features as providing the conditions of 'capacity and openness' that, in David Getsy's words, 'make queer life possible' (2019: 72). Abstraction, the works suggest, masks movement and kinesthesis – it literally means *withdrawal*. Abstraction can conceal affinities, dramatize chance encounters and organize spectators' interrelated movements, shaping their visions of the work and engendering a certain awareness of individual and mutual embodiment (Doyle and Getsy 2013: 65). The open form of an abstract work allows for lateral movements, aimless lingering and unfocussed, associative ways of engaging what appears on a video screen – dispensing with any sense of completion or destination (Ricco 2002: 7). The space of exhibition, under such conditions, does not train its audience's comportment and behaviour, but offers itself as a blank slate for emergent and indeterminate spatial orientations, putting into question spectators' relation to materiality and environment in general.

A queer architectural point of view might observe that an art object and the social environment it engenders cannot be separable in any meaningful way. Hence a mode of analysis that, as Halberstam advises, will 'reimagine the (re)constructed body as it intersects the coordinates of gender, the social constructions of identity and the familiar contours of the built environment' (2018). Thinking with Halberstam, we might conclude that Bradford's *Spiderman* is a work that is coded as both transgender and transformational. The character's moniker is an allusion to the way that bodies, subjects and environments form and reform, sometimes in the shadow of contemporary cultural references and sites of collective, even popular (as in 'pop') valuation: the name *Spiderman*, taken from the mutant comic book superhero, hints at a logic of pop appropriation and corporeal transformation. Bradford's practice is, in this sense, somewhat allegorical, as his recuperation of the outwardly awful and offensive Murphy serves as an example of work to be done across multiple spaces and mediated formats. Here it is instructive to engage the artist's larger oeuvre of abstract paper collages: he gathers material for these works by walking about the spaces of Los Angeles, tearing paper fragments from wheat paste posters, gleaning end papers from his mother's hair salon and even collecting littered cigarette butts. Importantly, however, this itinerant creative practice does not bely its situated origins – Bradford's background is never banished from the finished work but is richly present in fragments, scraps and traces (not only did he grow up in South Central Los Angeles, he worked in his mother's hair salon for many years). His description of this process as extraverted, transformational, difficult and in some ways private recalls Getsy's enthusiasm for abstraction's potential as a tool for recovery and renewal:

> Abstraction for me, I get it – you go internal, you turn off the world, you're hermetic, you channel something. No. I'm not interested in that type of abstraction. I'm interested in the type of abstraction where you look out at the world, see the horror – sometimes it is horror – and you drag that horror kicking and screaming into your studio and you wrestle with it and you find something beautiful in it.[8] (Bradford and Hill 2018: 18)

In Bradford's view, abstraction is a method of continual material and conceptual transformation. 'I'm a builder and a demolisher', he has said. 'I put up so I can tear down. I'm a speculator and a developer. In archaeological terms, I excavate and I build at the same time'. Bradford's use of abstraction does not end at a point of opacity or refusal, in other words; rather he utilizes the visual form of abstraction to scaffold and conceal a more daunting, at times messy and contradictory practice of mixing, disassembly and change. This same mode of clandestine invention and reconstruction, attuned to the conditions of ruined and neglected spaces and bodies, also clearly animates the conceit of *Spiderman*. The starting point is after all a scene of queer injury: a performance by a laughing, taunting comedian who targets gay men ('no faggots allowed', Murphy announced at the start of *Delirious*). In confronting this scene, Bradford could again be said to 'wrestle with' widespread feelings of disgrace and horror – specifically the feeling of generalized embarrassment he felt and witnessed when he saw Murphy perform – and to 'find something beautiful' via the reconstructive actions of queer appropriation and art-making. The work is not just a critique of Eddie Murphy's notoriously homophobic standup persona, in other words, but a confrontation with all that lies beneath: namely, in the words of Connie Butler, a 'masculinity so constricted by its own repression that it emerges from the other end of the intimate soliloquy, transformed' (2018: 105).

Why does this largely thematic gesture demand a spatial and material analysis? Indeed, it shows that radical performance practices, in the words of Fred Moten, can serve as a 'disruption of architecture' by way of disrupting the normative ordering of gender, sexuality, race and ability through disciplinary norms and modes of valuation (2017: 187).[9] Performances like those of Jarman and Bradford can be seen as contesting suppositions not just about who experiences a given space but how space itself can be experienced. I have suggested that Jarman's facility with art and institutional culture makes his oeuvre less of a challenge to aesthetic conventions than Bradford's – but Jarman's work too proposes such disruptions, perhaps not in regard to the problem of access to cultural capital, but in response to the Platonic character of museum display strategies. Of all Jarman's films, it is only *Blue* that eschews representation for what the filmmaker called the 'alchemy' and 'liberation' of abstraction. Why? Although Jarman was eager to produce a film about Yves Klein (he had made biographies of Caravaggio and Wittgenstein), it was his loss of sight that prompted him to pursue this particular project. The artist's visual impairment provides the most immediate explanation for many formal choices and perhaps for the film's apparent inaccessibility and difficulty. I do not mean that the work's unchanging blue field is a metaphor for Jarman's lost vision, but that the film acknowledges and explores the ways that differently abled bodies move through and experience the world. It calls attention to the way that perceptual capacities are 'culturally organized' through visual strategies that presume an 'unproblematic, collectively shared relationship to material space' (Boys 2018: 60). The work demands a modality of spatial perception keyed into these differences and their aesthetic possibilities – hence his reference to 'a blue-eyed boy in a system of unreality'. Certainly Jarman's visual impairment disorders his life ('your clothes are on back to front and inside out', a waitress has told him in an anecdote he reports at the start of the film), but does not mean the loss of his aesthetic faculties. Far from it. He suggests that decentring the visual as the modus operandi of cinema, painting and (as installed at the MFA) museological display will open other channels of sensory life, including those of touch, listening, proxemics and shifts in the registers of spatial and temporal apprehension (Jones 2021: 13). The grey zones of abstraction – the space of abstraction's differential effects on bodies, subjects and the minor architectures of relation – becomes a loose framework for moving with and in these possibilities, away from the supposition of occupancy and shared perception and towards something else which is not yet named.[10]

Conclusion

The purpose of these remarks has been to frame the minor architectural operations that *Blue* and *Spiderman* enable their audience to perform via formal strategies such as abstraction, withdrawal, refusal and opacity – strategies that operate under the protection of darkness rather than the scrutinizing light of day. These works create spaces in which to confront the injuries that arise from living in a homophobic, transphobic, racist and ableist social world and to remake these conditions in the grammar of irrepressible social difference and plurality. I hope to have shown the ways that minor architectures can exploit porous and sometimes dependent relationship with larger spaces, at times accounting for and correcting failures in normative disciplinary form – Jarman examining the logics of death and debility and Bradford transforming the waste of American culture into an expression of transformation and empowerment.

Notes

1   My enormous gratitude to Mark Bradford for granting me access to the video from his installation *Spiderman* and to Stewart Campbell at Hauser & Wirth for facilitating my request. Thank you also to the NEH, which purchased entry to the Museum of Fine Arts in Boston for fellows in its 2017 Summer Institute 'Space, Place, & the Humanities' (led by Elizabeth Maddock Dillon, Tim Cresswell and Sarah Kanouse).

2   Both authors define minor architecture as energies and movements rather than built structures. Stoner describes 'active verbs operating on concrete nouns' (2012: 4) while Ricco describes 'less a force than a form' (2002: xxxv). Although talk of the minor is strongly associated with Gilles Deleuze and Felix Guattari's discourse of 'minor literature' (1986) it has strong geographic and thus epistemological variants; Françoise Lionnet and Shu-mei Shih for example describe the minor as a 'uncontainable, invisible symbolic geography of relations that become the creative terrain on which minority subjects act and interact in fruitful, lateral ways' (2005: 2). For a recent summary of the minor across humanistic inquiry, see Maya Boutaghou and Emmanuel Bruno Jean-Francois, 'The Minor in Question' (2020).

3   The colour is the product of a chemical polymer called Rhodopas, that suspends particles of blue pigment to catch and reflect a light source. In Klein's words: 'I disliked colours ground in oil. They seemed dead to me; what pleased me above all were pure pigments, in powder, such as I saw them in the windows of retail paint-sellers. They had brightness and extraordinary, autonomous lives of their own. This was essential colour. Living tangible colourmatter. It was depressing to see such glowing powder, once mixed in a distemper or whatever medium intended as a fixative, lose its value, tarnish, become dull. One might obtain effects of paste but after drying it wasn't the same; the effective colour magic had vanished' (quoted in Wollen 2000: 124).

4   Tim Lawrence has emphasized the anti-representational character of Jarman's *Blue*: 'If reformists stress the normality of the person with AIDS and if queer theorists emphasize the same person's disruptive and defiant outlook, then Jarman incorporates both possibilities, with the metaphorical thrust of Blue militating against the existence of a 'single universal truth' about the epidemic, the meanings of which cannot be contained' (Lawrence 1997: 260).

5   Literature on the sensory and experimental dimensions of architecture can help us to place these operations in a disciplinary lexicon: for example, Barry Blesser and Linda Ruth-Salter describe the ways that sound can enclose or define a space, inducing 'feelings as exhilaration, contemplative tranquillity, heightened arousal or a harmonious and mystical connection to the cosmos' as well as components that might 'discourage social cohesion' (2009: 5).

6   'Anti-Portrait' is a word coined by artist Lorna Simpson to describe her works' ways of conveying resistance to objectifying portraiture.

7   Glissant's (1996) revocation of 'opacity' in the poetics of relation builds on Deleuzian theories of rhyzomatic networks to describe experiences of cross-cultural engagement. Opacity appears in contrast to the transparency and even empathy demanded by liberal cultural politics. Following Glissant, many Black critical theorists and Black artists have criticized the hypervisibility of Black bodies and Black culture, whether because they are commodified or subject to regulation. For a recent engagement with the question of relation vis-à-vis opacity, see Kara Keeling's *Queer Times, Black Futures* (2019).

8   'As a child in the hair salon, I never turned away from horror. I saw it all. There was so much strength and so much beauty too. The laughter in between the crying. I believe in that. For me, I was going to drag it all into the studio and then I was going to drag it out to the gallery. Yes, in a way it is social abstraction. The thing about Abstract Expressionism that fascinated me was the fact that so many African-American men and women have been left out. It was also really fun when they told me, 'Oh Bradford, you can't. Don't do that' (2018: 18).

9   Moten borrows from Masao Miyoshi's recognition that architecture discards its vital components once it becomes operative as a commodity or state planning project and thus calls for a radically open and imaginative modality of architecture which proceeds in light of fugitive social performance.

10 Moten refers to this prospect as 'an architecture set up to receive aninstrumental, anarchitectural doing, thinging, thinking' of and about the 'communal, anarchic, textural environment that is ecological, social and personal' (2017: 196).

References

Blesser, B. & Ruth-Salter, L. (2009), *Spaces Speak, Are You Listening?: Experiencing Aural Architecture*, MIT Press, Cambridge, MA.

Boutaghou, M. & Emmanuel, B. J. F. (2020), 'The Minor in Question', *Cultural Dynamics*, vol. 32, nos. 1–2, pp. 3–13.

Boys, J. (2018), 'Cripping Spaces? On Dis/abling Phenomenology in Architecture', *Log*, vol. 42, pp. 55–66.

Bradford, B. & Hill, A. (2018), 'Anita Hill in Conversation with Mark Bradford', in *Mark Bradford*, ed. Michele Robecchi, Phaidon, London, pp. 8–41.

Bruno, G. (2019), *The Moving Eye*: Film, *Television, Architecture, Visual Art and the Modern*, ed. Edward Dimendberg, Oxford UP, New York.

Butler, C. (2018), 'Focus: Spiderman', in *Mark Bradford*, ed. Michele Robecchi, Phaidon, London, pp. 104–17.

Cohen, A. (2015), 'AIDS, Abstraction and Absent Bodies: A Conversation with Mark Bradford', *Hyperallergic*, December 9, https://hyperallergic.com/260045/aids-abstraction-and-absent-bodies-a-conversation-with-mark-bradford/

Deleuze, G. & Guattari, F. (1986), *Kafka: Towards a Minor Literature*, trans. Dana Polan, University of Minnesota Press, Minneapolis, originally published 1983.

Doyle, J. & Getsy D. (2013), 'Queer Formalism', *Art Journal*, vol. 72, no. 4, pp. 58–71.

Getsy, D. (2019), 'Ten Theses on Queer Abstraction', in *Queer Abstraction*, ed. Jared Ladesma, Des Moines Art Center, Des Moines, pp. 65–75.

Glissant, E. (1996), Poetics of *Relation*, University of Michigan Press, Ann Arbor, MI.

Halberstam, J. (2018), 'Unbuilding Gender', *Places Journal*, October, https://placesjournal.org/article/unbuilding-gender/

Jones, C. R. (2021), 'Blue / Crippistemologies: In & Around Derek Jarman', *Art Papers*, vol. 44, no. 4, pp. 12–17.

Keeling, K. (2019), *Queer Times, Black Futures*, NYU Press, New York.

Klein, Y. (2000), 'The Specialization of Sensibility', in *Yves Klein: Long Live the Immaterial*, Delano Greenridge Editions, New York, originally published in 1958.

Lawrence, T. (1997), 'AIDS, the Problem of Representation and Plurality in Derek Jarman's *Blue*', *Social Text*, 52–53, pp. 241–64.

Lionnet, F. & Shih, S. (2005), Minor *Transnationalism*, Duke UP, Durham.

Ma, J. 2021, 'Deep in the Cave', in *Deep Mediations: Thinking Space in Cinema and Digital Cultures*, ed. K. Redrobe and J. Scheible, Minneapolis: University of Minnesota Press, pp. 57–69.

Moten, F. (2017), *Black and Blur*, Duke UP, Durham, originally published in 2016.

Muñoz, J. E. (1999), *Disidentifications*, University of Minnesota Press, Minneapolis.

Powell, R. (2020), *Going There: Black Visual Satire*, Yale UP, New Haven.

Ricco, J. P. (2002), *Logic of the Lure*, University of Chicago Press, Chicago.

Stanley, E. (2021), *Atmospheres of Violence: Structuring Antagonism and the Trans/Queer Ungovernable*, Duke UP, Durham.

Stoner, J. (2012), *Towards a Minor Architecture*, MIT Press, Cambridge, MA.

Wollen, P. (2000), 'Blue', *New Left Review*, vol. 6, pp. 120–33.

10

Queer space in a peripheral modernity*

Sarah Nicholus

Introduction

In my mid-twenties, I arrived in Natal, Brazil, to teach English at a federal high school/college through an international education and research programme between Brazil and the United States. Then, my interest in LGBT+[1] community was personal; I didn't know if I could or should be out about my gender or sexuality in a small, socially conservative city in the Brazilian Northeast, a region known for maintaining many rural, religious and traditional cultural norms. Now, after two years living in Natal and five years of extended visits throughout my PhD programme, I speak Portuguese with a Northeastern accent, I have written extensively on LGBT+/queer community in the region and I have developed a supportive local community in Natal. The spaces I examine in this chapter form part of my personal engagement in a transnational queer community. I follow the work of feminist geographers[2] to critically reflect on my positionality through narrative and storytelling while drawing from my experiences navigating Natal both as an outsider to Brazil and as an insider in the LGBT community to describe queer spatialities of the city. My inquiries reflect my own engagement with gender and sexuality across borders and my growth as a scholar of gender, sexuality and cultural studies in Latin America.

Acknowledgments: I would like to thank the editors for their comments, Lorraine Leu for the initial space to work on an earlier version of this text, and Susan Sage Heinzelman for her brilliant and generous review of this chapter in its final stages.

LGBT+ spaces in Natal are generally invisible to outsiders, hidden from the public eye and ephemeral in nature. They are a certain section of the beach on a Friday night, a residential plaza on a Wednesday evening, a party held once a year during the June Festivals. Unlike the large cosmopolitan centres of the Brazilian Southeastern regions, Natal does not have a gay neighbourhood or a gay zone. Due to its more conservative social context, Natal's LGBT+ community spaces are spread throughout the city with varying degrees of formality. In this chapter, I look at three spaces of LGBT+ interaction and socialization to demonstrate how these spaces function in queer ways. I use participant observation, online ethnography, close reading and spatial analysis to better understand the diverse spaces and cultural geography of the city. The merged methods of cultural studies allow me to interrogate the ways in which identities, positionalities and power relations are historically, socio-culturally and geographically contingent rather than fixed, stable or uniform.

Natal is the capital city of Rio Grande do Norte state in Northeastern Brazil – a region that the Brazilian national imaginary constructs as rural, conservative, religious (Albuquerque Jr. 2014) and not especially welcoming of LGBT+ people or communities. Yet to most people living in and around Natal, it is a modern, urban centre that offers both the opportunities and challenges of a big city. Indeed, Natal is home to a large LGBT+ community. Natal articulates what many postcolonial Latin American scholars refer to as a 'peripheral modernity', a space of underdevelopment and cultural hybridity conditioned by its position on the periphery of the world capitalist system that assumes different rhythms of modernity from developed areas (Rowe and Schelling 1991; Martins 2000; Schelling et al. 2000; WREC 2010). In Natal's peripheral modernity, cultural hybridity and dissimulation often interweave with conservative social values, such as traditional gender roles for men and women. For example, gay men might display the (foreign, expensive, imitation) Calvin Klein brand name of their underwear as a status symbol (appearing cosmopolitan, up-to-date and modern) while denigrating effeminate gay men (reasserting traditional gender roles). Natal embodies the contradictions of modernity in Northeastern Brazil and contextualizes the queer spatialities of the city.

In this chapter, I elaborate 'queer space' as ephemeral, fluid, flexible, subversive, radically inclusive and linked to the ways in which space functions in Natal's peripheral modernity. In order to mobilize queerness in a Global South context, I elaborate the concept as both a spatiality and a transnational politics.[3] I highlight the ways in which queer space functions as a collective and spatially informed, position relative to state, capitalist and colonial power. At once traditional and modern, urban and rural, Natal is a hybrid space that generates queer spatialities from its position at the margins of the world capitalist system. Expanding on the work of queer scholars (Cohen 2005, 2019; Halberstam 2005), I detach queerness from individual identity or isolated sexual acts and employ the term to illustrate how space functions in this sociocultural context. I argue that queer space troubles conventional understandings of space as static or physical, just as it unsettles colonial logics of market capitalism, state regulation, heteropatriarchy and white supremacy. In this way, I contribute to a transnational dialogue on anti-normative gender and sexuality and decolonial queer politics that pushes back against the north-normativity of queer studies and that highlights the ways in which Natal's particular socio-cultural setting generates queer spatialities.

Natal a geographical introduction

In mapping queer geographies in Natal, one must consider the ways in which patterns of development, social stereotypes and natural features not only form a mutable urban geography but also impact how people understand, navigate and locate themselves within the city, given multiple, intersecting subjectivities. Natal is formally divided into four zones: *Norte*, *Sul*, *Leste* and *Oeste*, which are imbued with local social-cultural meanings (Figure 10.1). The oldest neighbourhoods make up the city centre just south of the Potengi River[4] in the east. After the Second World War, the more cramped colonial architecture and layout of these areas contributed to their decline as the city developed a larger, more modern infrastructure. From the centre, Natal expanded south along the coastline. The current *bairros nobres* or upscale neighbourhoods of Tirol, Lagoa Nova, Candelaria and Capim Macio make up the central region of the city. These neighbourhoods are easily accessible and close to the city's modern commercial centres, including the largest shopping malls. The *Arena das Dunas* soccer stadium, built for the 2014 World Cup, is located in Lagoa Nova, not far from Natal's main tourist district of Ponta Negra in the South. The most distant, peripheral areas of Natal are the North and East Zones. These areas were incorporated as rural migrants moved in large numbers to the city in the 1970s (Chianca 2007). *Zona Norte* is the most peripheral and marginalized region as it is geographically cut off from the rest of the city by the Pontegi River. The *Igapó* Bridge was the only land route that connected *Zona Norte* to the city until 2007 when the Newton Navarro Bridge was constructed. Still considered peripheral, *Zona Norte* is home to Natal's poor migrant population and subject to many negative stereotypes that mark it as a potentially dangerous space. Most of Natal's urban workforce lives in this sector of the city.

Vogue Natal, Candelaria (Zona Sul) – a gay nightclub hidden in an upscale neighbourhood

Vogue, Natal's gay nightclub, is the most formal and established LGBT+ space in the city. It has been in business since 1996 but has significantly changed over the years. After over ten years in the working-class neighbourhood

FIGURE 10.1 *Natal's zones (North, South, East, West) and neighbourhoods (SETUR-RN, 2015).*

of Alecrim in Zona Oeste, Vogue moved to a new location in the upscale neighbourhood of Candelaria in 2008 (França 2018). It then began to cater to a wealthier demographic of gay men and tourists in the southern zone. Like most gay nightclubs, Vogue highlights young, masculine men in its advertising and features elements of gay culture such as drag queens, diva shows and go-go dancers. It has three distinct settings: an outdoor patio, a club dance floor and a live-music dance area where local artists play Northeastern music, such as *forró*. There are generally fewer women than men at Vogue and women tend to congregate in the live-music area closer to the entrance, as well as in the adjacent Donana Pub bar.

Vogue Natal's location speaks to both its homonormativity and its queerness. As a gay venue associated with nightlife and consumption, Vogue Natal is an example of the most familiar, formal and visible LGBT space in the city. It is literally on the map. Visitors can easily find it – centrally located just behind Sam's Club, which is visible from the highway connecting the tourist district of Zona Sul to the rest of the city. In fact, Sam's Club is the point of reference given to visitors. This geographical connection between a

US membership-only retail warehouse owned by Walmart Inc. and the club, Vogue Natal, is strangely appropriate given the ways the club reinscribes the association between normative gayness and the logics of global capitalism. Catering predominantly to young men over eighteen, the club has, like most gay clubs, flashing lights, a disco ball and high bar tables. Bartenders serve alcohol amidst popular club beats, including top hits in English. To enter Vogue, patrons must present a valid ID and pay a cover fee, which limits access for those without the fee and those whose IDs might be questioned, such as trans folks. One patron reviews Vogue on its Facebook page as a 'transphobic LGBT place' that 'doesn't respect the feminine identity of *travestis* and *transexuais*'. Rebecka goes on to attribute the transmisogyny she experienced to the club's change in location: 'I frequented Vogue for many years when it was in Alecrim and I loved it. . . . The problem was after it went to Zona Sul . . . it seems that it went to the managers' heads' (Rebecka 2014). Like many gay nightclubs, Vogue Natal often reinscribes normative hierarchies.

The move highlights how gender, age, class and race exclusions overlap and intersect with the geographical location of the club and its resulting spatialities. While Rebecka was not happy with the change, another patron, FOXX, comments on a gay blog that the move from a 'popular' neighbourhood to an upper-middle-class neighbourhood resulted in a positive change in the clientele:

> For Natalenses, gay or straight, Vogue was a club where only trashy things happened. It was the club that had a dark room . . . the club of the 'bread and egg' fags. It was the ugly people's club . . . the club frequented by drag queens. And everything changed. You could see it in the new faces we saw there. . . . Unlike the old space, a younger public now visits that foggy place. Some straight couples consider themselves hip for finding such a good spot in their city . . . various muscular guys taking off their shirts in a strange mix between 'barbies' and hipsters who got tired of the usual city night. (FOXX 2010)

Here FOXX replicates pejorative class and gender stereotypes, referring to the old Vogue as a lowbrow space for effeminate, poor and gender-nonconforming gays. He casts these bodies as 'ugly' and undesirable in contrast to the younger and more attractive '*barbies*', '*musculosos*' and '*moderinhos*' at the new location. The expression '*bichinhas pão com ovo*' [bread and egg fags] uses the diminutive, depreciative form of the word '*bicha*' (an effeminate gay) while referencing a simple, cheap food which everyone has eaten. FOXX's class implications and references to white culture from the United States racialize the clientele at Vogue's two different locations. For example, the '*barbies*' at the new Vogue are large, hairless, muscular men who present an idealized masculine body type. Like Ken Dolls, they are commonly white and light-haired. To prove his point, FOXX calls upon

mainstream heterosexual culture or '*casais héteros*' [straight couples] to give
the new location legitimacy. The new location and its spatial implications
allow FOXX to claim Vogue Natal as a space that melds with a globalized
white, straight, upper-middle-class, masculine and mainstream culture to
exclude those most marginalized within LGBT+ communities in Natal.
The old Vogue's location in a working-class neighbourhood allowed it to
hold space for marginalized folks – those who navigate the intersections of
multiple marginalized identities.

Despite all of its homonormativity, however, Vogue Natal remains a
'foggy place'. It embodies the paradoxical tension between normativity
and marginality that is characteristic of Natal's peripheral modernity. Its
historical persistence gives it legitimacy, yet this same permanence also
renders it inaccessible and unwelcoming to many LGBT+ folks, who do not
fit the normative stereotype. The club looks 'modern' without really being
'modern'.[5] It is both a carefully carved out, middle-class, white, gay zone
with all the trappings of dominant culture *and* yet still a marginal space in
a conservative social context. Its literal and symbolic proximity to global
capitalism (Sam's Club, nightclub culture) make it visible. Yet, it is spatially
and figuratively hidden, not only behind the warehouse but also behind
careful euphemisms: in a small, conservative city in which everyone knows
each other's business, Vogue patrons often refer to Vogue as 'VG'. Vogue
requires this dissimulation because it courts normativity. It is thus limited
in its potential to resignify space precisely because it wishes to assimilate.
Natal's peripheral modernity also produces, however, spaces that are fluid,
flexible, subversive, creative and radically inclusive. The spaces in Natal that
resist the reproduction of dominant (hetero/homo)-normative paradigms
are often informal, non-commercial and ephemeral spaces: these are queer
spaces. Their temporary and mutable locations, as well as their inclusion
of multiple, intersectional and marginal sexual subjectivities, subvert the
dominant practices of clubs like Vogue.

Praça Mits, Lagoa Nova (Zona Sul) – an informal, ephemeral space for LGBT youth in a residential plaza near a public high school/college

One of the most ephemeral spaces I encountered is the Praça Mits, an open-
air plaza in which LGBT youth used to, at one time, socialize on Wednesday
nights. An informal, auto-constructed space, it's not exactly clear when LGBT
youth began to gather in the plaza. Informal interviews with frequenters
revealed that a similar space, the Praça do Cei near the Federal University of
Natal (UFRN) in the adjacent neighbourhood of Lagoa Nova, was a popular

LGBT point up until the beginning of 2011, when I estimate the Praça Mits emerged within Natal's queer geographies. The physical space is a small rectangular area formed by four cobblestone streets, a sidewalk tracing the outer edge and a low wall, about the height of a bench, separating the inside from the outer walkway. Located in a central, upscale neighbourhood near a shopping mall, its proximity to the local high school/technical college made it an ideal space for students ages sixteen to twenty-two to gather after class.

The Praça Mits hosted anywhere from a dozen to over one hundred LGBT youth from approximately 2011 to 2014. As a young teacher at the technical school, my social circles often overlapped with those of the college-aged students.[6] I heard about the plaza by word of mouth and invited a couple of friends to visit with me. I wanted to observe the space while socializing with people my own age. While I didn't teach the younger students, I was interested in maintaining social distance given my age and position at the school. During the day, the plaza was relatively unoccupied, save a small food stand on the corner and occasional occupants. Medium and small trees provided much-needed shade over patches of grass and sandy soil. Tall security walls cut off the surrounding residences from the plaza, a common feature of urban areas of Brazil. In contrast to this hot, still landscape, the plaza came alive with movement on Wednesday nights. Young people arrived in small groups and mingled under the light of a few tall lampposts, their outlines melding with the dark trunks of the trees.[7] I conceive of the Praça Mits as queer: set within the peripheral modernity of Natal, the plaza represents a fluid, temporary and subversive space for LGBT youth. An auto-constructed, informal, non-commercial and ephemeral space, the plaza presents alternative LGBT geographies that intervene in stable and static understandings of time and space by unsettling the logics of market capitalism and state regulation.

If we disassociate queerness from individual identity, we can further appreciate how the plaza re-shapes conventional constructions of time and space.[8] The Praça Mits functions in queer ways in order to accommodate those on the margins, in this case, LGBT youth on the outside of the capitalist logics that so often drive globalized gay culture. Unlike commercial LGBT spaces, such as bars and clubs, the Praça Mits is free to enter. It does not have an opening or closing time and is constructed through the comings and goings of those who occupy the space. In her discussion of peripheral urbanization in the Global South, Theresa Caldeira characterizes auto-constructed urban space as operating within a temporality of 'always becoming' (2017). The plaza's ephemerality is part of its queerness. Defined by fluidity, movement and change, the plaza is a space by and for young people who themselves occupy a liminal time/space between childhood and adulthood, often seen as a dangerous, unruly and chaotic stage (Halberstam 2005). In his ethnography of Praça Mits (2016), João Batista Figueredo de Oliveira observes the youth that visit the plaza as ever-changing – in their styles, gender expressions, sexual desires. Rather than demonstrating fixed and stable identities, they embody movement and multiplicity. While Oliveira does not call this movement 'queer', his description aligns with formulations of 'queer' as movement 'against the grain'.[9] The Praça Mits holds space for ambiguity and fluidity and the young people who created it, by pushing back against what is often associated with adulthood: the desirability of stability and linear processes of becoming. By spatializing fluidity and change, the youth of Praça Mits not only make space for disruptions in temporality, life stages and capitalist economic practices that characterize queer life (Halberstam 2005) but also utilize place-making as a form of resistance.

Seeing the plaza as an act of resistance becomes even more plausible when one considers that the plaza's official name, Praça Dr. Amaro Marinho, pays homage to a local judge and law professor (Simonetti 2021). This type of official place-making reflects processes of ownership and belonging regulated by elite state actors (Alderman 2008). The name itself confers respect and prestige to educated men in Natal and those whose age, race, gender and class align with them. Actively resisting local histories and cultural landscapes that do not hold space for them, the LGBT youth laid claim to the plaza by renaming it. First dubbed Praça Mitsubishi, referencing a Mitsubishi car dealership visible to students arriving at the campus, the plaza's later, shortened name, Praça Mits, disassociated the space from the dealership. The new name both claimed and protected the space for LGBT youth – providing a way to locate the plaza while also protecting it from those who were not meant to find it. The Praça Mits unlike, for example, the Praça Amaro Marinho cannot be found on any official map. In his work describing the Praça Mits as a nomad space, Oliveira argues that the two names of the plaza represent two realities of the space: one of a physical location on a map and the other outside the confines of geography – a reality of transient existence (2016). An act of resistance to state ownership and authority, the renaming unfixes the identity of the plaza and configures it for the LGBT youth who occupy it.

The Praça Mits presents queer space as transient, changeable, subversive and inclusive of those excluded from normative LGBT spaces in Natal. While LGBT youth had stopped frequenting the plaza when I returned in 2015, the space that was once known as the Praça Mits could very well have moved to another location. Indeed, Praça Mits could have been a migration of the space that was once located in the Praça do Cei. Both the Praça Mits and Praça do Cei were near schools and mapped onto many of the student geographies of the city. While I've referred to this space as the 'Praça Mits', the specific geographic space, as well as the concrete, material and architectural contexts are not as relevant as the social practices that create the space. To be sure, the plaza facilitates the social practices that make the configuration possible, but the specific location of the plaza can change. As sites of community formation in Latin America, plazas represent the kind of transient LGBT spaces that produce the queer geographies of Natal.

Arraiá do GAMI, Redinha (Zona Norte) – a June Festival party for LGBT women in a rented space on the other side of the river

'There's going to be a trans *quadrilha* performance at an *arraiá* for lesbians in Redinha at the Nana Banana Space'. I checked my WhatsApp message again. I had been living and working in Natal for over two years, but I had never been to a space that was by and for women – lesbian, bi, trans, cis. I had never been to a radically inclusive LGBT+ space that centred women, trans folks, children, elders, Black and working-class people; one that did not rely on or replicate the exclusions I'd encountered in spaces more closely organized around globalized gay culture and capitalist exchange. As an outsider to Natal, my engagement with the LGBT community followed a spatially organized pattern: one that began in the southern tourist districts of Ponta Negra, moved to the nearby gay nightclub and continued in the upscale central neighbourhoods where I lived and worked. It took more than two years for me to connect to the feminist, anti-racist, radically inclusive LGBT+/queer community I sought.

The Affirmative Group of Independent Women (GAMI) is a non-profit feminist organization founded in 2004 that promotes sexual diversity, community engagement and women's empowerment through sports, culture and popular education in Natal. GAMI's target audiences are youth, women, LGBT folks and the Black population (GAMI, ND). GAMI's activities are not confined to a single, physical space; rather they rely on word of mouth, social networking and community engagement to create and define multiple ephemeral spaces for LGBT+ women in the Redinha neighbourhood of Natal's Northern Zone. *Zona Norte* is, itself, a marginalized geographic space. Located on the other side of the river, it is home to Natal's Black, working-class, rural and migrant population.

In 'Defiant Geographies', Lorraine Leu describes the long history of Black and Blackened subjects in poor communities in Brazil mobilizing their own spatial logics to introduce new ways of occupying the city (2020). Here, I argue that GAMI mobilizes a queer spatial logic organized around community networks (rather than stable, static or physical space) to produce queer space during the June Festivals. With colonial, religious and heteropatriarchal origins, the June Festivals often exclude LGBT+ folks at the intersections of multiple marginalized identities. At their annual party for LGBT+ women, GAMI utilizes alternate spatial organization, resistant practices and radical inclusivity to unsettle the colonial logics of white supremacy and heteropatriarchy and reclaim the traditional June Festivals as spaces of LGBT+ community formation.

While I've translated *arraiá* as 'a party', it is technically a small temporary space that hosts the events of the *festas juninas* – the popular June Festivals associated with the rural space of the Brazilian Northeast. Contemporarily, the June Festivals include informal social events which offer seasonal food, drink and partner dances as well as more formal religious processions and *quadrilha* dance competitions. Already situated within the alternate temporal and spatial organization of seasonal festivals, GAMI's 'strange temporalities' (Halberstam 2005) include configuring a multi-use space for the event and mobilizing the network[10] as a central organizing unit. The *arraiá* party happens once a year in the Espaço Nana Banana, a rented space in the Redinha neighbourhood of *Zona Norte*. A multi-use space with a large open-air patio, stage, dance floor and kitchen, it is necessarily fluid, flexible and adaptable to the events it hosts. Not only can different community groups use the space for a variety of events, but GAMI can also configure space for its annual *arraiá* party in a different location. In this way, GAMI provides an alternative both to conventional concepts of space as stable and static and to the organization of LGBT+space around permanent spaces, such as gay neighbourhoods, for-profit businesses and the gay clubs and bars of globalized, consumerist gay culture.

As a result of this alternate spatial organization, participants access the event via community networks. Indeed, I first became aware of GAMI's event through word of mouth and social networking.[11] As an outsider, I did not have the network capital[12] to access this type of space until I received my friend's WhatsApp invitation. Even once I knew there was going to be a 'June Festival party for lesbians in the Nana Banana Space in Redinha', I could not locate the space. The *Espaço Nana Banana* is not a business, nor does it have an address or commercial website. Without specific knowledge of Redinha or a familiarity with the bus routes to this peripheral zone of the city, I did not know how to find it. When I asked university friends for a ride, they discouraged me from going to a 'dangerous' part of town.[13] I ended up riding the bus with two friends and walking along Redinha's seaside boardwalk until a group of young people directed us to the Nana Banana Space. In many ways, the ephemerality and adaptability of GAMI's queer space integrated it with the local community and protected it from outsiders.[14] In essence, my white, middle-class, North-American cultural/ network capital did not give me easy access to the LGBT+community I sought. The willingness of friends and strangers to share their 'community cultural wealth'[15] (Yosso 2005) ultimately made it possible for me to attend the party.

Another way in which the GAMI configures a queer space is through resistant practices that make the event accessible to and supportive of a radically inclusive community. GAMI's 'eccentric economic practices' (Halberstam 2005) include an affordable and donation-based entrance fee. The first year I attended, the arraiá cost five *reais;*[16] the following year, GAMI collected toy donations, instead of a fee. Proceeds from the event supported GAMI's functions and went directly to the community. Both years, GAMI invited a local street vendor to sell foods associated with the harvest time of the *festas juninas* and featured local artists in the entertainment.

In addition to these economic practices, the *arraiá*'s temporal configuration supported 'imaginative life schedules' (Halberstam 2005), such as those who have non-traditional families, those who manage odd work hours and those excluded from typical LGBT+ spaces. The event began on a Sunday afternoon and extended through the evening to accommodate day and night workers. In 2014, it drew close to 150 people, including children, teenagers, middle-aged women and elders who are often excluded from the bar and club scenes of typical gay life in Natal. Activities included *pescaria* (a fishing game) for children in the afternoon, a *carimbó*[17] dance performance by community elders in the late afternoon, a concert hosted by local artists in the evening and a drag *quadrilha* dance performance at night.

As celebrations of the harvest, fertility, marriage and the Catholic saints whose feast days fall in June, the *festas juninas* often replicate colonial, religious and heteronormative structures. The *arraiá*'s configuration around alternative, ephemeral networks and its use of resistant economic and temporal practices intervene in the symbolic meanings of the June Festivals[18] and centres the local community, thus resisting global capitalist logics. The *arraiá* also challenges moralistic, patriarchal and heteronormative values associated with rural Northeastern culture. In this space, cultural workers reclaim the festivals as an important space for LGBT+ community formation. While normative scripts cast rural, traditional and religious regions, like the Brazilian Northeast, as conservative and not especially welcoming of LGBT+ people, GAMI demonstrates how traditional cultures hold space for radical LGBT+ communities.

Conclusion

In June 2016, I gathered in international solidarity with a group of LGBT activists on a downtown street in Natal after the mass shooting at Pulse Nightclub. It was one of the last events I attended before returning to the United States. As the day passed into evening, we lit candles that illuminated our hands and faces and the crosses we laid in the street. Aside from Natal's modest LGBT pride parade a few years earlier, I'd never been out in this type of exposed space in the city. I was not only struck by the way in which our act of solidarity with Orlando bridged space between continents, but I was also cognizant of the direction of this transnational political alliance. Standing openly in the street, during the day, with signs and symbols of our community, I was aware of what it means to take up this space in Natal. Situating LGBT+ politics and queer identities within modern, cosmopolitan and urban centres of the Global North does not consider the ways in which LGBT+ people in traditional, rural and hybrid sociocultural settings create space for themselves.

As a queer, nonbinary, feminist scholar, I have become familiar with inhabiting the undefined spaces in-between. My experiences living and working across cultures centre my scholarship in this space. While I am not from the Global South, I have seen and felt the limits of traditional Euro-American academic inquiry that does not interrogate its own epistemological, geographical and spatial normativity. As such, I am interested in how transnational queer theorizing can intervene in the persistence of US/Western exceptionalism within queer studies. I am also interested in the ways in which culture, theory and the body traverse traditional borders and subvert the clean binaries of north/south, centre/periphery, normal/abject and academic/popular to re-territorialize our bodies of knowledge.

A region with histories of slavery, colonization and uneven processes of development, Latin America's experience of modernity is peripheral (Schelling et al. 2000). Brazilian modernity pushes back against Western culture, appropriating, consuming and deconstructing external influences to produce something new,[19] something I name as queer. Brazil's hybrid modernity and its position at the margins of global capitalism organize LGBT+ spatialities in Natal, producing queer space and time. A hybrid, urban space in a rural, conservative region, Natal's culture integrates seemingly disparate cultural influences: at once traditional and modern, urban and rural.

To frame queerness as anti-normative, as 'movement against the grain' (Valentine 2018), we must investigate how political and cultural workers in the Global South create new worlds by claiming and reconfiguring space for LGBT+ community formation. Queer space is that which is adapted for use by those at the intersections of multiple margins – women, youth, LGBT+ folks, communities of colour, working-class people and those at the margins of the world capitalist system. Thinking from spatial contexts in the Global South, we can better understand how space functions within different histories of urbanization, modernization and LGBT+ community formation. By interrogating multiple sites of normativity, we can come closer to transnational coalitions in which solidarity, transnational dialogue, knowledge production, methods of intervention and valued lived experience move from the south to the north, as well as north to south.

Note: All translations by the author. The original Portuguese text is not included due to word count limitations.

Notes

1   I use the acronym 'LGBT/LGBT+' (lesbica, gay, bi, trans/travesti/transsexual) to respect the umbrella term most widely used in public, activist discourse in Brazil.

2   See (England 1994; Kobayashi 1994; Brown et al. 2010; Faria and Mollett 2016).

3   For more on decolonial queer politics, see (Puar 2002; Browne 2006; Lugones 2007; Oswin 2008; Costa 2012; Costa and Alvarez 2014; Miskolci 2014; Cohen 2019; Pereira 2019).

4   The Potengi River was named by the indigenous Potiguar people. Portuguese settlers took over their land and eliminated most of the potiguares. 'Potiguares' or 'shrimp-eaters' is also an informal nickname for people from Natal.

5   To borrow Martin's phrasing (2000: 259).

6   The fluidity of my position in terms of age and social circles resonates with the other blurred distinctions I describe. There were times I was a teacher/researcher (with the social/cultural capital to enter and exit these spaces); other times, I was part of the social environment.

7   For a detailed description of the plaza, see Oliveira (2016).

8   See 'In a Queer Time and Place' (Halberstam 2005).

9   See Valentine (2018) and Lugones in Valentine (2018).

10 For more on network configuration, see Castells (2010) and Nicholus (2019).

11 For more on how lesbian, bisexual and queer women configure space through community networks, see Rothenberg (1995); Valentine (2000); Cattan and Clerval (2011); and Browne and Ferreira (2015).

12 'Network capital' involves 'the capacity to communicate, travel, find places to meet up and when things go wrong, compensate and make up for system failure – requiring high levels of network capital' (Urry 2006).

13 Conversely, I was offered a ride to Vogue Natal within my first weeks in the city and I was able to return multiple times on my own. Familiarity with central transportation networks, socio-cultural patterns of gay clubs and mechanisms of a permanent business made it easier to plan my night and arrive at my destination.

14 In contrast, Vogue Natal is separated from residential areas and relegated to a more hidden, night-time space. It is also one of the first spots LGBT tourists visit.

15 Tara Yosso's concept of 'community cultural wealth' values the knowledges and networks of marginalized groups and communities of colour that are not valued in traditional interpretations of cultural capital.

16 Five Brazilian reais is just over US$2. Vogue Natal's entrance at the time was 20 reais.

17 Carimbó is a dance and a music genre from Northern Brazil with Indigenous origins mixed with African and Iberian elements. It often represents social themes such work and class inequality.

18 See Nicholus (2019). GAMI creates new community formations through cultural and spatial anthropophagy: that is, devouring, absorbing and hybridizing different cultural influences and types of space.

19 See Islam (2012) and Neto (2015); Nicholus (2019) on Brazilian cultural anthropophagy and queer anthropophagy.

References

Albuquerque Jr., D. M. de (2014). *The Invention of the Brazilian Northeast*. Durham: Duke University Press.

Alderman, D. H. (2008). 'Place, naming and the interpretation of cultural landscapes'. In eGraham, B. and Howard, P. (eds), *The Ashgate Research Companion to Heritage and Identity*. London and New York: Routledge.

Brown, G., et al. (2010). 'Sexualities in/of the Global South'. *Geography Compass*, 4(10), pp. 1567–79. doi: 10.1111/j.1749-8198.2010.00382.x.

Browne, K. (2006). 'Challenging queer geographies'. *Antipode*, 38(5), pp. 885–93. doi: 10.1111/j.1467-8330.2006.00483.x.

Browne, K. and Ferreira, E. (eds) (2015). *Lesbian Geographies: Gender, Place and Power*. Farnham, Surrey, UK; Burlington, VT: Ashgate.

Caldeira, T. P. (2017). 'Peripheral urbanization: Autoconstruction, transversal logics and politics in cities of the global south'. *Environment and Planning D: Society and Space*, 35(1), pp. 3–20. doi: 10.1177/0263775816658479.

Castells, M. (2010). *The Rise of the Network Society: The Information Age: Economy, Society and Culture*. 2nd ed. Chichester, West Sussex; Malden, MA: Wiley-Blackwell.

Cattan, N. and Clerval, A. (2011). 'A right to the city? Virtual networks and ephemeral centralities for lesbians in Paris'. *Justice Spatiale | Spatial Justice*. Translated by C. Hancock 3, pp. 1–16.

Chianca, L. D. O. (2007). 'Quando o campo está na cidade: migração, identidade e festa'. *Sociedade e Cultura*, 10(1), pp. 45–59.

Cohen, C. (2019). 'The Radical Potential Of Queer?'. *GLQ: A Journal of Lesbian and Gay Studies*, 25(1), pp. 140–4. doi: 10.1215/10642684-7275334.

Cohen, C. J. (2005). 'Punks, Bulldaggers and Welfare Queens'. In Johnson, E. P. and Henderson, M. G. (eds) *Black Queer Studies: A Critical Anthology*. Durham and London: Duke University Press, pp. 21–51.

Costa, C. de L. and Alvarez, S. E. (2014). 'Dislocating the sign: toward a translocal feminist politics of translation'. *Signs: Journal of Women in Culture and Society*, 39(3), pp. 557–63. doi: 10.1086/674381.

Costa, C. L. (2012). 'Feminismo e tradução cultural: Sobre a colonialidade do gênero e a descolonização do saber'. *Portuguese Cultural Studies*, 4, pp. 41–65.

England, K. V. L. (1994). 'Getting personal: reflexivity, positionality and feminist research'. *The Professional Geographer*, 46(1), pp. 80–9. doi: 10.1111/j.0033-0124.1994.00080.x.

Faria, C. and Mollett, S. (2016). 'Critical feminist reflexivity and the politics of whiteness in the 'field'. *Gender, Place & Culture*, 23(1), pp. 79–93. doi: 10.1080/0966369X.2014.958065.

FOXX (2010). 'Estórias Do Mundo: PRESENTE: Vogue! Vogue!' 16 March. Available at: https://soumundano.blogspot.com/2010/03/presente-vogue-vogue.html (Accessed: 11 June 2018).

França, R. de (2018). *Transcedendo Terrirórios: A Geografia da População LGBT no Estado do Rio Grande do Norte, Violências e Vivências*. Natal, Rio Grande do Norte, Brasil: Instituto Federal de Educação, Ciência, e Tecnologia do Rio Grande do Norte.

GAMI (no date). 'Gami Natal – about, facebook page'. Available at: https://www.facebook.com/pg/mariagorettigomes.goretti/about/?ref=page_internal (Accessed: 25 November 2016).

Halberstam, J. (2005). *In a Queer Time and Place: Transgender Bodies, Subcultural Lives*. New York: New York University Press.

Islam, G. (2012). 'Can the subaltern eat? Anthropophagic culture as a Brazilian lens on post-colonial theory'. *Organization*, 19(2), pp. 159–80. doi: 10.1177/1350508411429396.

Kobayashi, A. (1994). 'Coloring the field: gender, "race" and the politics of fieldwork'. *The Professional Geographer*, 46(1), pp. 73–80. doi: 10.1111/j.0033-0124.1994.00073.x.

Leu, L. (2020). *Defiant Geographies: Race & Urban Space in 1920s Rio de Janeiro / Lorraine Leu*. Pittsburgh, PA: University of Pittsburgh Press (Illuminations: Cultural Formations of the Americas).

Lugones, M. (2007). 'Heterosexualism and the colonial/modern gender system'. *Hypatia*, 22(1), pp. 186–219. doi: 10.1111/j.1527-2001.2007.tb01156.x.

Martins, J. de S. (2000). 'The hesitations of the modern and the contradictions of modernity in Brazil'. In Schelling, V. (ed.) *Through the kaleidoscope: the experience of modernity in Latin America*. New York: Verso (Critical studies in Latin American and Iberian cultures), pp. 248–74.

Miskolci, R. (2014). 'Queering the Geopolitics of Knowledge'. In Fabrício, B.F. (ed.), *Queering Paradigms IV : South-North Dialogues on Queer Epistemologies, Embodiments and Activisms, Queering Paradigms*. Peter Lang GmbH, Bern, Switzerland: Internationaler Verlag der Wissenschaften, pp. 13–30.

Neto, J. N. (2015). 'Anthropophagic Queer: A Study on Abjected Bodies and Brazilian Queer Theory'. CUNY Academic Works. https://academicworks.cuny.edu/gc_etds/1071.

Nicholus, S. (2019). 'Queer anthropophagy: building women-centered LGBT+ space in Northeastern Brazil'. *Journal of Lesbian Studies*, 24(3), pp. 240–54. doi: 10.1080/10894160.2019.1678327.

Oliveira, J. B. F. de (2016). *Corpos em mutações—Cartografia das sexualidades nômades na praça mits*. Universidade Federal do Rio Grande do Norte. Available at: https://repositorio.ufrn.br/handle/123456789/24850 (Accessed: 25 August 2021).

Oswin, N. (2008). 'Critical geographies and the uses of sexuality: deconstructing queer space'. *Progress in Human Geography*, 32(1), pp. 89–103. doi: 10.1177/0309132507085213.

Pereira, P. P. G. (2019). 'Reflecting on decolonial queer'. *GLQ: A Journal of Lesbian and Gay Studies*, 25(3), pp. 403–29. doi: 10.1215/10642684-7551112.

Puar, J. (2002). 'A transnational feminist critique of queer tourism'. *Antipode*, 34(5), pp. 935–946. doi: 10.1111/1467-8330.00283.

Rebecka (2014). 'Vogue Natal | Facebook, Recommendations & Reviews'. Available at: https://www.facebook.com/VogueNatal/reviews/?ref=page_internal (Accessed: 4 June 2016).

Rothenberg, T. (1995). '"And she told two friends": Lesbians creating urban social space'. In Bell, D. and Valentine, G. (eds), *Mapping Desire: Geographies of Sexualities*. New York: Routledge, pp. 150–65.

Rowe, W. and Schelling, V. (1991). *Memory and modernity: popular culture in Latin America*. New York: Verso.

Schelling, V., et al. (2000). *Through the Kaleidoscope: The Experience of Modernity in Latin America / Edited and Introduced by Vivian Schelling ;*

Translations by Lorraine Leu. Edited by V. Schelling. New York: VERSO (Critical studies in Latin American and Iberian cultures).

Simonetti, D. B. (2021). 'AMARO DE SOUZA MARINHO FILHO—NATAL: AMARO DE SOUZA MARINHO FILHO'. Amaro de Souza Marinho Filho—Natal. Available at: https://jm-amaromarinho.blogspot.com/2021/02/amaro-de-souza-marinho-filho.html (Accessed: 30 August 2021).

Urry, J. (2006). 'John Urry on social networks | global public media'. [mp3]. Available at: http://old.globalpublicmedia.com/transcripts/824 (Accessed: 7 February 2017).

Valentine, D. (2018). 'Intersectionality: origins, contestations, horizons by Anna Carastathis (review)'. *Critical Philosophy of Race*, 6(1), pp. 120–33.

Valentine, G. (ed.) (2000). *From Nowhere to Everywhere: Lesbian Geographies*. 1st ed. New York: The Haworth Press, Inc.

WREC (2010). 'Peripheral modernism and third world aesthetics, warwick research collective—project description'. Available at: http://www2.warwick.ac.uk/fac/arts/english/research/currentprojects/collective/project/pmtwa/ (Accessed: 7 March 2017).

Yosso, T. J. (2005). 'Whose culture has capital? A critical race theory discussion of community cultural wealth'. *Race Ethnicity and Education*, 8(1), pp. 69–91. doi: 10.1080/1361332052000341006.

11

Music as a site of transing

Simona Castricum

Oh, the night is my world,
City light painted girl,
In the day nothing matters,
It's the night time that flatters.
I, I live among the creatures of the night

LAURA BRANIGAN, 'Self Control' (Bigazzi et al. 1984)

I'm often asked: 'How is architecture transphobic?' Architecture as an institutional silo, a practice and a built environment upholds essentialist, normative, binary frameworks of gender: male and female. As architecture creates, defines and controls gendered spatial boundaries, the very nature of binary gender and cisnormativity works to disproportionally affect spaces produced by trans and gender-diverse people. In their book *Transgender Architectonics: The Shape of Change in Modernist Space*, Canadian author and trans scholar Lucas Crawford observes: 'the public sphere itself is a series of architectures that sometimes seem designed to keep others vigilant in their surveillance of [transgender] bodies' (Crawford 2015).

To speculate on futures in architecture means imagining conditions beyond our wildest dreams and diving deep into our worst nightmares. To begin articulating the utopias that might sustain radical ways of living, we must first understand the dystopian realities we might also find ourselves in. For trans and gender-diverse people these dystopias are a daily struggle of systemic transphobia, enacted through a series of interpersonal, political, administrative and geographical agents that ultimately diminish their ability to meaningfully participate in civic life. Yet, the radical utopias imagined by trans and gender-diverse people throughout their lives can lead to the very worlds that have sustained gender-nonconforming lives and communities against those ongoing conditions of hostility, contest and risk applied by the cisnormative paradigm. While these worlds we imagine might seem unachievable and implausible, it's a radical act to believe they might one day become a reality. In this chapter I present 'transing' as a process, a critical tactic of survival, that trans and gender-diverse people have fashioned throughout time as they manifest the worlds they require – to realize their identities, build relationships, create community and achieve their full potential.[1]

The practice of transing is a radical act of world-building that destabilizes the overarching hegemony of cisnormativity and heteronormativity. Being gender-nonconforming within the dominant cisnormative gaze is a revolutionary act of living, yet trans visibility is often paired with conditions of risk, contest and surveillance. My interdisciplinary practice in architecture and music looks to unpack the dystopian conditions of my own lived experience, to imagine futures where my visibility and existence are not threatened: where safety, belonging and permanence lead to greater participation in civic life. My creative and speculative methodology of 'world-building' imagines and renders these utopias and dystopias through media, performance and event architecture. I argue that alternative architectural methodologies are necessary to materialize the radical change required to realize our future tactile and virtual worlds, particularly beyond the existing gender binary.

In this chapter I present music as a site of transing through musical creation, performance and events in live venues and clubs within a trans and gender-diverse framework. Drawing upon my lived experience in music and performance, together with architecture, I connect my practice to existing transgender epistemologies to establish how trans-spatial production in underground culture occurs in both music and architecture – each understood as events in space. In defining production, I refer to Sophia Psarra's use of 'production sites' – where 'sites' are understood as assemblage of physical spaces and conceptual constructs which acquire meaning through the intersection of 'physical and mental, collective and individual, material and social' worlds. Critical to Psarra's concept of production sites is the 'process of making and explaining buildings, the sources of inspiration and media used in these processes, the persons and social groups involved in their production' (2019: 2). I am particularly interested in how trans and, by extension, queer experiences of architecture manifest as sites of production through music and performance, as drawn from my own experience as a performer. From this process, I identify a trans design methodology that draws from an existing conceptual lineage framing the stage as a site of queer and trans-spatial production. Using both spatial tactics and strategies of performance, I aim to make better outcomes possible for trans and gender-diverse people, while increasing visibility and providing a space for inclusive storytelling.

My creative practice is grounded in guiding principles of speculative futures through trans-feminism and abolition feminism which shapes a methodology for architecture in its central role in the imagination, delivery and building of the worlds we live in. Angela Y. Davis, Gina Dent, Erica R. Meiners and Beth E. Richie in *Abolition. Feminism. Now.* (2022) recognize abolition feminism as a conversely applied social justice practice that 'incorporates a dialectic, a relationality and a form of interruption' (Davis et al. 2022: 2). Abolition and feminism act together with transing and queering as practices of 'world-building'. In combination they become agents of change. Through radical methodologies they work to critique the dystopia and to imagine the radical utopias that might accommodate the radical futures we need. For Davis et al.: 'we will dream our way out; we must imagine beyond the given' (2022: 16). Liam Young's *Planet City* (2020) applies a speculative architectural methodology that utilizes storytelling and rendering of worlds so unreal and radical that 'narratives of imagined cities help us to visualize other possible futures that sit outside of the one that all too often feels inescapable. As we write stories, we write the world – and in this way storytelling can be considered a critical act of design'. Given these precedents, I reflect upon my own methodologies in an architectural and musical practice that renders the dystopias and utopias that I experience or imagine both as sites and events. For this is not about the despair at or abandonment of architecture, but rather how its practice offers hope. Avoiding a dystopian list of grievances, the utopian exercise of 'world-building' serves to propose a set of conditions that might offer solutions to those grievances beyond our wildest dreams.

My trans awakening happened while I was studying and working in architecture and engaging with the queer club and rave scene on Wurundjeri land around Naarm-Melbourne and Wathaurong land in Djilang-Geelong, Australia. Specifically, through two periods in the late 1990s and throughout the 2010s, Thursday nights through to Sunday mornings always ushered with them a sense of opportunity and discovery. Queer entertainment spaces seemed familiar to me from the popular culture of my childhood, as evoked in 1980s popular music. Laura Branigan's music video for her Italo-disco hit 'Self Control' echoed the queer, drag and fetish clubs I frequented as a musician, a DJ and a reveller in my early adulthood. The music video for 'Self Control' blurs the realm of sexual fantasy and reality, somewhere within the liminal spaces of permission, denial, shame and pleasure. Upon its release, deemed too sexually explicit for mainstream television by MTV, Branigan reluctantly edited out the video's simulated group sex scenes (Laura Branigan Forever, 2019). Yet, the version that eventually received airtime was enough to visualize something that I would soon understand as queer and trans space. I identified with Branigan's role as protagonist in her song, where the daylight hours felt like a world within which she edited her true self.

Nightfall ushers in the opportunity to reject the control of the heteronormative and cisnormative world, to grant oneself permission to transgress external controls of sexuality and gender. Inspired by Branigan's song, I saw myself as a protagonist in my own world – a creature of the night. As a nonconformist, I sounded out like-minded souls in search of safer worlds within which to transgress sexual and gender norms deeply rooted in my relationship to music. In a world where popular culture seemed the only place to see my transness reflected, Branigan's song and music video, served as a meaningful allegory. This imprint informed my very own tactics for navigating sexuality and gender exploration within the context of music.

In my young adulthood I was forced to move in and out of visibility for my own safety. During this period, my experiences in cities and urban spaces informed my tactics to mitigate risk in public space as a transgender person. This also informed my methods of interrogating architecture and deploying architecture through a trans lens. As I became involved in the organization and promotion of clubs, music events and solo performances, I drew upon my experience in architecture to produce space expressly for queer and trans people. This understanding resonated strongly for me during a conversation between myself and New York-based architect A. L. Hu, which was recorded and televised as a keynote for the 2019 symposium *Transformations*, which took place in Naarm-Melbourne. During the course of this conversation Hu considered my practice, observing that: 'for you, it's like music creates the conditions within which to practice architecture' (Castricum et al. 2019).

Upon reflection, I began to understand a queer world as described by Cuban American performance studies scholar José Esteban Muñoz, who, in his book *Cruising Utopia: The Then and There of Queer Futurity*, argues that queerness is a 'rejection of the here and now and an insistence on potentiality or concrete possibility for another world' (2009: 1). This queer futurity offered a world where music and architecture presented the conditions to emerge into my transness as it intersected with community and practice. To further establish a context of transing architecture, I read Hu's observation alongside Susan Stryker, Paisley Currah and Lisa Jean Moore's theory on transing as 'a practice that takes place within, as well as across or between, gendered spaces' (Stryker et al. 2008: 12). Vic Muñoz views this idea further in a First Nations context, suggesting that transing is 'a negotiation with the way things are; changing ourselves through a constant study of what could be' (2014).

Transing architecture might be understood as a development of queering, specifically as the practice by which gender-nonconforming people destabilize both the gender binary and the monolith of cisnormativity as it is produced in architectural space. It's a practice that creates fluid stages not only of being and possibility but also of safety, belonging and permanence – allowing trans individuals and enclaves to flourish in urban environments. Beyond inclusion and diversity, transing architecture is a negotiation with the dominant cisnormative paradigm to present liminal spaces and futures beyond the control of the binary. In their book *Black on Both Sides: A Racial History of Trans Identity*, C. Riley Snorton explains Dionne Brand's use of 'transversality', describing it as 'a tear in the world', 'a rupture in history, a rupture in the quality of being' (2017: 9). Where strategies of queering allow ways to seek a pathway to the realization of queer futurity, through the 'quagmire of the present', they work synonymously with transing and transversality to reimagine life upon the threshold that binary conditions enforce upon gender-nonconforming people (Muñoz 2009: 1).

With strategies of queering and transing at the centre of my creative methodology, I began to investigate my idea of 'world-building', exploring further in creative practice by presenting and analysing my trans narrative through the media of performance, songwriting and video. Music sat at the intersection of architecture, sexuality and gender to articulate portrayals and visions of queer utopias and dystopias. It manifests as public site of trans and queer performativity. Trans event spaces exist more broadly to curate representative artistry, enact safer space practices, destabilize sexual normativity and the gender binary and reflect a broader queer politic. Transing architecture serves as a methodology to break down myths, assumptions and stereotypes that undermine gender-nonconforming people and lead to futures of safety, belonging and permanence. By safety, I refer to individual and physical safety. In belonging, I speak of connection to the community. Permanence refers to the enshrined rights of trans and gender-diverse people beyond partisan contest. By interrogating architecture and space against these three virtues, I uncover ways in which architecture can work to facilitate greater life chances and inclusion for trans and gender-diverse people in civic life.

My own lived experience of queer and trans nightclubs is that they are places of personal connection, resistance, celebration and community building for and by sexual- and gender-diverse people. Events and the immediate urban precincts they are produced within, inspire a sense of how music, urbanism and architecture might act together as a multidisciplinary queer practice. These underground trans and queer club spaces are produced outside of the formal frameworks of architecture, yet they are no less architectural in their organization and production. Like any other functional space, they are conceived with a vision, have a programme, have a budget and require people to produce, install and operate that space. They are etched into the urban fabric, albeit temporarily. But the unique character of queer and trans-spatial production is how it uses temporality to its advantage through adaptive use and installation. This adaptivity ensures its ongoing survival.

Over time, as my cognitive map of queer cities began to evolve and consolidate, I wondered how queer and trans people might experience this same mapping process, individually and collectively. Queer performance spaces are often produced within an architectural context of adaptive reuse within gritty urban infill developments. Performance venues that repurpose decaying or abandoned space (the underground basement, the loft, the factory, the warehouse), the underutilized space (vacant lettable spaces) and edge conditions (the street, the gutter) made significant sites for music, queering and indeed transing.

This activation of queer and trans sites within urban infill spoke to me about how queer space is produced within hostile urban conditions of heteronormativity and cisnormativity. It formed an inquiry: Why, how and what activates these sites? I observed them as places of resistance, survival, visibility and celebration within a dichotomous context of safety and risk. I saw that the liminal and transitional spaces of the city, for example, streets and public modes of transport, present risk to trans people who are vulnerable to violence and abuse from the surveillance and gaze of the cisnormative paradigm. The nightclub offers a safe haven from the scrutiny of the cisnormative gaze. This speaks to my overarching question: What if safety becomes permanent? It's important to recognize that no place can be completely safe. Queer and trans spaces are not immune from enacting harm among their communities, projects and organizing (Davis et al. 2022: 10).

Jack Halberstam's framework of the 'transgender gaze' establishes interactions where gender variance means trans and gender-diverse visibility brings a specific relationship to conditions of personal risk (Halberstam 2001: 294–8). In *Queer City: Gay London from the Romans to the Present Day* (2017), Peter Ackroyd observes that queer clubs and bars have historically been situated upon a threshold of risk and pleasure, 'as furtive as their clientele, [these] public houses that somehow survived by bribery of the police, 'cottaging' in always dangerous situations, clandestine street encounters were the order of the night' (2017: 216). Openly public vernacular cultures of gender nonconformity have long emerged in urban centres. Still, they have done so within a proximity all too close to the edge of legality, sending them largely underground. This underground condition gives queer and trans musical sites their edge. At sites and events of transgression are the very ideas of futurity and resistance that flourish as creative sexual and gendered expression.

Such were the very sites I frequented studying architecture on Wathaurong land in Djilang-Geelong and working as a designer for a major student-led international architecture conference called 'morphe:nineteen97'. My involvement in this organization committee bridged a period of immersive participation in architecture, graphic design and event planning. I eventually moved to Naarm-Melbourne to complete my architecture degree. A required text for me at the time was one in Lewis Mumford's *The City in History* (1961), which argued that one of the great opportunities for architecture lies in the urban: 'the city itself provides a vivid theatre for the spontaneous encounters and challenges and embraces of daily life' (Mumford 1961: 653). I wondered, both then and now, if Mumford's prospects for the city included queer and gender-nonconforming lives.

As a student in 1996, my first architectural project was for a dancefloor at a Deakin University architecture student ball at the Eureka Hotel in Djilang-Geelong. A temporary fit-out to the existing downstairs bar and dancefloor, its most striking feature was a DJ booth forming the centrepiece for the room. Installed into the front half of an old white Ford utility vehicle (or ute as they were locally known) were two turntables and a mixer, installed in the dashboard overlooking the bonnet. This ute dashboard repurposed into a DJ console was the ultimate representation of white Australian cisnormative, heterosexual patriarchy. Usually hosting DJs playing top-forty and pub rock music, this ute was a shrine to the very toxic masculinity and misogyny that permeated the streets of Geelong in 1996, that I grew to fear and from which I hid my true self to escape homophobic and transphobic violence. I also read this ute as a symbolic cultural reference to Bachelor and Spinsters Balls which, as the term suggests, are regular dance events in rural Australian communities where single male farmers dined and danced with unmarried farmers' daughters (Law 2010: 16–17). Benjamin Law observes how single men would travel to these balls on utes like the one in this club – complete with nationalist, sexist and racist paraphernalia adorning them. These balls had a reputation for being 'feral', with men largely outnumbering women and they most often descended into drunkenness and sometimes violence (Law 2010: 16–17).

Given these cultural, political and social cues, my design response was to subvert – indeed to trans – these symbols of nationalism, cisnormativity and heterosexuality. With the consent of the venue, I simply made the white Ford ute my submissive and dressed the room in fetish wear by lining the entire room and the DJ consul in black sheets of polyvinyl chloride (PVC) and gaffer tape. The use of PVC served as centrepiece material to queer and trans the existing space. While PVC is often used in building for waterproofing, it is a staple clothing material for fetish wear and haute couture in queer, kink and bondage (BDSM) culture. Gaffer tape also serves as an ideal utility for bonding and re-enforcing PVC, while in BDSM, it's used for concealing, binding, gagging and tying. The walls and bar, dressed in PVC from floor to ceiling, represent a made-to-measure act of fetish clothing and gender transgression. The white Ford ute, the embodiment of cisnormative heterosexuality, sat in the middle of the room wrapped, bound, severed and gagged in PVC and gaffer tape. Submissive now to its new hosts and context, its symbolism is subverted: stripped bare and denied its former cultural, political and social status. The result was a black darkroom that evoked the fetish clubs, bondage dungeons and sex-on-premises venues I had frequented or seen in magazines. Creating a musical space informed by my queer and trans lens felt liberating. Within architecture and building, students could not only celebrate their annual ball in a transgressive space but my queer friends could feel safe and reflected through its materiality, its artist curation and organization. In the queer spirit that Esteban Muñoz writes of, it felt like a place of possibility, of futurity, of exploration (2009: 1).

Music as an immersive component of stage, dance and theatre has long been a site for performance and storytelling that historically play a significant part in trans and gender-diverse public life. C. Riley Snorton's study of a French music hall postcard *c.*1900 '[Black Couple]' posits how queer and trans musical history in the Black diaspora at the turn of the nineteenth century 'represents not an origin but an entry point' to understanding gender-transgressive countercultures outside the Western Global North trans lens (Snorton 2017). Halberstam observes how glam and new wave musical movements of the late twentieth century, championed by Prince and David Bowie, ushered with them a critical era in music and gender nonconformity's relationship to visibility (Halberstam 2018: xiii). As influential as they were, Prince and Bowie aren't too far removed from the localized underground queer punk and post-punk scenes Esteban Muñoz uses to establish his understanding of the musical stage as a site of queer performance (2009). For Roberta Perkins, the trans enclaves of drag queens and kings, showgirls, sex workers, clubs and bargirls of Sydney's Kings Cross at the turn of the 1980s reveal a twenty-four-hour trans ecosystem that survived in deeply hostile urban conditions (Perkins 1983). House music DJ and producer Terry Thaemlitz recalls of New York City's Midtown transgender district at the turn of the 1990s: 'house isn't so much a sound as a situation'. For Thaemlitz, house music was born out of a dystopia of police brutality, racism, hate crime, a crippling HIV/AIDS epidemic, 'black market hormones' and houselessness – with gender nonconformity at its epicentre (2008).

Eight years on from 'the transgender tipping point' (almost arbitrarily declared by Katy Steinmetz in *Time* magazine in 2014), the Western transgender civil rights landscape has experienced some positive generational change. Still, anxieties and struggles remain ever-present. While the human right to space and citizenship for trans and gender-diverse people globally continues as a partisan debate, the permanence of transgender and gender-diverse rights in architecture remains subject to acute contest. Trans people still hold the burden of anxieties – collectively, intergenerationally and in their nuanced lived experiences.

Many contemporary trans and gender-diverse performers, musicians, DJs and producers at the turn of the 2020s conceive their artistry within this socio-political framework. Anohni, SOPHIE, Honey Dijon and Mykki Blanco exemplify this manifestation of trans-spatial production within the context of music. The tactile and virtual nature of their musical production and consumption creates complementary conditions and technologies for music as a site of transing – more so than for their predecessors. The utilization of digital streaming platforms and their nuanced relationships to musical content presents malleable and curated sites for the construction and performance of the body and gender identity. SOPHIE's song and music video for *Faceshopping* with the line 'My face is the real shop front, I'm real when I shop my face' describes a methodology of body shaping and facial reconstruction as much as it does a commentary on gender-affirming surgeries (2018). For SOPHIE, 'transness is taking control to bring your body more in line with your soul and spirit so the two aren't fighting against each other and struggling to survive. . . . It means you're not a mother or a father – you're an individual who's looking at the world and feeling the world' (Beaumont-Thomas 2021). Anohni's live production of *Swanlights* is an extension of sonic, virtual and physical space as sites of transing to connect with audiences on a cathartic level. Performing on stage as a solo visible figure against a backdrop of triangular lasers and projections, accompanied by the 44-piece Melbourne Symphony utilizing her back catalogue to expand upon themes of feminism and ecology. Anohni's creative methods inspire me to reflect upon how this expansion of trans artistry through intersections of digital and physical sites creates connections with queer and trans audiences through visibility and catharsis.

In 2020, I released my third studio album, *Panic/Desire*, the soundtrack compendium to my PhD thesis at the University of Melbourne titled 'What If Safety Becomes Permanent? Music and Architecture as a Site of Transing'. Comprising ten songs, *Panic/Desire* acts as a world-building tool, rendering architecture and urban space much like any traditional visualization method – only though music, conceived as itself a site of transing. I appeal to the listener to experience this world not by seeing it but by feeling it. I utilize lyrics, composition, sonic arrangement and performance to construct a soundtrack to an urban gender-nonconforming underground as I experience it.

The world of *Panic/Desire* is rendered with contradictory forces: themes of risk, pleasure, hostility, connection, futurity, archive, resistance and surveillance. Rather than a series of grievances about architecture, *Panic/Desire* seeks to engage the listener in an empathetic relationship. I offer my vulnerability as a means for understanding this world viscerally through imagination and feeling – to walk the streets of this world in my shoes as I hear it. I hope that together we can imagine futures beyond binaries or contests. While I articulate an urban condition characterized by conflict and hostility, I look for hope in identity, safety and belonging. Using autoethnographic methods as a starting point and embedded within a trans epistemological framework, *Panic/Desire* explores my urban cognitive map, a trans urban morphology, an archive of lived experience and its affective conditions.

The work concentrates on four themes: transphobia and space (*Borderline Spaces, Panic/Desire*), relationships (*The Half Light, The Good in You*), community (*Supertouch*) and resistance (*The Present, Monolith*). These themes form a reference point to explore and interrogate sites within the city where trans and queer life exist through my lived experience. Exploring liminal spaces with themes of risk, pleasure, panic and desire, the work connects my academic research with autoethnographic investigations into the trans and gender-diverse experience of architecture, place and the city.

Panic/Desire is the narrative through which I construct the relationship between personal archives, affective responses and analysis. The importance of creative content acting in concert with theoretical methodology extends Jill Bennett's inquiry into the role art plays in processing trauma and the experience of conflict and loss (Bennett 2005: 16). It could sit in a university library or academic journal. Still, a five-minute pop song can speak about this work to more people through its performance at a festival or broadcast on radio. Of the subversive power of pop music, Depeche Mode stands as a significant influence of mine for their capacity to destabilize gender and sexuality through synthpop and queering. Guitarist, vocalist and songwriter Martin L. Gore observes: 'we did get accused at certain times of being like a very subversive pop band and I do think that we did get away with some stuff that was probably risqué for the radio, just because we used it in a pop context – in our early career, songs like "Master and Servant"' (Whalley 2009). The medium of pop music has always proved a curious, experimental vehicle for the message in my practice. This became evident after a live performance at the Golden Plains festival in Meredith in Wadawurrung Country in 2020. After I finished my show, an audience member whom I'd never met before remarked that 'I found out way more about the experience of transgender people through your show than I could have imagined'. This feedback speaks directly to Gore and Bennett's understanding of art's potentiality to communicate on a visceral and subversive level to build essential relationships with its audience for insight, representation and shared catharsis (Bennett 2005: 16).

Trans awakenings are not linear, nor are they singular events tied to a moment in time. Much like transition, awakenings are ongoing and involve times of flux.[2] My formative experiences of embracing my femininity in the late 1990s led to experiences of fetishization, social isolation, violence and sexual assault. By the turn of the millennium, I saw myself moving back into the shadows of androgyny for my personal safety, ultimately presenting as masculine to maintain the social and intimate connection I had lost through my attempts at transition. Yet, my perceptions of architecture and urbanism continued to accrue, only now as a gender-nonconforming subject in hiding. My cognitive map of the city as a queer space evolved, informed by my personal archives of delight and trauma, hope and sorrow. Queer event spaces continued as my centre of gravity, offering microcosms and visions of queer utopia.

Yet it still felt like I didn't fit in, as my transness and queerness were unreadable. Unable to see architectural practice as a method of world-building, I looked further to music and soundtracks. Inspired by Wendy Carlos and Vangelis, I found something cinematic in my imagination of queer and architectural futures. My composition of music during the 2000s was sketched as soundtracks to visions of my future, as well as archives of trauma. Music and architecture became a language to articulate both spatial and effective conditions of my queer and trans life. The events that defined them are liminal places of my imagination: liberation, connection, discovery and hope – of vision and inspiration.

Of my experiences of significant queer and trans club nights in Naarm-Melbourne in the 2010s, the laneway seemed to be one of the most important spaces. The edge conditions of laneways purposed as functional non-places for smoking and egress became critical for the chaotic spontaneity of queer life: chance meetings for deeper connections and retreat spaces that gave respite from the dancefloor (Weiner 2018). There were many nights I didn't even bother entering a club, as I could socialize with up to fifty people for a prolonged period outside the venue. Simply through your visibility and ability to catch up with friends, you had ostensibly been at the club. Hanging out in those adjacent laneways and gutters with friends and chosen family was the experience. These rear lanes present club venues with a discreet entry point, away from highly visible and trafficable main streets. For queer and trans club nights hosted at the loft and underground clubs such as Hugs'N'Kisses, Liberty Social or Boney, the laneway served as a critical buffer zone between the hostility of the city and the sanctuary of the club. In the context of transing space, these were places in which trans and gender-diverse people organized socially. They also provided a sense of entry, a midnight welcome mat, a farewell into the early morning and a place of negotiation for where to go next – 'kick-ons'. For some revellers, the gutter facilitated covert consumption of alcohol (often cheap cask wine known as 'goon' or beers purchased at takeaway bottle shops) and drugs rather than buying expensive drinks at the bar. The gutter is therefore repurposed to suit both the economic and social conditions of queer life. For many queer people, this makes the social functions of clubbing somewhat more accessible. The gutter, something most would understand as a harsh utilitarian threshold, a metaphor for waste, disposability and trash to be washed away from the streets, became a liminal space that harboured queer and trans life – an entire universe within which to exist, indeed, to perform gender.

The role of urban entertainment and nightlife have been central to localized LGBTIQA+ cultures as a place for queer identity and subcultures to thrive and survive. It's not by chance that the very inner-city entertainment strips that house clusters of sex shops, strip clubs and brothels are often in close proximity to vibrant queer neighbourhoods. While this might paint a picture of a queer and trans utopia, this collective and individual experience cannot be understood in a vacuum, outside of the hostility of a cisgender heteronormative dominant paradigm. Beyond any nightclub club edge condition, there is an urban environment that is hostile to many cohorts of the broader community, with trans and gender-diverse people particularly singled out for vitriol. Navigating safe passage between home and the club presents unique anxieties. Once trans and gender-diverse people venture across these liminal spaces, their safety becomes compromised. Thaemlitz recalls New York City cab drivers randomly dropping trans women deep in the outer boroughs of New York to fend for themselves (Nation 2021). In Australia the deaths and disappearances of trans women in the 1970s through to the 1990s resulting from abductions from the city's entertainment and nightclub precincts remain unsolved to this day (Moor 2010). Nightclubs themselves have been sites for significant violence trauma, particularly the 2016 Pulse Nightclub shooting in Orlando, Florida, which remains the deadliest mass shooting on record in the United States. Of the Forty-nine LGBTIQ+ revellers killed, 90 per cent were Latinx (Torres 2016). These tragic events present only the recent histories that comprise part of the collective intergenerational trans trauma.

The cisnormative world presents a daily negotiation for trans and gender-diverse people, as they work through conflict in family, community, relationships and workplace settings. In the public realm, resistance to cisnormativity often manifests as contestation – of spaces and events, which poses inherent dangers to gender-nonconforming people, such as surveillance and becoming a target of violence and discrimination. While trans and gender-diverse people might engage in tactics of survival such as risk assessment or hypervigilance, the impetus for these tactics is informed by bodily imprints of trauma, which often manifest without explanation as acts of instinct (Van der Kolk 2014: 127). When your primary consideration moving through the built environment is surviving transphobia and only secondarily navigating space, the capacity to enjoy the public domain is diminished. Meanwhile, for gender-nonconforming people, simply navigating through any urban public realm is an experience often characterized by the expectation of violence, rejection or discrimination based upon societal stigma (Rood et al. 2016: 151). It is also an experience of being under the constant gaze of surveillance, policing and profiling. This public scrutiny comes from a place of curiosity and suspicion, as transgender and gender-diverse people are widely perceived by the dominant paradigm as different, deviant, suspicious or non-compliant: bodies and identities that defy normative ideas of male and female (Beauchamp 2019).

This system leads to compromised experiences in public spaces for trans and gender-nonconforming people (Beauchamp 2019). They are subject to daily interactions rooted in fear of or prejudice against transgender and, more broadly, gender-nonconforming people. Often the confrontation is intended to victimize and discriminate and this contest results in one or several undesirable outcomes for trans people, denying their personal safety and citizenship. This brings into question their right to identity and access to space. The result is that gendered spaces for trans and gender-diverse people become inherently contested on a daily basis. Hostile events can result in direct conflict: specifically experiences of vilification (verbal abuse, ridicule), discrimination (policing, victimization, erasure, inaccessibility) and ultimately extreme violence (murder, aggravated assault and sexual assault) (TMM 2020).

While the cisgender gaze is as much an attempt to satisfy the fascination cisgender people have for gender-nonconforming people, it also stems from the fact that society has been historically conditioned to administer gender – to facilitate population control; and segregate gender – as a means of access to public space and amenity, bathrooms, schools, incarceration or health care. Regardless of recent gains made in trans and gender-nonconforming rights, representation and acceptance, individuals who do not conform to gender norms are still frequently met with hostility and inquisition. As the US scholar Toby Beauchamp observes, the very systems of governance and surveillance that regulate public space are conditioned to separate people into normative categories of male and female. Beauchamp, read together with Australian criminologist Bianca Fileborn on how gender and sexuality are policed in entertainment venues, show that trans and gender-diverse people are subject to harsh facial and body recognition techniques through advanced biometric tools that act in concert with human observation, institutional administration, policing and law enforcement (Fileborn 2016). Liquor licensing laws are inextricably linked to entertainment security personnel, who play a critical gate-keeping role in ascertaining gender. This has direct consequences on how critical venue infrastructure and spaces are policed, including identification, bathroom amenity and points of egress.

My experience in architecture and music, together with my lived experience as a transgender woman, has put me in a fortunate position to consult on policy and governance on creating safer musical spaces. Through using music and architecture to render both the utopia and dystopias of my lived experience, as I had done with the Architecture Ball and *Panic/Desire*, I looked to deploy this knowledge in service to my trans and gender-diverse musical community at a time when gender nonconforming artists and audiences were beginning to emerge out of queer venues into local live-music venues and night clubs. There was an evident community and industry need for a policy document that sustained more healthy relationships between transgender and cisgender stakeholders.

While on Music Victoria's Women's Advisory Panel from 2017 to 2019, I co-authored the *Gender Diversity Draft Strategy for Best Practice Guidelines for Live Music Venues* (2021). This process involved sourcing existing reference materials from creative institutions to inform similar policy documents to advocate for queer, trans and gender-diverse artistic communities. Spence Messih and Archie Barry's co-authored guideline document for Australian gallery institutions served as a precedent guideline to inform best practice examples for musical settings (Barry et al. 2019). It provided a detailed outline for the proposed Music Victoria section, serving as a 'return briefing' document and managing the expectations of the Music Victoria board, which commissioned the guidelines.

The objective of the guidelines was first to provide a publicly accessible resource on trans and gender-diverse needs in music industry settings. Secondly, the strategy serves as an educational tool to ensure music venues are culturally safe for the trans and gender-diverse cohort. Producing detailed guidelines meant imagining live-music and club settings in their different experiences for trans and gender-diverse people. More than a document that existed for artists, it spoke to the needs of all trans and gender-diverse people who might be present in a venue, musicians, technical staff, music-adjacent workers, venue staff (bar staff, bookers, security) and to revellers. The guidelines provided information to music venues on methods security and staff can use to mitigate violence against trans and gender-diverse people and advice on spatial planning, public egress and amenity provision. It also provides guidance for staff on inclusive language and encourages respectful attitudes towards trans artistry.

Understanding the needs of trans and gender-diverse creative, worker and audience cohorts requires considering the key relationships and interactions in event settings. One of the most critical settings to test the document against was how it could be applied to venues across the spectrum of gender and sexuality. A crucial takeaway from the guidelines was that venues need to understand that trans and gender-diverse artists, workers and patrons exist in space whether there is a queer event or not. While some venues exist to serve an exclusively LGBTIQA+ audience, cisgender and trans and gender-diverse people coexist in all entertainment settings. Meanwhile, spaces with multiple events, settings and programmes running simultaneously serve different cohorts. Here, the needs of heteronormative, cisnormative, queer, trans and gender-diverse cohorts are purportedly in conflict. The Gender Diversity Draft Strategy acts not as a comprehensive solution to this challenge but rather as a starting point to understand the needs of trans and gender-diverse cohorts in live-music and club settings.

The *Transgender and Gender Diverse Inclusion for Best Practice Guidelines* demonstrate to the music industry the value of trans and gender-diverse cohorts' contribution and participation, not only in music and entertainment venues but in broader understandings of night-time and 24-hour economies and ecosystems. Critical to ensuring the policy document served the community was engagement with trans and gender-diverse advocacy groups – namely Transgender Victoria and Queerspace through Drummond Street Services. This also included further peer review from trans and gender-diverse artists in Victoria. Further, recommendations for the report's evolution include prioritizing further peer review and authorship with queer and trans Aboriginal and Torres Strait Islander people.

To affect real change in trans lives, more significant agitation and advocacy are required at higher levels on issues of legislation, codes, policy and governance. When building codes make no provision for trans and gender-diverse people to design spaces that reflect their autonomy of self-identity or when building codes use discriminatory language to identify trans and gender-diverse people or when legislation provides protection to those who seek to discriminate and enact violence on trans kids and adults, those who uphold it and those who remain silent are complicit in administrative transphobia and its violence. Those who enforce the mis-categorization of the trans and gender-diverse community are complicit in administrative transphobia. The suffering of indignity becomes enshrined in policy and law, reflecting a regime that cares little for trans lives. When ideas for buildings are imagined, architecture has an opportunity to embody the identity, values and aspirations of a client group, their stakeholders or its specific and adjacent communities. Through this role, architecture is uniquely positioned to be part of transformative cultural shifts that bring people in from the margins and take concrete steps towards ending transphobia and discrimination against gender-nonconforming people.

No matter how wild our utopias may seem or how dire our dystopias are, we must be bold enough to believe in the worlds that will sustain the change necessary for people to reach their full potential in civic life. Trans and gender-diverse people have proven this through their survival and endurance.

Notes

1 'Queering' refers to how LGBTQ+ space and identity is produced: 'reconfigured, performed and contested through the technologies and spatial politics of diverse ethnic cultures' (Ramos, Mowlabocus 2021: 1).

2 By transition, I refer to Julian Carter's description as 'ways in which people move across socially defined boundaries away from an unchosen gender category' (Carter 2014: 1).

References

Ackroyd, P. (2017). *Queer City: Gay London from Romans to Present Day*. London: Chatto & Windus.

Barry, A., Messih, S., Sayed, B., Gill, E. O. (2019). *Clear Expectations: Guidelines for Institutions, Galleries and Curators Working with Trans, Non-Binary and Gender Diverse Artists*. Sydney, Countess: NAVA.

Beauchamp, T. (2019). *Going Stealth: Transgender Politics and U.S. Surveillance Practices*. Durham and London: Duke University Press.

Beaumont-Thomas, B. (2021). 'Sophie, acclaimed avant-pop producer, dies aged 34'. *The Guardian*. Retrieved from https://www.theguardian.com/music/2021/jan/30/sophie-acclaimed-avant-pop-producer-dies-aged-34

Bennett, J. (2005). *Empathic Vision: Affect, Trauma and Contemporary Art*. Stanford, CA: Stanford University Press.

Bigazzi, G., Piccolo, S., Raf (1984). 'Self control' (Recorded by Laura Branigan) [Song]. Self Control. United States, Atlantic.

Carter, J. (2014). 'Transition'. *TSQ: Transgender Studies Quarterly*, 1, 235–7

Castricum, S., Hu, A. L. (2019, 14 Nov). 'Beyond the binary'. Paper presented at the Transformations: Action on Equity, Melbourne, AU.

Crawford, L. (2015). *Transgender Architectonics: The Shape of Change in Modernist Space*. Burlington: Ashgate.

Davis, A. Y., Gina, D., Meiners, E. R., Richie, B. E. (2022). *Abolition. Feminism. Now*. Dublin: Hamish Hamilton.

Fileborn, B. (2016). *Reclaiming the Night-Time Economy: Unwanted Sexual Attention in Pubs and Clubs*. London, UK: Palgrave Macmillan.

Halberstam, J. (2001). 'The transgender gaze in Boys Don't Cry'. *Screen*, 42(3), 294–8.

Halberstam, J. (2018). *Trans*: A Quick and Quirky Account of Gender Variability*. Oakland, CA: University of California Press.

Laura Branigan Forever - Matty. (2 April 2019). Laura Branigan - [cc] Interview About Self Control Music Video Controversy - ET (1984) [Video]. https://youtu.be/836TObjuj0I.

Law, B. (2010). 'Bush love'. *The Monthly*. The Monthly Pty Ltd, (May 2010), 16–17.

Moor, K. (2010, July 27). 'New evidence implicates several former police officers in Adele Bailey murder'. *Herald-Sun*. Retrieved from https://www.heraldsun.com.au/news/victoria/new-evidence-implicates-several-former-police-officers-in-adele-bailey-murder/news-story/

Mumford, L. (1961). *The City in History*. London: Penguin Books.

Muñoz, J. E. (2009). *Cruising Utopia: The Then and There of Queer Futurity*. New York: New York University Press, 1.

Munōz, V. (2014). 'Tatume'. *TSQ: Transgender Studies Quarterly*, 1–2, 213, 216.

Music Victoria (2021). 'Transgender & gender diverse inclusion, best practice guidelines for live music venues'. Retrieved from https://www.musicvictoria.com.au/resource/best-practice-guidelines-for-live-music-venues/transgender-and-gender-diverse-inclusion/

Nation, P. (Writer) (2021). *Terre Thaemlitz: Give Up On Hopes And Dreams* [Documentary]. In P. Nation (Producer). United Kingdom: Resident Advisor.

Perkins, R. (1983). *The Drag Queen Scene: Transsexuals in Kings Cross*. Sydney: George Allen & Unwin.

Psarra, S. (2019). *The Production Sites of Architecture*. New York: Routledge.

Ramos, R., Mowlabocus, S. (Ed.) (2021). *Queer Sites in Global Contexts: Technologies, Spaces and Otherness*. Oxford: Routledge.

Rood, B. A., Reisner, S. L., Surace, F. I., Puckett, J. A., Maroney, M. R., Pantalone, D. W. (2016). 'Expecting Rejection: Understanding the Minority Stress Experiences of Transgender and Gender-Nonconforming Individuals'. *Transgender Health*, 1, 1.

Snorton, C. R. (2017). *Black on Both Sides: A Racial History of Trans Identity*. Minneapolis: University of Minnesota Press.

SOPHIE. (2018). 'Faceshopping: on oil of every pearl's in—insides'. MSMSMSM INC / Future Classic.

Steinmetz, K. (2014). 'America's Transition'. *Time Magazine*, 183(22), 43

Stryker, S., Currah, P., Moore, L. J. (2008). 'Introduction: trans-, trans or transgender?' *WSQ: Women's Studies Quarterly*, 36, 12.

Thaemlitz, T. (2008). 'Midtown 120 blues'. Retrieved from http://www.comatonse.com/writings/2008_midtown120blues.html

Torres, L. (Ed.) (2016). 'In remembrance of the Orlando Pulse nightclub victims'. *Latino Studies* (Vol. 14). UK: Palgrave Macmillan.

Transrespect versus Transphobia Worldwide (2020). 'TMM update trans day of remembrance 2020'. Retrieved from https://transrespect.org/en/tmm-update-tdor -2020/

Van Der Kolk, B. (2014). *The Body Keeps Score*. UK: Penguin Books.

Whalley, B. (Writer) & Whalley, B. (Director). (2009). Synth Britannia.

Weiner, S. (2018, July). 'The final night of hugs & kisses'. *LNWY*. Retrieved from https://lnwy.co/read/the-final-nights-of-hugs-kisses/

12

Queer reading in queer lodgings

Naomi Stead

This is a tale of two rooms: first, the bedroom of my young son and, second, my own bedroom, as shared with my partner – his other mother. It's also about two books, read respectively but very differently within those rooms: a classic fantasy adventure novel beloved by children and an acclaimed book of lesbian poetry. It's about ambivalently queer spaces and practices and more particularly, it is about queered *domestic* spaces and *reading* practices, complicated by motherhood and childhood, performance and utterance of story. Why is it interesting to consider these things? Well, as Donna Haraway famously notes,

> It matters what matters we use to think other matters with; it matters what stories we tell to tell other stories with; it matters what knots knot knots, what thoughts think thoughts, what descriptions describe descriptions, what ties tie ties. It matters what stories make worlds, what worlds make stories. (Haraway 2016: 12)

What worlds are made in a child's bedroom, what stories are told to tell other stories, what matters in the matters that we use, as queer parents and the spaces where this all takes place? And to what extent can we even call this domestic milieu a queer one? Olivier Vallerand, among others, has pointed out the problematics of how 'queer' has been understood within much architectural discourse – as an unproblematic umbrella term referring to anyone who is non-heterosexual (Vallerand 2020). Queer space, by extension, has been understood by some simply as the spaces that such folk either frequent or design, an understanding which has at times veered dangerously close to essentialism. Vallerand makes a distinction between how 'queer' is variously defined in architecture in terms of activism, theory and identity-based approaches and notes in particular how discussions of queer space have tended to play into normative conceptions of private and public space as a binary opposition.

My hope with this chapter is to trouble such distinctions. To examine how even in the domestic realm and even its seemingly most intimate and inner sanctum of the bedroom, in the loaded activity of care for a child – how politics and the political intrude. Likewise in these spaces forms of criticality and citizenship are also enacted – transgressing and confusing any kind of binary opposition. More importantly, my hope is to demonstrate how spaces themselves are performed and enacted, not only by human actors but also by the assemblages and contexts of things and beings that constitute them, including books themselves. Even as my own dwelling provides housing for a queer family, it is the setting and staging of our rituals and practices, our modes of occupation and being together, that really constitute the space – in all its variable and complex queerness.

Reading to the boy, or, bedtime and bedplace

So here I am, reading to the boy. He is ten years old. Every night we, his mothers, take it in turns to put him to bed – an elaborate routine which he insists must be followed nightly and exactly with the same actions and sequence. It might even be called a 'queer' ritual, in the weakest and oldest sense of that word, because it is idiosyncratic and particular and habitual – there's nowt as queer as folk's bedtime routines. We all enjoy it or let's say we do now, more than when it used to be even more extended and energetic and take hours to accomplish. These days he completes his ablutions and gets into pyjamas and then he and whoever is the designated mother for the evening convene in his bedroom, shut the door and read. His other mother reads him a different book. The two books interweave. I am reading him *The Hobbit*.

It's an oft-unspoken thing that different stages of parenting are differently enjoyable. My partner very much enjoyed the period when the boy was a baby and sure it was blissful and all, but it was also monotonous. For me it's greatly improved over time until now, when he's ten, it is complemented by a distinct and pleasurable sense of having my own childhood over again but this time as a boy. This, too, is a queer moment, a moment of my own triumphant retrospective embrace of the gender nonconformity I didn't dare back then; a vicarious appropriation of all that I wanted but was out of reach for me, now embodied 'naturally' and 'innocently' in the boy.

What's more, I am reading to him the books that I read at his age – reliving them for myself and also through his eyes, in a literary triangle that is also an intimate ritual. After ten years, we've really read a lot of books.

And for ages I've been looking forward to reading *The Hobbit*, working up to it, waiting until he was old enough to follow the plot, understand the vocabulary and be interested enough to care about the characters. Finally, he's ready. We are both enjoying it. I find it has a rhythm and cadence well suited to being read aloud. This time around I'm more attentive to the prose itself: it is elegantly written, the sentence construction graceful. Previously, of course, I had been focused on plot and character. Reading it again, while I remember most of the adventures, some I have forgotten altogether. The book has aged fairly well; while there are objectionable aspects (e.g., the almost complete lack of any female characters whatsoever – something I did not notice as a child, but which troubles me greatly now) on the whole the values are sound.

Queer intrusions and substitutions

But then it happens, for the first time: I am reading along and I encounter the word 'queer'. It's used of course in the old sense, as an adjective, to mean strange, wrong, sickly, ill-fitting, uncanny. It's not surprising that I encounter the word per se – the book was published in 1937, after all; at that time it was more simply a usefully multivalent word, rich in connotations, even if they were of a somewhat bilious kind. As a writer, I can see the appeal of such a word – it has great connotative depth and piquancy. Turns out that Tolkien used it many times throughout *The Hobbit and* even more frequently in the *Lord of the Rings* trilogy that followed; a trilogy which is of course much darker – the affect more 'queer' overall.

So it's not surprising to have encountered the word. What *is* surprising is that, at the point of these encounters, when reading aloud, I substitute it with another: seamlessly and without note. I erase it and just keep intoning so the boy won't even notice. 'Strange', I swap in or 'odd', sometimes 'weird' although that's patently historically inappropriate.

It keeps happening, again and again: right at the beginning, Gandalf the wizard scratches 'a queer sign on the hobbit's beautiful green front-door' (Tolkien 2001 (1937): 15). Later, when the journeying party prepares to venture into Mirkwood, they are warned by their ally Beorn – himself able to speak in 'a queer language like animal noises' (Tolkien 2001 (1937): 98) – of a general air of strangeness and danger in the wood: 'in there the wild things are dark, queer and savage', they are warned (Tolkien 2001 (1937): 103). Sure enough – in the forest they encounter 'queer noises . . . grunts, scufflings and hurryings in the undergrowth' (Tolkien 2001 (1937): 109). There is a furtiveness here, not just strange but secret.

The first few times I encounter the word I don't give it another thought: slip in a substitute and just barrel on. But then I start to think: What am I doing here? Why am I doing this? What do I achieve by trying to protect the boy from the negative connotations of this word – trying to quarantine the pejoratives away from his queer mothers, his queer family and his rainbow self. He already well knows the history of the word – knows that it was originally an insult to people seen as outsiders, deviants and all kinds of wrong. And he knows that the tables turned and those same deviants re-appropriated the term, embraced their supposed perversion and oddity, switched the value system and showed that there are other norms and values, other ways to live and that they are heroes and progenitors for a queer community which today is flourishing and thriving and proud and open and which also, importantly, includes our own rainbow family. And yet, I still censor the term; and I wonder why.

The 1980s reappropriation of the term 'queer' was more militant than its use today. It was designed to mitigate against complacency, against an apolitical forgetting of 'how we are perceived by the rest of the world' (Vallerand 2020: 4) – that is, how we are perceived negatively, even sometimes through an appearance of neutrality. To use the word 'queer' at that time was to specifically recall prejudice, to raise and wield it – a mirror and an activist action. Certainly things have changed since then, but not entirely and not for everybody. Perhaps what I am refusing in the erasure of this pre-re-appropriated word is the intrusion of activism into the bedroom: the civic domain into domestic intimacy.

Odd, bent and twisted

In the essay-form prelude to her later book, *Queer Phenomenology*, Sara Ahmed muses on the history of 'queer' as a word and how its multivalency continues into present use and how in fact that is useful: 'It is important to retain both meanings of the word queer, which after all are historically related even if irreducible to each other. This means recalling what makes specific sexualities describable as queer in the first place: that is, that they are seen as odd, bent, twisted' (Ahmed 2006: 565). The boy and I, in our nightly reading sessions, are seeing the full range of these connotations, implications and inferences.

'At the best of times heights made Bilbo giddy', we hear; '[h]e used to turn queer if he looked over the edge of quite a little cliff; and he had never liked ladders, let alone trees' (Tolkien 2001: 86). As a term and a concept here, queer seems to be remarkably multivalent – an atmosphere and a mode of behaving, that which is unfamiliar but also frightening, unusual but also freakish, a departure from normality yes, but in a highly particular, unsettling and creepy way – a few steps down the path to disgusting. Except on those occasions where it is used quite neutrally – and these are, in some ways, the most striking of all.

Still, the most common use of 'queer' in *The Hobbit* is adjectival – the noises are queer or the wild things or an unfamiliar language. But sometimes it is a comment on the person and disposition of the progenitor

Bilbo Baggins himself who, 'although he looked and behaved exactly like a second edition of his solid and comfortable father, got something a bit queer in his make-up from [his mother's] side, something that only waited for a chance to come out' (Tolkein 2001 (1937): 13). It does indeed come out, which is what enables Bilbo to embark on his adventure, where his more 'natural' hobbit-like tendencies (homeyness, placidness, love of food and comfort, limited evidence of bravery or intrepidness) are at war with his 'queerly' bold and adventuresome streak. Seems that sometimes it's good – even if only equivocally – to depart from the norm in a queer direction.

So then the question is, why am I not using this as a teachable parental moment, to remind us both about the history of queer oppression and resistance, a history of prejudice that we must never forget but still actively resist, every day, as we go about our lives as a queer family. Perhaps I simply can't be bothered. It's surprisingly easy to censor or even completely change a story as you read it, imperceptibly and I have often had to do this for the boy over the years, to avoid stories or details or descriptions that would likely lead to fear and nightmares. I've also done it to add more female characters (swapping the gender of animals, in particular, which are almost universally gendered male, in a way that irritates me intensely – changing them just like that, at the flip of a pronoun) or to skip over explicitly racist and sexist remarks – which are surprisingly common in historical children's literature. So maybe I censor because I can – and can pretend ours is a world where children's books as a general category *don't* enshrine the worst kind of stereotypical, discriminatory, heteropatriarchal typecasting in forms which range from the wildly gratuitous to the sneakily insidious.

Maybe I censor because I'm also tired of my life and family and even my son himself all lending themselves to be or being appropriated as, teachable moments for others, opportunities for a lesson on diversity – see, that boy has two mommies and he seems clean and sane and fairly normal. Perhaps, for us, that gets boring and exhausting. Or perhaps one can tolerate this most of the time, in most places (the schoolyard, for example or the workplace) but in the fastness of one's own house, in the very *bedroom*, one hesitates to interrupt the nightly book with the intrusion of the political or worse, the didactic. Perhaps it just seems like *work*.

Or perhaps we are trying to protect him, in his most private moments, from having to see himself as exemplary of anything, of particularly standing for something; perhaps this is a desire to provide a simple intimacy, a bedroom, a bed, with stories, that don't require him to be alert to how the world perceives him (as aberrant). Because in fact he is, by the virtue of his family, already always marked in the eyes of others (albeit sometimes positively, these days – it's amazing how many children seem envious of the ones with two mommies). And in this intimate interior space of his bedroom and with a fantasy novel being read for him, as a parental performance and enactment and embodiment of love, we want to preserve for him the experience of any child – to imagine himself somewhere else, someone else – not an example to others.

Other queer lodgings

Time passes, we read on and I continue to switch, erase and ponder. Perhaps it's because this reading is all happening in his bedroom. *The Hobbit* is peppered with references to queer looks, queer sights, queer fits, queer feelings, queer creatures and queer lodgings. And this last one, in particular, gets me thinking. Because as it happens, just over the hallway in my own bedroom, the one I share with the other mother in this equation, indeed in my *bed* – that most symbolic of furniture items, the most freighted with ideas of (queer) intimacy and sexuality, the object of torrid conjecture and fantasy on the part of mainstream society, all of which have long been framed as inimical to parenthood or the care of a child – in this bed I am also reading a queer book. Actually and more correctly it's a lesbian book: *C+nto and Othered Poems+* by Joelle Taylor. Winner of the TS Elliot Prize, this is a remarkable evocation of the butch lesbian counterculture of 1980s and 1990s London, in an unforgettable poetic voice that is equally raging and elegiac.

This one is poetry not prose. It is history not fantasy. It is allusive and lyrical and fragmentary, not driven by plot. It's an affirmation of LGBT+ life and identity and joy and kinship and defiance, rather than an instantiation of the historic prejudice built into the very word and concept of queer. But there are also commonalities: both books are evocative, enthralling, transporting the reader to another affective world. They are both emissaries, in their own ways – bringing those other worlds into the bedroom. Both set you dreaming.

I don't read *C+nto* aloud: I read to myself and only myself, internally, in my own mind's interior. Perhaps it's this internalization, as well as the contrast with the out-loud performance of the childhood rituals immediately preceding it, but it seems bizarrely incongruous to be reading *C+nto* tucked up in bed, my wife beside me, way over on the other side of the world from its London setting and some three or four decades later, thinking of violence that lurks, for people like me, in the dark: 'because dead names haunt living rooms' (Taylor 2021: 111). As I read each night, before sleep, I am struck by the very particular quality of this book's rage: its lament which is also a rallying cry, a protest, an act of defiance, an incantation and carrying of the names of the dead: '& what is a closet but the body' (Taylor 2021: 107). Reading this book makes my own bedroom, the place of reading, into an entirely distinct kind of queer space.

Taylor opens with statistics: the seventy-two countries which still criminalize same-sex relationships and the '11 jurisdictions that support the death penalty for lesbians and gays' (Taylor 2021: 15). Taylor writes (and speaks, as a celebrated performer) from a position not often seen in the public domain and declares it as such: 'There is no part of a butch lesbian that is welcome in this world. It was bad when I was a teenager. It is as bad today' (Taylor 2021: 14).

For this reason, it's perhaps not surprising that *C+nto* is a book strikingly focused on interiors ('A fluorescent strip light undresses & the white tiles watch' [Taylor 2021: 65]). The public domain of London, at the time when these poems are set, was a violent and dangerous place for a butch lesbian woman. Interiors were spaces of refuge.

Of the book's spaces, the smallest scale is the vitrines with which it opens, in an imagined present, each of them displaying some fragment of bygone LGBT+ culture. From these vitrines turned to the tourist eye, to rooms and spaces, to the streets of the city itself, there is a layering of interiority in the book, a recursive, mutually imbricated sense of queer interiors tucked within queer interiors.

The rooms are mostly lesbian clubs, nights and bars, although there are also many other spaces in the built environment – boxing ring, cemetery, backroom, bathroom, haunted house, 'a cathedral of girls / snuffed like candles' (Taylor 2021: 110). But the bars are the most richly drawn, the most inhabited and layered with affect. Spaces where people dance, euphoric and joyful, performing and uttering kinship, protecting one another, all in the shadow of fearsome prejudice and marginalization, just outside the door, sometimes spilling inward.

It's very powerful, this book. It is not a book for children. The violence makes sure of that, also the fist fucking. But mostly it's the sadness, the rank injustice of it all: if I was to tell the boy even a very mild version of this story, even without the trauma, I know he would look at me with intensely worried disbelief – that such prejudice could have existed, against people like his own mother, in his own mother's lifetime. I can't tell him this because it would scare him and damage his faith in humankind. This is another kind of censorship, as protection. What's queer here, to his eye, is not the lesbians but the prejudice.

Alongside *C+nto* I've been reading Maggie Nelson, who in turn quotes Ahmed: 'The moment of queer pride is a refusal to be shamed by witnessing the other as being ashamed of you' (Nelson 2015: 22). Could it be that while in my own bed I am reading about spaces of queer refuge, over there on the other side of the hall I am building my son's bedroom into a kind of closet itself, enclosed and with the queerness kept safe inside, protected from all this sorrow and pain, this history into which he has been born. But a queer space is one in which, despite every layer and level of enclosure, the political always creeps in: bleeding through the walls and seeping through the floor. For queer families in queer spaces the distinction between the private and public domain shows itself to be not binary at all but diaphanous: complicated by motherhood, childhood, relived childhood and gender identity; performative reading and reading aloud as a form of care; bedrooms and their various forms of intimacy; the bedroom as a form of protective closet; censorship and erasure; didacticism and politics (both personal and public); literature and its historicity; poetry and place; connotation and the history of words or rather *a* word, namely 'queer' itself.

In Haraway's terms, these two books in two bedrooms represent the stories that make worlds, the worlds that make stories. They are the matters that matter – read (sometimes aloud, sometimes silently) by particular people, within particular spaces – variously and complicatedly private and public, queer and normative. Perhaps indeed they are *normally* queer – in a quotidian, everyday, banal sense. And perhaps there is something in that: in the very weakness and contingency and specificity of a single voice, telling stories; of a queer reader, a queer mother, reading aloud, at night, in the bedroom of a child.

References

Ahmed, Sara, 'Orientations: Towards a queer phenomenology', *GLQ: A Journal of Lesbian and Gay Studies*, vol. 12, no. 4 (2006), 543–574 (565).

Haraway, Donna, *Staying with the Trouble: Making Kin in the Chthulucene*. Duke University Press, Durham, 2016.

Nelson, Maggie, *The Argonauts*, Graywolf Press, Minneapolis, 2015.

Taylor, Joelle, *C+nto & Othered Poems*, The Westbourne Press, London, 2021.

Tolkien, JRR, *The Hobbit: Or There and Back Again*, HarperCollins, London, 2001 (1937).

Vallerand, Olivier, *Unplanned Visitors: Queering the Ethics and Aesthetics of Domestic Space*, McGill-Queens University Press, Montreal and Kingston, 2020.

IV

Pedagogies

13

[Spatial] pedagogic readings of queer theory

Experimental realism and opportunities for teaching and learning

Gem Barton

This chapter aims to establish an understanding of approaches to queer theory via the teaching and learning of spatial design subjects in higher education. Introducing 'experimental realism' as a pedagogical approach to (speculative) spatial design subjects, the chapter will discuss the relational binaries of architecture and interiority through an understanding of identity discourse and map the relationships between key interpretations of queer theory. In addition, it will consider the impacts that speculative design, diegetics/mimetics and equitable futures could have on teaching and learning in spatial design. Ultimately the chapter aims to serve as a provocative catalyst for queer theory and queer pedagogy to be read spatially and/or architecturally: as Oliver Vallerand has written, '[d]espite most of the thinking about the relation between queerness and architecture taking place in the academic world, its impact on architectural pedagogy has been quite limited. However, to be transformative, the acts of queering space and of queering design should be thought about at the root, in design schools' (Vallerand 2018: 141). In education specifically, the *queering* of archetypal architectural teaching practice, process and product may offer an opportunity to interrupt heteronormativity at its inception. Acts of queering in the educational context open new avenues of thinking and practice that go beyond the narrow confines of identity politics, towards making space for equitable and desirable futures.

I will therefore argue here that interiority and the pedagogies that shape it, should be defined by process rather than output, focusing on how design propositions are imagined and how educational processes can be designed to facilitate that. I will do this by introducing *Speculative Spatial Design* (SSD) – a spatial derivation of the well-known Critical Speculative Design (CSD) coined by Dunne and Raby in 2005. SSD is understood here as the application of speculative design processes and methodologies to spatial design subjects and the relationship this can enact between interiority and queer theory.

The future is already queer; it's just not evenly distributed

In this chapter as in my practice, queer is not meant (only) as a signifier that represents LGBTQIA+ identities. In this I follow bell hooks who once described 'queer not as being about who you are having sex with, that can be a dimension of it, but queer as being about the self that is at odds with everything around it and has to invent and create and find a place to speak and to thrive and to live' (hooks 2014). Likewise, when I use 'queer' it is not understood through a white gay male lens, as some earlier queer theory in architecture has been (Betsky 1997): showcasing how mostly rich white gay men experimented with their domestic space. As a queer woman, queer is most definitely an identity for me, but I also identify as an author and academic and for that side of me, queer (as the verb rather than the noun), holds the greatest power: *do*-ing queer (while also *be*-ing queer) in an academic context, operating (as many do) on the margins of a male-dominated discipline while deploying methodologies which depart from the dominant model. As Bryson and de Castelli write:

> Clearly, the distance from queer theory to queer pedagogy is great. [. . .] Queer pedagogy could refer here to education as carried out by lesbian and gay educators, to curricula and environments designed for gay and lesbian students, to education for everyone about queers or to something altogether different. Queer pedagogy could refer to the deliberate production of queer relations and to the production of subjectivities as deviant performance – that is to say, to a kind of postmodern carnivalesque pedagogy of the underworld, as agitation *<implemented deliberately to*

interfere with, to intervene in the production of so-called normalcy in schooled subjects> (Bryson and de Castelli 1993).

There are differences in expectation and allowance for 'being queer', 'doing queer', 'teaching queer' and 'learning queer' – the tolerated trend being acceptance through co-existence, as a curiosity, an alternative offering, rather than a serious critical endeavour worthy of a stand-alone practice. The academe is still introducing itself cautiously, from a safe distance, to the full spectrum of queer pedagogy, requiring a greater level of ambition than many schools of architecture appear ready to embrace.

It is important to clarify that identity and action are not exclusive; one can *be* queer and not *do* queer, equally one can be straight-identifying and still embody queer practices – as such, queer pedagogy is not *only* for queer pedagogues. As Susanne Luhman writes:

> Progressive pedagogies are already queer theories. What queer theory does to gender and sexuality discourse progressive pedagogy is doing to mainstream education. Both critically examine processes of normalisation and reproduction of power relationships and complicate understandings of presumed binary categories. (Luhman 1998)

My own design, teaching and writing practice is deeply informed by my lived experience (as a queer woman, with many intersections). But not all queer women design, teach or write in the same manner. A queer identity (as with many minority representations) seems to bring with it a subversive desire, born from repression, to deform and reform mainstream standards. This aligns especially well with the field of the arts, less so with the architectural profession and less again with the bureaucracy of academia. Arcidi wrote that 'as a gay man or a lesbian you can consider yourself a person on the margins, critical of or at least distant from, the norms that most people take for granted. But in a medium as complex as architecture, the sexuality of the designer can rarely be identified in the product' (Arcidi 1994). Meanwhile, twenty-five years later (2019) Adam Nathaniel Furman writes that:

> It is human instinct to externalise our identities through the form and decoration of our environments and buildings. Architecture has a duty to reflect the nature and make-up of those who produce it and those it contains. Alternate taste or cultures from those of the mainstream have an equal right to presence in the urban context. Within architectural circles, it is, to a degree, acceptable to be queer in your life but it is not and has never been, acceptable to express this through the architecture you produce. You will be tolerated, not accepted. (Furman 2019)

We might say that in architectural practice it is OK to *be* queer but not *do* queer. Similarly, in schools of architecture it appears OK to *be* a queer academic, have queer students, even discuss queer theory to some extent, it is far less OK to *do* queer: to queer institutional systems or structures. Nevertheless, that has been part of my journey throughout a teaching career of more than a decade.

Intentionally unknowable and (un)knowably intentional

The 1990s, the period Arcidi writes of, was a time in architecture when queerness was strongly identified and reacted to. In 1994 Betsky writes in the *Architectural Record* about gay architects being labelled as 'sensitive' or 'decorating minded' and tells of Seattle-based architect Jeff Harris, 'I was a project architect until I came out of the closet [. . .] Then I found myself where all the other openly gay architects in the firm were, designing tile patterns for elevator lobbies'. It could be that the perceived subservient position of interior design in the architecture industry contributed to the formalization of interior architecture as a subject of its own. Almost a century earlier, Edith Wharton was, in 1897, the first person to reference the term in the book *The Decoration of Houses*. Conflating all three aspects of interior work – design, decoration and architecture – into one whole, she named it Interior Architecture. The first intellectually prescient publication referencing Interior Architecture came almost seventy years later in the May 1966 issue of *The Architectural Review*. What is more quintessentially queer than adopting a term previously jostling for value and space and defining your own community when you are not accepted or respected by that which already exists? Interior Architecture's unknowability, being free from the regulations, controls (and formal identity) of architectural chartership provides the chance to redefine and experiment with its meaning and processes, ensures an open-ended opportunity to develop its cultures of practice, research and education.

In order to contextualize the research informing this chapter, I first introduce a series of interrelated concepts, processes and entities developed during my time as course leader for the BA (Hons) Interior Architecture programme (2015–21) at the University of Brighton. Beginning with the overarching structure of this course, these constructions include a *pedagogy*, a *studio* (in a sequence of iterations), a *think tank* and the particular use of the *scenario* for educational purposes. Figure 13.1 illustrates the interrelationships of the key components of the pedagogy – Experimental realism,[1] which aims to be socio-spatial, mimetic, speculative and protopian[2] in both pedagogy and curriculum.

The concept and method of experimental realism originated in the testbed of a design studio titled the Near Futurists' Alliance[3] (the *studio*), which I led and co-taught with set designer Amelia Jane Hankin[4] from 2017 to 2021.

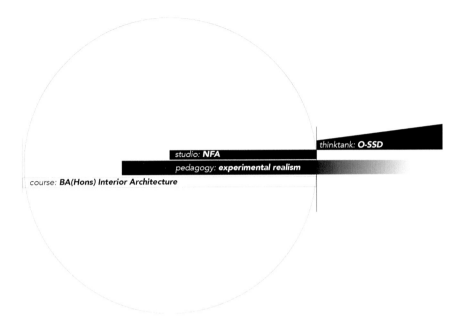

FIGURE 13.1 *Diagram showcasing the strategic interrelationships of/between the course (interior architecture), the design studio (Near Futurists' Alliance), the pedagogy (experimental realism) and the think tank (O-SSD).*

Over 4 years approximately 100 undergraduate students were part of this educational journey. The Near Futurists' Alliance (NFA) is now associated with the Office for Speculative Spatial Design (O-SSD,[5] the *think tank*), where research-led design projects enable my collaborators and I to consider three core areas of human behaviour and discover their interrelationships with space. Through these projects and consideration of these behaviours, we hope to contribute to policy change towards a more just and inclusive society.

Our main educational method is the scenario: through imagined scenarios we are able to speculate on the ways in which relationships and interaction; pleasure and entertainment; genders and identities (and all the many intersections of these) could change in the near future. We use the insights generated from these developed scenarios to study potential spatial impacts and requirements, culminating in the exploration of emerging programmes of use and new spatial typologies (Figure 13.2).

As we conceive it, experimental realism is intentionally unknowable. The term has previously been primarily used in the field of social psychology, where it refers to 'the extent to which situations created in social psychology experiments are real and impactful to participants' (Aronson and Carlsmith 1968). In a pedagogical context, 'experimental realism' reframes the experimental (adjective) as a method of testing, as well relating to something new and untried and sees realism (noun) as both a practical understanding of

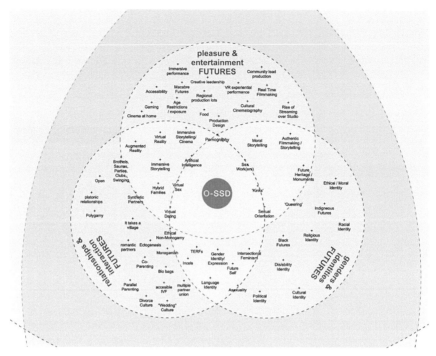

FIGURE 13.2   *Office for Speculative Spatial Design core research themes*
mapping. O-SSD operates through the femme-queer lens of; relationships and
interaction, pleasure and entertainment, genders and identities (www.o-ssd.com).

life and/or a simulation – building upon the currency of the present to design for
new/different problems/situations of the future, as this is *always* an unknown.

The apparent opposition in the title is intentional: 'experimental /
realism' speaks to the inherent challenges of design and indicates the equally
fragile and agile position of the designer. As a queer pedagogue, I face this
juxtaposition head-on, along with the friction and possible awkwardness it
brings – underscoring the need to engage in speculation, testing convention
and playing (un)safely within the limitations of projected reality. Students and
staff working together, as NFA, have sought a space safe enough for learning
and dangerous enough to enable speculation, guided by lived experience as
well as other ethical, political, social and cultural understandings.

Speculative Design, with its dozens of wanderingly disparate definitions,
was pioneered by Anthony Dunne and Fiona Raby, founders of the MA
Design Interactions course at the Royal College of Art (2005–15) and
authors of *Speculative Everything: Design, Fiction, Social Dreaming*. This
seminal book proposes design as a tool not only to create things but ideas but
also to speculate about possible futures. One way of describing speculative
design is in relation to 'typical design'. Where typical design tackles small
problems with design solutions, speculative design could be said to address

big societal issues with design processes and systems. According to Dunne and Raby, designers should not only be concerned with the issues of today but also consider future societal challenges and how design might play a part in these. With academic and student collaborators I work to imagine what SSD might offer to a future world, through the lens of spatial, architectural, interior systems and structures – a future designed to be free from the current limitations of space, technology, culture, politics and regulation. In exploring such speculations, my collaborators and I operate with an intentional focus on the 'near future' as an entity relatable to students; a timeframe near enough to follow and more importantly connect, to the trajectory or acceleration of an idea, while being far enough into the future to suspend disbelief and shed the shackles of probability. To assist in this process, creative prose in the form of a poem is written to set the scene for a project intention or brief; acting as both an accessible synthesis of ideas as well as a provocation (Figures 13.3 and 13.4).

The pleasure hunt

The freak shows once marvelled, are now scorned upon
The romanticised allure of blood sports now gone.

The sting of Punch and the bruise of Judy,
Domestic violence once infantilised, now rightly, unruly.

But that was the past, what's next for me and you?
A life of power and control? Striving for what's true?

Will we create a world that drowns in its sadness
A place where joy is found in fickle madness?

Will we create a world full of meaningless flirtation?
A space where thrills comes from more exploitation?

Swipe left, Swipe right, how will you vote
In an automated world it is impossible to gloat?

Imagine a world without elation only pain.
From the things you enjoyed, you now must abstain.

We live in a world that's bitterly salty.
Be careful what you wish for, cos it's perfect though faulty.

It's your turn to take charge, to lead from the front
So join the Alliance on our righteous Pleasure Hunt.

Gem Barton
Near Futurists' Alliance
18-19

FIGURE 13.3 *Poems written as part of the Near Futurists' Alliance design brief, set as both synthesis of ideas and provocative prose.*

The next original

From packhorse librarians, who carted books to the hamlets,
To downloads in milliseconds, direct to your tablets.

Is it change, is it progress, must we be open to the new?
Fly-over, crawl-under, swim-past, drive-thru?

-

Some say, respect, honour the intention of tradition!
Others say, that's regressive, but what is your position?

What survives, what doesn't, how is it decided?
To take part, to play the game, do you have to be invited?

-

Some projects live forever, in the mind of the designers,
Others make it out, win prizes, big head-liners.

To challenge the truth and question the divine,
You will create, with your hands, a monumental shrine.

-

Delve deep into history its stories and ruins,
But remember it's designing for the future you are doing!

It's your turn to take charge, to revel in the mystery,
So join the Alliance and start making [future] history!

Gem Barton
Near Futurists' Alliance
19-20

FIGURE 13.4 *Poems written as part of the Near Futurists' Alliance design brief, set as both synthesis of ideas and provocative prose.*

Queer as non-normal, interiors as non-architecture

The approach to experimental realism examines 'genders and identities' as one of three key research foci of the O-SSD, subverting conventional approaches to teaching design, not least through teaching students to imagine and design for near-future uses of space (rather than focusing on present-day commercial and/or normative uses) – and looking to actively subvert accepted power relationships and presumed binaries in the design process. This resists archetypal approaches to architectural education, including, for example, the syllabus of the Weimar Bauhaus (1923) which centres, quite literally, on the building as product, not process and noun, not verb. In comparison, experimental realism centres on pedagogy rather than curriculum, stimulating students to think beyond the world as it is and consider the world as it might be. The ultimate aim is to teach students how to think forward – to speculate and take responsibility for the decisions they make; where the 'design' of the proposition is a staging post and not the end point.

Vallerand writes that '[q]ueering design pedagogy means multiplying points of views, opening the discipline to not only other disciplines, but to the everyday and thinking about how our experiences as human beings, impact and transform our designs' (Vallerand 2018: 141). But it also means expressing discomfort through design process, setting briefs designed to be tackled with questions rather than answers. In many ways it was these ambitions that lead to the development of experimental realism – which holds human behaviour at the core of its design intent and process. This can be demonstrated by exploring in more detail the three themes of the O-SSD.

The first theme is the future of relationships and interactions. The definition and structure of 'relationship', 'family' and 'love' are evolving as are the ways in which humans interact, date and display passion and commitment. The historic fluidity of identity and expression is being exposed and polyamory and ethical non-monogamy are a growing desire for many. The word 'parenting' is being redefined: What does that concept mean for domestic space and the home? Our research asks whether and how spaces designed for the archetypal family will become redundant. How will design allow for and celebrate future union ceremonies or multiple parents and/or partners? Will there be a growing desire for synthetic companions? In this we investigate possible scenarios: Consider a world in which holiday resorts are no longer restricted to stag and hen do's but provide a unique way to holiday for the growing polyamorous population. Or a new norm of 'wedding' venues catering for multiple partner unions with aisles that allow a procession from three to fifteen. Or a time when ectogenesis becomes the most favourable way of having children, a new equality in parenthood that dismantles the gender hierarchy and completely changes the nature of human reproduction and thus the structure of our working and private lives. Students are invited to imagine the spatial futures that might accompany these social and behavioural shifts – if perceived as positive, students may design for the inclusion and encouragement of such scenarios or if negative, students may choose to use their design skills to communicate the trauma and confusion that could play out.

The second theme explored in our experimental realism pedagogical model is the future of pleasure and entertainment. As individuals, the places and experiences from which we derive pleasure change throughout our lives. The same is true of society: once upon a time the people derived pleasure from the macabre – freak shows, blood sports and public humiliation, but these are seen as distasteful or even immoral in contemporary times. Common pleasures today may seem more humane – but are they? What do the things we enjoy (or find taboo) say about us as individuals or as a society? In our teaching we have explored the part that design plays in this process, with our research questioning the relationship between humanity and gratification through the vehicles of architecture and design. We speculate about the future proponents of [dis]pleasure and the design they require or desire. Possible scenarios students are asked to consider are the design of a world where humanity has reached pleasure-saturation, where the only way forward is to design a factory for the creation of synthetic joy. Or the design of a secret HQ for a group of rogue pleasure-seekers from which they challenge strict authoritarian agendas. Or the design and execution of a new government-owned Instant Gratification Unit.

The third and final theme is the future of genders and identities. Here we posit the idea that space is gendered and gender is spatial; likewise, that space is political and politics is spatial; and that space has identity while identity is spatial. We propose that as society grows and transforms, so do the ways in which individuals behave in and experience the space around them. There are over sixty different terms to describe gender, identity and expression and those identifying with every one of these and their combinations, experiences space in a different way. Our research looks to explore the spatio-human experience, speculating upon future identification and recognition through spatial design, within the built environment. Students are encouraged to consider possible scenarios, including a world where softness and femininity are not interchangeable and skyscrapers are not phallic. Students imagine a process of de/re-gendering our spaces and imagine a truly intersex-tional city.

Experimental realism as continuous pedagogic queering: the queer-over

Experimental realism is a hybrid of other, more well-known pedagogies developed by psychologists, notably including constructivism (see Piaget and Vygotsky), behaviourism (see Skinner) and liberationism (Freire 1987). In general, pedagogic approaches are often described in terms of the direction of the learning, that is learner-centred or teacher-centred (instructional) learning. In the conception of experimental realism I have developed over the past decade and embodying lessons from Greene's (1996) three differential 'readings' of queer theory, through adjective, verb and noun; and Morris's (1998) three 'types' of queer theory: subject position, politic and aesthetic sensibility – I have developed a pedagogic code of conduct for teaching spatial design subjects via 'queer-overs'. In this I embrace possibility over prediction, empathy over ego, co-discovery over instruction, inclusion over elimination, experience over representation – the queered open alternatives to more traditional closed approaches – as follows.

Possibility over prediction

As Frederick Greene has written, '[q]ueer theory doesn't argue for a reversal of privilege or a revolution that puts what was subordinate on top; instead, it insists on other possibilities, refusing to be trapped or limited by an oppositional stance' (Greene 1996). In a similar way to future thinking, which centres multiplicity and plurality over singular visions, spatial design can be taught through Socratic methods rather than solution-centric problem-solving. If as the poem by Jezebel Delilah suggests 'femme is queer queering queer' (Lewis, n.d.) then I argue for a similar assertion that *speculation is design designing design*. Speculative design is inherently queer in its plurality and multiplicity. As educators we must focus on opening up dialogue, opposing and subverting affirmative approaches to design centred around finding single solutions to specific problems.

Empathy over ego

We must formulate a learning environment where students are encouraged to design and build from personal lived experiences. This recognizes the fact that to think critically is itself a privilege – for some who come from unsafe or culturally diverse backgrounds, these attributes are not taught nor do they come naturally. As educators we must nurture the ability to imagine in safe ways, providing empathic and democratic classrooms where open discussion is encouraged. Educators and students need to be willing and comfortable to have difficult conversations, to explore and navigate these together, without fear of judgment. This requires educators getting to know their students and curating learning opportunities to give all a chance to recognize their voice and unique point of view.

Co-discovery over instruction

We must disrupt the archaic hierarchy of architectural institutions, the model of the 'tutor as master' and 'student as apprentice' and move towards a democratic model of education: a profoundly respectful, collaborative pedagogy, focusing on co-discovery and co-creation, a natural home for speculation, for pure futures (theory) and applied futures (practice). This requires embracing the notion that there are infinite possible futures and these cannot be 'taught' as fact. Closing the loop of co-discovery involves mutual feedback and learning between student and tutor.

Inclusion over elimination

Depictions of the future are powerful. Given this, educators in speculative design, those who create and enable fictions and other visions of the future are in an extremely privileged position – one which must be taken with the weight that it deserves. There are many challenges to consider: future fatigue, future shock, academic navel gazing with a weak appetite for real action, the dangers of utopian ideals, the fascist history of some of the Futurist art movements and not least the fact that research and development has to date been the focus of the privileged – those who have access to education, to university tuition and those who are invited to participate and to speculate. Thus, the role of the educational institutions and educators themselves is to change this – it is time for a more relatable, more inclusive, more hopeful and more careful reflection of humanity to engage in speculative design and futures thinking.

Experience over representation

Borrowing from the cinematic world and strands of design fiction, we must encourage the use of mimetic and diegetic prototypes in student works, such as utilizing narrative props and designed dramatic experiences to illustrate ideas/concepts/designs instead of relying solely on the more traditional language of a package of drawings.

As David Kirby writes, '[t]he presentation of science within the cinematic framework can convince audiences of the validity of ideas and create public excitement about nascent technologies' (Kirby 2010). He observes that science fiction films typically have science consultants and technology consultants who provide expertise on the communication of technological innovations and how they might coexist in society – but there are few such opportunities for a similar role advising on the future design, use and inhabitation of space. Kirby continues:

> Fiction's lack of constraints and film-makers' creative assistance provides an open, 'free' space to put forward speculative conceptualizations; it also embeds these speculations within a narrative that treats these ideas as already actualized within a social context. The key to cinematic diegetic prototypes is that they allow scientists and filmmakers to visualize specific methods and technologies within the social realm of the fictional world. (Kirby 2010)

In this way we can see that diegetic and mimetic prototypes for visions of the future in popular culture can impact the ways we see and imagine what is possible through design. This is one core aim of experimental realism: to be a powerful force in creating and framing the desire for socio-spatial advances. These 'queer-over' values are delivered through research-led design projects in a three-phase process: first via a catalyst based on analysis of human behaviour; second a structured methodology of speculation; and third an output, namely a spatial design proposition.

Ultimately, spatial design is the design of space and its uses and it comes in many forms. Using the experimental realism method and within the

Near Futurists' Alliance we do not seek closed-loop solutions but rather a multiplicity of possibilities. Drawings and models are not representative of solutions but instead open-ended questions. We use narrative props, spatial diegetic and mimetic prototypes and film to explore spatial potentials: to test concepts, express possibilities, present our findings and share our ideas.

By deploying this approach, between 2015 and 2021 undergraduate students have produced research-led design projects pushing at the boundaries of traditional building typologies. These include: a honeymoon suite in a hotel designed specifically for polyamorous relations, a set for a post-industrial reality TV shows where contestants compete for employment, digital graveyards, test facilities where bankruptees pay their debts to the government through medical trials, dining labs where food-derivatives are used to manipulate dream experiences, rebel education environments lead by the Covid home school generation and innovative environments for sex workers to provide experiences for those with pandemic-induced intimacy anxiety. All these projects demonstrate and manifest various ideas and ideals of queer spatial pedagogy, for which I offer the following manifesto:

> Queer spatial pedagogy is not unsettled by structural biases – it is democratic in structure, supporting an equilibrium of multi-directional feedback between students and staff – enabling the mutual sharing and examination of life and lived experience, enabling empathetic thinkers, design, questions.

Queer spatial pedagogy is a continuous, growing, breathing, subversive process; it is responsive and reactive and will always be moving. It goes beyond queer visibility (Neto 2018) for educators and students and transgresses into adjacent disciplines. For the field of interiors this means engaging with film and game design as the liminal space and fantasy threshold between the two blurs into submission.

Queer spatial pedagogy is the facilitation of imagined futures through the lens of spatial practice, designed outside of today's limitations of space, culture, technology, hegemony and normativity. For the education in interiors this means questioning the spatial impacts of our behavioural changes. For example, what impacts might a generational wave of ethical non-monogamy have on the way we design and/or use interior space? Or the introduction of a universal basic income? Or the ready availability of lab-grown meat?

Queer spatial pedagogy does not accept the problem-solving design proposition as the summation of learning and is instead an advocate for Socratic question-asking and question-seeking academic design endeavours. For teaching in interiors, the most radical outcome of such a pedagogy might be the making of a design to produce a brief rather than the writing of a brief to produce a design. 'Design' can instead be a means to a more sophisticated process of fostering intelligent and inclusive practice where we construct in order to deconstruct – focused on the interrogation of human behaviour, speculation and inhabitation of space.

Notes

1 Experimental realism as pedagogy embodied by the practices of Near Futurists' Alliance uses cinematic storytelling and ficto-critical approaches to imagined events and environments, absorbing the extremes of 'fact-as-truth' and 'untested fiction' as fuel for fantastic yet grounded speculative processes and products. The Experimental realism digital platform www.experimentalrealism.com which offers an archive of student projects and a global mentoring scheme. The Experimental realism book, published by RIBA Publishing 2022).

2 Protopia set out by Kevin Kelly in the book *The Inevitable: Understanding the 12 Technological Forces That Will Shape Our Future* defines the state between the fight for survival (dystopia) and perfection (utopia). Monika Bielskyte, founder of the Protopia Futures [framework] takes a 'significant departure from the original framing of "better futures" via the route of technological innovation to proactive prototyping of radically inclusive futures that shifts the gaze from technological panaceas to focus on future cultural values and social ethics'. https://medium.com/protopia-futures/protopia-futures-framework-f3c2a5d09a1e

3 Near Futurists' Alliance embraces the speculative, the unreal, the theatrical, the processes of narrative and storytelling, personification and characterization. With no pressures for its outputs to exist in the concrete world, it can be described in the following way: facilitating students through speculative design projects to question, test and simulate the ways in which our physical, emotional, societal and intellectual behaviours could change in the future. Looking at the multiplicity of ways in which that impacts the ecologies of spatial design practice.

4 www.ameliajanehankin.com Amelia is a London-based set and costume designer. She completed a year as a trainee designer at the Royal Shakespeare Company 2014–2015. Previously Amelia graduated from RADA in 2013 with a Postgraduate Diploma in set and costume design. Amelia initially trained in architecture and her first-class BA (Hons) in architecture was received from the University of Nottingham in 2009. Amelia has designed a variety of theatre ranging from new writing, devised, touring theatre, immersive, site-specific and theatre for young people.

5 Office for Speculative Spatial Design (www.o-ssd.com) co-founded with Amelia Jane Hankin in 2021.

References

Arcidi, P. (1994). 'Defining gay design'. *Progressive Architecture*, 75: 36.

Aronson, E., & Carlsmith, J. M. (1968–1970). 'Experimentation in social psychology'. in G. Lindzey & E. Aronson (Eds.), *The Handbook of Social Psychology* (2nd ed., Vol. 2, pp. 1–79). Reading, MA: Addison-Wesley Pub. Co.

Betsky, A. (1994). 'Closet conundrum: how "out" can the design professions be?' *Architectural Record*, 6(182): 36.

Betsky, A. (1997). *Queer Space: Architecture and Same-Sex Desire*. New York: William Morrow.

Bryson, M. and de Castell, S. (1993). 'Queer pedagogy: praxis makes im/perfect'. *Canadian Journal of Education / Revue canadienne de l'éducation*, 18(3): 285.

Furman, A. N. (2019). 'Outrage: the prejudice against queer aesthetics'. *The Architectural Review*, 27 March 2019, London: EMAP Publishing.

Greene, F. (1996). 'Introducing queer theory into the undergraduate classroom: abstractions and practical applications'. *English Education*, 28(4): 325–39. Retrieved July 20, 2021, from http://www.jstor.org/stable/40172908

hooks, b., (2014). 'Panel talk'.—https://livestream.com/thenewschool/slave/videos /50178872https://livestream.com/thenewschool/slave/videos/50178872

Kirby, D. A. (2010). 'The future is now: diegetic prototypes and the role of popular films in generating real-world technological development'. *Social Studies of Science* 40(1):41–70.

Lewis, V. R. (n.d.). 'Untitled'. *Queering the Game of Life*. Retrieved from http://queerandpresentdanger.tumblr.com/post/140493287149.

Luhmann, S. (1998). 'Queering/querying pedagogy? Or, pedagogy is a pretty queer thing' in W. F. Pinar (Ed.), *Queer Theory in Education* (pp. 141–56). Mahwah, NJ: Earlbaum.

Morris, M. (1998). 'Unresting the curriculum: queer projects, queer imaginings'. In W. Pinar (Ed.), *Queer Theory in Education* (pp. 275–86). Mahwah, NJ: Earlbaum.

Neto, J.N. (2018). 'Queer pedagogy: approaches to inclusive teaching'. *Policy Futures in Education*, 16(5): 589–604.

Vallerand, O. (2018). 'Learning from . . . (or 'the need for queer pedagogies of space')'.*Interiors*, 9(2): 140–56.

Wharton, E. (1897). *The Decoration of Houses*. Milton Keynes: Lightning Source UK Ltd.

14

Teacher/student

Queer practices to dismantle hierarchies in studio culture

A. L. Hu

Preamble

When I think about the potential to learn from queerness to transform architectural education, I hold two truths together: that I cannot remove myself and my personal experiences from my analysis and that there exist in the world multiverses of countless dimensions of experiences. What I write fits into a long, storied history of queerness in architecture and design.

My nonbinary transgender queerness tints how I perceive the world and seeps into my everyday work. I use broad umbrella terms to describe my identity because they provide fluidity and expansiveness that more specific words preclude. Being a nonbinary queer person is a way for me to refuse the cis-tem while living within its clutches: to resist essentialism or assimilation through repeated performances and to recognize that processes – relationships, research, feedback loops – matter as much, if not more, than products.

The personal is political is practice. These are stories of how my queerness shapes my teaching and how my experiences as a student and a teacher shape my queerness.

Teacher-student

At the core of architectural education is the design studio, an immersive environment structured around a design project that becomes more refined during the course of the semester. Studio culture constitutes the experiences, habits and patterns found within the architecture design studio as both a space and a pedagogy. Like many architecture students in the United States, I plunged into the world of design studios blindly as an undergraduate college student, enraptured by the allure of beautifully designed schemes and the mystery of how buildings were produced. Unlike 'regular' college classes, design studios feature direct access to professors via desk crits, where students receive immediate feedback on their designs. Studio culture offered a focus on iterative production, experimentation, a level of intellectual freedom that couldn't be found in a traditional lecture or seminar.

In a typical design studio in the US context, a group of five to ten or more students are given a site on which to design a building, using methods that are taught by the teacher. Methods vary from teacher to teacher, but there are common elements of an architecture design studio project. Site analyses often barely brush the surface of the histories and socio-political contexts of place, focusing on physical elements that shape the form but not the concept. Programming studies are informed by the site analyses and provide the spatial requirements to which students design. Form-finding is often the primary focus of the studio, with representation of the form through drawings, renderings and physical models as a close second.

These elements themselves are not problematic and are necessary pieces of any architectural puzzle – it's in the ways they are often taught that produce studio culture. While 'culture' can refer to a 'cultivation' of shared practices, architecture studio culture emphasizes more of the 'cult' aspect. Paolo Friere, a noted Brazilian educator and philosopher, describes the 'banking model' of education: students are considered empty vessels into which knowledge is 'deposited' and stored. Students have no agency in their education because they are there to learn; teachers use curriculum to 'deposit' information as unquestionable facts, stable and true because students do not know how to question the information they are given (Freire 1972: 72). Studio culture relies on the banking model of education to assimilate students into the cult of architecture. By the end of the semester – or even sooner – most students have been indoctrinated in the principles of studio culture.

This hierarchy between the teacher, whose methods cannot be formally questioned or changed and the student, who may provide feedback but cannot effect change, is designed to maintain the power of the teacher over the powerlessness of the student. 'Deposits' are received as a matter of course, even welcomed as fresh knowledge. The teacher-student hierarchy in studio culture is a manifestation of patriarchal domination in architectural pedagogy, disguised as forward-thinking innovation. As an undergraduate student and an empty vessel, I readily succumbed to the unspoken rules of design studio, believing I was passionately producing something new and exciting at the bleeding edge of design.

The norms of studio culture are starkest in the shared trauma among architecture students. Everyone's experiences are specific to their school, time and place, but there are common themes that are nearly universal: pulling all-nighters to finish modelling and rendering a project; becoming upset during a pin-up or a review in response to a harsh comment from a critic; feeling paralysed with anxiety when making design decisions; and lacking confidence that what you've produced is enough, just to name a few (Koch et al. 2002). Though topics, tools and aesthetics have drastically changed since the Beaux Arts era, new forms and methods of creating them do not mean that processes of culture have shifted. Jeremy Till (2009: 15) writes that '[because] things look different, from school to school and from year to year, the assumption is made that the formative educational processes are equally different and equally evolving'. That assumption is wrong.

There are common positive experiences as well, to be sure. But the existence of so many shared traumatic experiences combined with the heavy shroud of mystery surrounding them is what Freire (1972: 106) calls a 'culture of silence': everyone in architecture school knows what's happening, but no one can confront it. And so, the rigid norms of studio culture persist, undisturbed and mutate into new forms as technologies change. This is not to say that I did not learn anything in the fourteen design studios that I participated in as an architecture student. Oh, I collected my teachers' 'deposits' like a dragon hoarding treasure in its lair – and it has taken me much time and space to be able to reflect on my experiences in order to critique them. I absorbed, mirrored and internalized what I was taught because I was a student immersed in studio culture, but I now understand that such culture is socially constructed through the back-and-forth between student and teacher. I am able to analyse how I acquired my knowledge in order to change the process.

    . . .

The brief for one of the design studios during my tenure as a student called for a commercial bank building in a gentrifying neighbourhood. Eight different studios working with the same theme interrogated the physical space of banks in relation to concepts ranging from building cores to the global art market to real estate. I opted to join the 'culture bank' studio, excited to immerse myself in what seemed like a broad area of research, to examine the spatial implications of repeated social behaviours in the acts of deposit and withdrawal.

Despite espousing a critical framing around 'divergent definitions' of culture and exploring the physical manifestation of social networks, the studio quickly devolved into an uncoordinated series of form-finding experiments that had no connection to the promised thematic of 'culture'. If the results of the formal exercises did not fit the critic's aesthetic, students were sent back to the drawing board. The 'banking model' of education

played out on many levels. From the very beginning, the studio instructor –
or teacher – chose the curriculum content and methods of inquiry and we,
the students, adapted to it. The teacher gave instructions ('deposited') and
we had the illusion of acting ('received'), by following the actions of the
teacher. If we responded as though the teacher did not know everything, for
example by questioning design advice, we were disciplined by the teacher
in the form of stricter rules or less engagement. Often, the teacher confused
their authority of knowledge with their own professional authority, creating
an authoritarian environment where the teacher always had the final say
and restricted students' inquiries and explorations. All of this meant that the
teacher, not architecture or design, was the subject of the learning process,
while we students were mere objects. These manifestations of the teacher-
student hierarchy actually serve to blunt rather than add to students'
creativity and growth (Freire 1972: 73).

Despite the risks of disobeying studio culture norms, several of my
studiomates and I took it upon ourselves to research our own interests
beyond the boundaries in which our teacher tried to contain us. Early in
the semester, a banker came in to give a lecture about the world of finance. I
could not stop thinking about people who are under- and unbanked – folks
who do not possess enough wealth to store in checking or savings accounts,
who rely on predatory payday loans and check-cashing operations to stay
afloat, who are targeted by city-led economic development programmes but
lacked physical spaces to gather. Throughout the semester, one question
remained persistent: What would a bank for the unbanked look like?

At the final review, I was last to present my 'culture' bank and I spoke
with a fervent urgency informed by my semester-long research. I proposed
a five-floor hybrid library-community centre with classrooms, a computer
lab and communal workspaces. A grand staircase that functioned both as
circulation and meeting spaces would foster a culture of personal connection
outside of formal and often exclusionary, educational spaces. The ground
floor housed a cafe and a gigantic public lobby, which would be open to
community functions in the evening. Instead of fortress walls and hidden
vaults, the glass curtain-wall façade invited interaction with passers-by on
the street and welcomed curious onlookers to step inside.

Fifteen seconds of silence ensued – thick, heavy, foreboding dead air –
before a member of the final review jury asked something along the lines of,
'Why are you so angry?'

At the time, I did not understand why my presentation elicited such a
gruff, dismissive response, but clearly, studio culture set us – both students
and teachers – up for disappointment. The 'banking model' of education left
no room for students to express or pursue passions that did not fit into the
teacher's predetermined framework. Add to studio norms the complexity of
presenting as a nonbinary person in a dominantly cis-male space – and it is
no wonder that I was faced with hostility towards my perceived emotional
state. Though my design work was put to the side while my feelings were

up for critique, I do believe that my resistance was worth it – but the norms of studio culture stunted the educational potential from the first day to the final review.

In a studio about 'culture banks', a critical analysis of studio culture would have been fitting. Such self-reflective examination could have been the source of 'critical consciousness' (Freire 1972: 71), which is required for educational practices to break free from the 'banking' model, towards education as a practice of freedom. In the context of the architecture design studio, pedagogies that seek to liberate rather than dominate necessitate recognizing the effects of the teacher-student hierarchy. Queerness, which Sewell describes as a discursive site for contestation and refusal of 'the order of things' (2014: 294), provides a starting point for transgressing the norms of studio culture. Queer architectural pedagogy, then, draws from queer practices in order to complicate, dismantle and reconstruct the power differential between teachers and students.

Student-student

Teachers possess knowledge and wisdom through experience and their guidance is absolutely necessary for architectural education. But what of the relationship between students? Because the teacher-student hierarchy is critical to maintaining studio culture, another key norm dictates that students are in competition with one another, each individually striving for the best design in the eyes of the teacher (Koch et al. 2002: 16). Care is not explicitly valued or taught as a part of the learning process, even in group projects. Instead, because success is measured by the students' understanding and reflection of their teacher's language and frames of reference, students compete against each other to achieve good grades. Since the teacher-student relationship is so dominant in architectural education, student-student relationships fall to the wayside.

Teachers are important as facilitators of learning, but their time with students is limited; students' interactions with each other form the bulk of their design studio experiences. Students cumulatively spend more time with each other than with their teachers, whether actively working on group projects or passively by working on similar projects together – sometimes, even in the same physical studio space. In this context, I am specifically examining relationships between students based on relational care: *care with* or acting in solidarity, in recognition that supporting one person supports everyone. Joan Tronto, a scholar of the ethics of care, describes 'cultures of care' as extending beyond familial bonds to communities, peers and strangers and encompassing actions taken to 'maintain, continue and repair' our bodies, selves and environments so that all who live there can thrive (Fisher and Tronto 1990: 40). The care between students is invisible to the field and discourse of architecture because it cannot be readily seen in sketches, renderings and models, but it is the bedrock of the success of architectural education.

As a group of people experiencing studio culture together, students *care with* each other in order to survive. It is not uncommon to cut your work short or prolong your stay in the studio so that you can head home with a fellow student at 2 in the morning. Sometimes you skip a meal, consciously or not, because you're so engrossed in your work, but someone in your studio has extra food to share with you. Yet another student has brought an electric kettle to the studio, which is used by multiple people for tea or instant noodles. You're able to borrow materials to finish building a physical model because the art store isn't open on Sundays. Besides *caring with* through sharing material things, student-student learning happens when skills are shared – both technical ones, like connecting surfaces in a 3D model and non-technical ones, like explaining a design decision with clarity. It would seem that this type of care is not welcome in the design studio, a space of hyper-individuality and competition, but such rigid normality necessitates *caring with*: because studio culture would tear the social fabric of the educational environment apart, student-student relationships based on care are essential. Students who *care with* each other form bonds of solidarity together, increasing the odds of mutual success. Imagine subsuming current surface-level manifestations of care in architecture with relational forms of care – starting with a foundation of intentionally cultivated relationships.

For cultures of care to thrive in the design studio, the definitions of care – what it looks like to care in different contexts, as well as the value of care – need to expand and practices of care need to proliferate. Queer conceptions of care have always reached beyond the boundaries of the nuclear family, always been promiscuous in practice. In the 1987 essay 'How to Have Promiscuity in an Epidemic', ACT UP activist and art historian Douglas Crimp (1987: 237–71) defines promiscuity not as casual or indifferent but as experimental in the ways that gay men were intimate with and cared for each other. Drawing upon this queer reading, promiscuous care in the design studio could redefine students' and teachers' orientations to one another to become based on *caring with*. Acknowledging and intentionally building upon the caring and solidarity practices that already exist in the studio could expand avenues for participation and, in turn, everyone's abilities to *care with*. Perhaps, if the notions of care in architectural education could expand through queer theory, then the measures of success could also change. Under this framework, promiscuous care is just the start of transformative relationships.

. . .

All of my all-nighters are a blur of fuzzy memories, blending together into one long dream. There came a point in my student career when I stopped counting how many I'd pulled that semester – and as soon as a semester was finished, it was time to forget and think about the next one.

The details are spare but bright: energy drinks and snacks before midnight; wild, winding conversations and roaring laughter as the tiredness sets in; working standing up to stay awake; feeling bone weary; upbeat music blasting from laptops; absolute silence and wired alertness in the early morning.

I've looked up from my computer screen to watch a fellow student place the finishing details on their sixteenth-scale model with tweezers held by gloved hands.

I look down again to see my own model-making disaster, a mess of chipboard, broken blades and tacky glue.

Five minutes later – or did three hours somehow slip by? – a group of students and I are gathering around a computer to troubleshoot an error-ridden 3D model.

I'm rotating a PDF back at my desk and holding my breath as I click Print.

Birds outside are starting to sing, even before the sun rises.

Least fragmented are my memories of how it felt to experience *care with*. Studio culture during college amplified competition to such an uncomfortable degree that when I started working late and working late turned into pulling all-nighters, I did it to stay in the game, to conform to what was 'normal', to fit in. Before long, though, the student-student relationships in the studio grew stronger than the competitiveness we performed in the daylight.

A feeling that nearly captures my experiences of mutual trust and support in student-student relationships is *belonging*, but its connotations suggest notions of citizenship, statehood and Othering (Yuval-Davis 2012). The promiscuous care that I practised with my studiomates transcends the construction of boundaries between 'us' and 'them' or even the need to find essential similarities as a precondition for solidarity. The feelings of *caring with* were so strong that students would bring their non-architecture friends to the studio and they would be immediately welcomed. Promiscuous care practices between students embodied *caring with* by respecting and honouring different ways to exist in relationship with one another. Engaged in mutual relationships of care I was free to explore and establish my own boundaries, to assert my own will. I knew myself in relation to the students in the studio.

Years later, during graduate architecture school, I experienced and practised promiscuous care in a more specific way as I began the process of coming out as a queer nonbinary person. Because coming out is an ongoing series of events, not a singular event, my process started even before I was consciously aware of my queerness. When I started my grad programme, I identified as a cisgender woman and was deeply entangled in a long-term relationship with straight, cisgender man. These facts about me did not impede my fast friendships with queer students in my cohort. When my identity began to morph and shift as I took the space and time to reflect on its social construction, I felt like my world was turned upside down – on top of trying to stay afloat in the design studio. My queer studiomates *cared with* me, not because I had something to offer them in return or because I could boost their grades, but because they considered me, a flailing, fledgling queer, as in need of their promiscuous care. I owe much of my emotional and psychological well-being to our mutual openness, acceptance and trust. They nudged me to continue, to find beauty in the upside-downness, to never forget to *care with* myself throughout the process.

Like the sparse details that linger of all-nighters, only flashes of late nights in graduate design studios remain, but one thing is clear: the queer, promiscuous care of student-student relationships sustained me as I wrestled with architecture school and my queerness.

Student/teacher

I had the chance to shape my architectural pedagogy even as I was wading through it: one of the ways I could make money as a graduate student was to be a teaching assistant (TA). This, in hindsight, was a conundrum to me, because how could I, the student, be an effective teacher if I was still a student? How did I transform from a student into a teacher? Was I still a student while I was a teacher? According to the 'banking model' of education, I could play either 'depositor' or 'receiver', but not both at once. As a TA, it was known that I was still a student but in a different role with more responsibilities and power. Even if I was not responsible for structuring the entire course, I was a conduit for its values, principles and curriculum, an enforcer of the teacher-student hierarchy.

But because I was still a student, still very much mired in studio culture and in the middle of becoming an architect, I had some latitude in my role. *Becoming* in queer theory is an ongoing process, as one does not simply flip a switch and 'become' a different person. Sociologist, educator, writer and activist Angela Jones (2009: 14) writes that '[becoming] queer is not about crafting a fixed identity or culture. . . . Becoming queer . . . cannot be envisioned as a collective project with programmed visions of how we need to perform queer'. There is no script to follow when *becoming* queer – in fact, queerness comes in the rejection of fixed identities, performances or procedures. Embracing this queer reading, my role as a TA meant that I was a student *becoming* a teacher and then *becoming* a student again, in a nonlinear fashion. And in *becoming* a teacher while still a student – in this grey area of processes – I was able to resist some of the norms of the teacher-student hierarchy.

If studio culture is maintained, in part, by the teacher-student hierarchy, we could trace the lineage of architectural pedagogy through unbroken cycles of student trauma and normalization. These processes and practices in the design studio have changed over time, but have not fundamentally, radically shifted, because they are inextricably connected to the power located in societal systems. The rigid norms that first appear in studio culture permeate the longer, broader process of becoming an architect. There is a clear 'script' to follow and ideals to aspire to; the pathways to becoming an architect are so well-worn as to be mythic. To break the cycle, architectural education needs to deconstruct this stable identity of the archetypal architect and teach different ways of *becoming* an architect in order to break down the teacher-student hierarchy and, in effect, studio culture.

It may seem that students and teachers have very little power to affect the systems in which we participate – that nothing short of a revolution is necessary to upend the system. However, revolution is not merely a singular event but an evolutionary process. Asian American intersectional feminist, activist and writer Grace Lee Boggs (1974: 19) says that 'most people . . . think of a revolution in terms of 'Instant Revolution' rather than in terms of a protracted struggle'. Just as the queer notion of *becoming* does not happen in one instant but in ongoing instances, revolution is not a momentary change or rebellion. In the context of transforming studio culture, revolution is *becoming*, the process of change as practices evolve. How, then, do we enact ongoing revolutions within the design studio so that the process builds towards radical, sustainable change in the teacher-student hierarchy? How might we practice *becoming* as a pedagogy within architectural education to challenge and abolish the rigid normality of studio culture, which threatens to co-opt, engulf,[1] and normalize our revolutionary efforts?

Becoming, in the queer sense of the term, requires fluidity between the roles you are striving for and the role you are currently playing. Think of yourself as water changing from solid to liquid to gas but still made of the same molecules. Fluidity means change is a constant. It means not only opening yourself to change and difference but also letting yourself change the process. It means bringing your whole self – uncertainties and questions and warts and all – to the process of *becoming*, rather than cutting parts of yourself off because you don't fit the norms of the current system. Fluidity stretches territorial and disciplinary constraints, eroding the strict norms that limit our imaginations on who we *could* be, instead of conforming ourselves to who we *should* be.

The space and time to practice fluidity, to *become* in radically different ways, to resist the hierarchies in studio culture, exists regardless of your current role. Being both a student and a teacher – literally, in my case – embraces the transformative power of fluidity.

. . .

My first formal teaching role at an architecture school was during my third and final year of graduate school. I was a TA for a required first-year course that introduces the conventions and attempts to spark innovations of 2D projections, 3D renderings and visual narratives.

The first-year cohort of students typically arrive with mixed design backgrounds: about half have earned undergraduate degrees in architecture or related environmental design fields, while the other half have studied subjects as varied as math, film, anthropology and economics. The course for which I was a TA is the great equalizer, an intensive apply-as-you-go skills and theory course that is a steep learning curve for some, a chance to refine familiar workflows for others. A legible and beautiful computer-aided drawing often requires multiple steps, from 3D modelling, to cleaning up linework and line weights, to colour and texture touch-ups. Learning that process requires immersing completely within the digital software.

As a TA, I was a teacher to the incoming first-year students. My own experiences with the teacher-student relationship were front-of-mind when I sat in on lectures and gave feedback during pinups. But it was the time that I spent in the studio, meeting with students one-on-one at their desks, that opened my eyes to the complexity of being student/teacher simultaneously.

Students were assigned a semester-long study of a building of their choice from a list curated by the professors – the building would be the constant as they learned how to draw plans, sections, perspectives, diagrams and details. Each student was tasked with crafting a narrative of their chosen building from drawing-based analysis. Quite literally, the floor was open to interpretation. Students were free to focus on aspects of the architecture that interested them – from the structural system, to the circulation routes, to the history of the project, to the ideologies that the design represents – but both the building and the narrative had to be expressed through three modes of drawing through the course of the semester: 2D sketches and axonometrics, a physical model in three dimensions and an animation that added the fourth dimension of time. These were exquisitely layered drawings, dense with information and meaning, evolving organically as students' skills and explorations grew deeper each week.

As part of my responsibilities as TA, I visited my students at their desks every week, sometimes for thirty minutes, sometimes just for five. The shorter desk crits were to-the-point and driven by students who already had a firm grasp on the functions of the software. These students' questions focused on the details of the assignments' deliverables or aesthetic choices that did not alter their analyses. The more technical prowess a student possessed, the more time they had to think about the conceptual framing of their narratives, the more self-assured they were in their ability to create architectural drawings.

In contrast, the longer desk crits often started off with discrete software tutorials or troubleshooting but, sooner or later, spun off into broader conversations about the students' feelings. For students who had trouble learning software, falling behind decreased their confidence to continue learning the myriad technical skills at the breakneck speed that architecture school requires. Figuring out how to model stairs in 3D virtual space could start out as a conversation about orthogonal lines and the sequence of keystrokes to produce volumes, but morph into commiseration on frustrations, joys and fears – sometimes ending in tears.

As a student/teacher, my role crossed the boundaries of architectural education into the territory of emotions, vulnerability and everything that makes us human. This is not usually the case in the 'banking model' of teaching, wherein students are objectified as 'empty vessels into which [knowledge is poured]' (hooks 2003: 129). The focus is on sharing facts and information without regard to students' emotional wholeness. *Becoming a teacher while I was still a student and practising fluidity between rule-setter and a shoulder to learn on challenged the stability of the teacher-student hierarchy. The boundaries that delineate the teacher-student hierarchy are actually fuzzier and more blended than they appear – in fact more like student/teacher – and emotional processing is just as important to architectural education as facts and technical skills. Those boundaries are meant to be traversed; the territory is meant to shift.*

Teacher/student

I began this chapter espousing the crucial role of personal experience in affecting politics, which constitutes the practices we choose to employ day-to-day. *The personal is political is practice.* Though my stories are just the trace outlines of what queering architectural pedagogy could look like, this work of remembrance and critical reflection must be done in order to transform practices.

Studio culture as it exists now tends to punish and traumatize students for their failures rather than foster environments conducive to learning, experimentation and growth. Queering studio culture means normalizing queer practices to dismantle the rigid norms that uphold the teacher-student hierarchy, the power differential that underwrites the architectural design studio. Through practices of promiscuous care, students sustain relationships with each other, despite the destructive forces of studio culture. Promiscuous care between students has the potential to rewrite solidarity as a studio norm and break down unhealthy competition. Through recognizing that teachers' roles are fluid and extending that grace to students as well, teacher/students resist defaulting to the 'banking model' of education. 'Soft skills' and expressing passion are devalued and penalized under the status quo's capitalist, patriarchal architecture profession; holding space to process emotions does not exist in the critical path to completion. In this way, our emotional lives exist within a political context. As a teacher/student, bearing witness to students' emotional expressions and addressing them as urgently and seriously as design questions dismantles the structures that uphold the cis-hetero-patriarchy within architecture.

Normalizing these queer practices will require love – not in the sense of romantic love or infatuation, but, as James Baldwin (1963: 102–3) writes, 'in the tough and universal sense of quest and daring and growth'. bell hooks (2003: 131) defines love's core principles as 'a combination of care, commitment, knowledge, responsibility, respect and trust' that work interdependently, regardless of the relational context. In this sense, teachers practice love in their pedagogy through promiscuous care and fluidity in their role, creating the optimal conditions for learning in the studio. And if the personal is political is practice, then teachers will need to extend this love to themselves, as well, for the trauma they experienced in their time in design studios. Self-love is the balm for scarred hearts and negative memories, the key to re-orienting the personal – and thus the political and practice – towards care and fluidity. Moving beyond surviving to thriving as a practitioner of queer architectural pedagogy requires creating learning environments that are based on love – building the world you wish you lived in.

This is not a prescription for establishing a new set of rigid norms but for creating a culture through queer practices of promiscuous care and role fluidity that embraces a plurality of norms. Alex Shotwell describes this as the concept of 'open normativities':

> If normativity can be understood as facilitating a too-easy collapse of complex subjectivity into one or two options, forming new orthodoxies is an important part of the collective work to forge more capacious and diverse ways of being. 'Open normativities', then, name those normativities that prioritize flourishing and tend towards proliferation, not merely replacing one norm with another. (Shotwell 2016: 154–5)

Whereas in current studio culture everything is black or white, right or wrong, rewarded or punished, open normativities allow a range, a gradient, of many different norms to be understood as valid simultaneously. This opens up the space for the co-creation of studio culture norms that are accessible and beneficial to both teachers and students and that can change over time.

In the same way that queer *becoming* is an ongoing process, normalizing queer practices to dismantle studio culture as we know it will require ongoing vigilance and action. Recognizing that teachers and students are relationally interdependent and necessitate reciprocal care is the first step. Queering the 'cult' of domination in architectural culture on larger and longer scales will involve creating open normativities that expand over time, in solidarity with work against white supremacy through Design Justice; abolitionist work through transformative justice; and disability justice's struggle for universal access. For what is a culture of open norms if not a practice of freedom that transforms architectural pedagogy from a closed system into a flexible, accessible culture, one that grows our collective capacities for as-of-yet unknown, caring, loving, exciting futures?

Note

1 For more on the use of 'engulf' in the context of the production of global space through racial knowledge and power, see Denise Ferreira da Silva's *Towards a Global Idea of Race* (University of Minnesota Press, 2007).

References

Baldwin, J. (1963). *The Fire Next Time*. London: Michael Joseph.

Boggs, J. and Boggs, G. L. (1974). *Revolution and Evolution in the Twentieth Century*. New York: Monthly Review Press.

Crimp, D. (1987). 'How to have promiscuity in an epidemic'. *October*, vol. 43 (Winter) [online]. Available at: https://doi.org/10.2307/3397576 (Accessed: October 24, 2021).

Fisher, B. and Tronto, J. C. (1990). 'Towards a feminist theory of care' in Abel, E. K. and Nelson, M. K. (eds.) *Circles of Care: Work and Identity in Women's Lives*, 36–54. Albany: State University of New York Press.

Freire, P. (1972). *Pedagogy of the Oppressed*. Middlesex: Penguin Education.

hooks, b. (2003). *Teaching Community: A Pedagogy of Hope*. New York: Routledge.

Jones, A. (2009). 'Queer heterotopias: homonormativity and the future of queerness'. *Interalia: A Journal of Queer Studies*, vol. 4 [online]. Available at: http://dx.doi.org/10.51897/interalia/PQBF4543 (Accessed: October 24, 2021).

Koch, A., Schwennsen, K., Dutton, T. A. and Smith, D. (2002). *The Redesign of Studio Culture* [online]. Available at: https://www.aias.org/wp-content/uploads/2016/09/The_Redesign_of_Studio_Culture_2002.pdf (Accessed: October 24, 2021).

Sewell, J. I. (2014). '"Becoming rather than being": queer's double-edged discourse as deconstructive practice'. *Journal of Communication Inquiry*, vol. 38(4), pp. 291–307 [online]. Available at: http://dx.doi.org/10.1177/0022002714553900 (Accessed December 28, 2021).

Shotwell, A. (2016). *Against Purity*. Minneapolis: University of Minnesota Press.

Till, J. (2009). *Architecture Depends*. Cambridge: The MIT Press.

Yuval-Davis, N. (2012). 'The Caring Question: the Emotional and the Political'. in *The* Politics of Belonging: Intersectional Contestations [online]. Available at: http://dx.doi.org/10.4135/9781446251041.n6 (Accessed: October 24, 2021).

15

Taking architecture from behind*

Colin Ripley

We start and end with failure. As Jack Halberstam reminds us, failure is endemic to queerness, a defining feature of the queer (Halberstam 2011). A queering of architecture must first of all dispense with the teleological pretensions of architecture. We are not trying to draw realizable buildings, let alone produce a better world: we understand that to achieve these goals would be to give up on the promise of queerness. Queer exists not in the hope of victory but in the joy of the struggle. As I have said before, not even a queer architect can design a queer house (Ripley 2018). And yet: we keep trying.

Queering architecture is an impossible exercise. I don't mean, in making this opening statement – one that is unlikely to be popular among readers of this volume – that queering architecture is merely difficult nor indeed that it is difficult at all. Nor am I suggesting, not for a moment, that queering architecture is not a vitally important endeavour. Rather, my thesis here is a strictly formal one: architecture cannot be queered because queer is already an architectural effect.

Queer, after all, is at its root a certain type of exteriority, that which lies outside the norm. We cannot think the exterior or an exterior, without a simultaneous consideration of the interior, that is, without recognizing the couple interior/exterior, that is, without architecture. One of architecture's most basic moves, perhaps following the production of the binary through the drawing of a line, is the production of enclosure, of inside and outside, us and them, normal and abnormal. Queer cannot exist without architecture and architecture cannot exist without queer.

What strategies and tactics might we develop then in order to do the impossible? How can we think the queerness of architecture? In this chapter

I will discuss the background, pedagogical positions organization and outcomes of an architectural drawing project based loosely on the work of Jean Genet that I have been conducting since 2017. For those who are interested in the drawn outcomes and I hope you are, the full archive of the project can be found at www.houseofthethief.com.

Learn to love your cell. The modern world starts with the prison cell: this is Foucault's position and it's hard to deny. The cell is the primary unit, the primary void, that defines in turn its corollary, the individual self and these two become the basic building blocks of modernity. The cell transforms into the room, agglomerates into the house or the apartment – the unit in contemporary language – and the individual self becomes the primary economic unit that moves capital, the primary political unit that moves democracies, the primary medico-erotic unit of the pharmacopornographic world. Learn to love your cell: escape is impossible. Escape is the only imperative for the queer.

To think queerness in architecture we need to look from outside of architecture, ignoring of course that to be outside is already to be inside the structure of architecture. We start from architecture's outside – as architecture itself, as a discipline, defines its outside. We need to find a way in which to penetrate its walls, to infest or occupy or break into its body: we need, in short, a thief.

The thief in this story, in the project I am presenting in this text, is Jean Genet, 1910–86, French orphan, homosexual, thief, novelist, playwright, essayist and activist.

Genet's life and work cover beautifully the period in question here, that is, the period from roughly 1840 to the present, starting indeed with the opening of the Mettray colony in 1840, an event which Foucault points to as the inauguration of the carceral society (Foucault 1977).[1] Genet's work chronicles for us the heroic modern period of the 1920s and 1930s, the Second World War, the intellectual 1950s, the unrest of the 1960s, the beginnings of globalization in the 1980s and, through recent extensions of his work, to the pornographic era of late capital.

From a direct point of view, Genet had little to do with architecture. In his extensive work there are only, to my knowledge, two short essays, 'That Strange Word . . .' and 'Chartres Cathedral' that can really be said to touch on architectural thinking (Genet 2003). If we look a little more closely, though, a concern for architecture permeates both his work and indeed his life, a concern that we can see in his descriptions of institutions such as prisons and brothels. He also designed and built some houses, at least one of which he gave away as a wedding present to his younger lover, despite never, as an adult, living in a house himself. For me, in this work, Genet – and the world of literature and philosophy that centres around him – operates as a guide or rather as a thief, helping us to break into the house of architecture, perhaps to steal some well-hidden secrets. Genet allows us to look at architecture from its outside, from the corner of our eyes, to see things that are never presented head-on.

A second text, interrupting the first, invading the spaces between lines and words. Winding its way through like a wisteria winding its way around a white marble piloti column. Disrupting, interfering, transposing meaning. But how should we read this second text? Is it manifesto or operating instructions? Does this text constitute (n + 1) points for a queer architecture? That seems too much. Maybe this second text (but which text, after all, is first and which is second? And are there other texts we should be discussing, texts that maybe appear only elsewhere or elsewhen or are simply not acknowledged?) is merely a description of the current situation, seen askance, through queer-coloured glasses, a fleeting view, through a peep-hole, of what is behind the (architectural) image – what is the behind of the image.

But as much as we need to see architecture from outside, we need to work from the inside. A step outside, a step inside: we heretics work like a virus, using the mechanism of architecture itself to do our work. We cannot really hope to queer architecture, to address the question of what it could possibly mean to queer architecture or to understand the queerness that is always already present in architecture, unless we approach it through the techniques and processes of architecture, through design. This project, *The House of the Thief*, is therefore first of all a design project and like a fifth column our little band of malcontents makes use of the traditional processes of architectural design – drawing, modelmaking and their extensions in the twenty-first century – in order to produce not buildings as such, but knowledge, to break into the house of architecture using its own techniques, to uncover hidden agendas and mechanisms. We undertake a perversion of what we have been taught to think of as architecture, a subversion of architecture from within (see Ripley 2020). With all respect for Audre Lorde, we recognize that all tools are in the end the master's tools and especially so in the world of architecture. We use instead the tactics of the prisoner: the tactical reappropriation of the strategies of the master. We sharpen our sabots, cut extra pockets into our trousers. We use architecture to betray architecture.

In other words, we take architecture from behind.

Jump into the void. Draw from inside: remember the presence of the three primary voids of which our lives and our selves are composed: cell, closet (or its Genet-ic formulation, the brothel) and tomb. Design is a matter of designing our (queer) selves: architecture wants us to forget this, this is why we have to betray architecture. Architecture presents a false and impossible exterior view. We queerly draw from inside the void.

Behind and especially taking from behind, is an important concern in the klepto-genetics of architecture.[2] First of all, the idea of taking from behind has clear and inescapable connections to queer and especially gay male culture through the practice of anal intercourse. Especially, but not only: Paul B. Preciado bases his *Counter-sexual Manifesto* in the liberatory potential of anal sex, since everyone – men, women and those who refuse this binary – has an asshole (Preciado, Dunn and Halberstam 2018: 30). Leo Bersani, in his discussion of Genet's *Funeral Rites*, finds a perverse futurity in anal sex, as the two participants are looking not in each other's eyes but rather are looking together towards the horizon (Bersani 1996: 166).[3] Taking from behind also has resonances of cowardice (shooting in the back) and of betrayal and we will need to take both of these into account.

Jam a dildo in the machine. We need to shatter gears, disrupt fluid and capital flows, break the architectural apparatus. Detangle the organs of pleasure from the organs of (re)production. Sever the connection between penis and phallus, in a permanent castration of architecture. This is of course a moment of the purest comedy and the saboteurs laugh and dance, drunk on their pleasure.

Aside from its connotations of anal sex, taking from behind also has a useful history in philosophy. I'm referring here to Deleuze's comments on his own process:

> I suppose the main way I coped with it at the time was to see the history of philosophy as a sort of buggery or (it comes to the same thing) immaculate conception. I saw myself as taking an author from behind and giving him a child that would be his own offspring, yet monstrous. It was really important for it to be his own child, because the author had to actually say all that I had him saying. But the child was bound to be monstrous too, because it resulted from all sorts of shifting, slipping, dislocations and hidden emissions that I really enjoyed. (Deleuze 1995: 6)

I'm referring also to Žižek's appropriation of the same concept in his discussion of Deleuze in *Organs without Bodies*. For Žižek, we should understand Deleuze's philosophical buggery not as an attempt to shock, we should not approach it with 'an obscene, condescending and dismissive sneer' but with 'completely naïve seriousness' (Žižek 2015: 42). And despite the understated but clearly present tone of scepticism or even of moral disapproval of this technique of buggery legible in Žižek's text (the necessity that Žižek feels, for example, to point out our need to take this approach with 'naïve seriousness' or even to insist that this seriousness must be naïve, that is, not exactly mature or considered), Žižek is also clear to point out that taking from behind remains a matter of producing an intimate relationship:

> While Derrida proceeds in the mode of critical deconstruction, of undermining the interpreted text or author, Deleuze, in his buggery, imputes to the interpreted philosopher his own innermost position and endeavours to extract it from him. So, while Derrida engages in a 'hermeneutics of suspicion', Deleuze practices an excessive benevolence towards the interpreted philosopher. (Žižek 2015: 42)

So, while Deleuze's buggery remains 'much more violent and subversive' than Derrida's deconstruction and while it 'produces true monsters', it remains, even in Žižek's description, an act of love and intimacy. One might ask, of course, why it is that taking from behind, anal intercourse, buggery, needs to be violent, subversive and productive of monsters? Might we focus instead on the pleasure that is produced in this activity, pleasure of course for both the buggerer and the buggered and consider the offspring of this union not so much as monsters (although they may be beautiful monsters), but as hitherto unrecognized and unseen pleasures? Could we say that taking from behind involves a pure pleasure, a pleasure unencumbered by productive outputs, pleasure with no strings attached, a pleasure that does not entwine us into the machine of the law?

And behind, of course, has an inescapable relationship to architecture, to that art form that only and always shows us a front, even if that front is now a three-dimensional surface. What more complete betrayal of architecture could there be than to demand to see what architecture hides from us, to see what is behind the architecture image, to uncover and let loose the ob-scene, that which Genet calls 'the off-scene of the world' (Genet 1987: 301)?

Be an abject object. To follow this agenda, to escape the prison cell of queer and straight, to queer architecture, we have to take on an impossible manoeuver: to need to become other to ourselves, to eject ourselves from our selves, to become fully abject. This is an inevitable end state, the final position of the already-abjected queer. We need to push this logic of abjection to its limit, to turn ourselves inside out like a glove, to be neither inside nor outside the line of enclosure but behind the drawing, behind the screen, behind architecture, inhabiting the ob-scene.

The House of the Thief is an architectural drawing project, funded primarily by the Social Sciences and Humanities Research Council of Canada, based, as I have mentioned earlier, loosely on the work of Jean Genet, that has operated in parallel to the production of my written doctoral dissertation, *On the Klepto-Genetics of Architecture* (Ripley 2021). The project team comprises groups of graduate design students, with anywhere from four to eight active in any given semester. About half the students have been paid for their work, as research assistants, while the other half received a mandatory research credit; the choice of credit or salary was up to each individual and the work was organized in chunks equivalent to about one credit (roughly eighty hours of work). It is important to note, I think, that none of the students were assigned to this work or required to take it on.

The project was not explicitly framed as a pedagogic endeavour but as a research activity. For the primary granting agencies in Canada, including SSHRC, the use of graduate students as research assistance is justified (in addition to the obvious mandate of providing income for students) as training of HQP (Highly Qualified Personnel). A similar objective could be claimed for the component, unique to our M.Arch. programme that provides the research credit mentioned earlier: to provide students with the opportunity to engage in a mature design-research project, that is, one led by experienced professionals, prior to engaging in their own design-research thesis. The project has been highly successful on those grounds, with a number of the participating students going on to produce remarkable theses.

On the other hand, there were and are a number of critical pedagogical tactics at play in *The House of the Thief*. The framing as a research project provides a certain amount of cover that allows more radical positions to be addressed and has allowed me to bring issues of queerness into the curriculum in a way that has flown below the radar of curriculum committees, workload assignments and so on. I have come to consider these tactics *counter-pedagogies*, as they are intended to counter the official pedagogies both of the institution and of the discipline of architecture. Unlike the formal mechanisms of institutional pedagogy, with their Learning Outcomes and Degree Level Expectations or for that matter the training methods of HQP, these tactics were never formalized or even acknowledged (until now). In retrospect, we can identify three overarching pedagogical objectives.

The first objective was to counter the understanding, produced by a heavily rules-based education guided by regimes of accreditation and the expectations of professional practice, of the architect as a technician. That is, I wanted to trouble a pervasive belief among students in the objective instrumentality and universality of architecture by insisting instead on developing a direct and personal connection to the work. For most of the students involved, this was the first significant opportunity to consider seriously the role of the personal – of *their* personal – and even the sexual in the production of architecture. I should point out that not all the students involved identified as queer, indeed I suspect the majority did not, although the question never actually came up; still, every student seemed to be struggling with questions of how their own personal beliefs and fears might work their way into architecture.

Masturbate on your drafting board. Architecture is always filled with sex, drawing is fornication. Queering architecture means to understand and participate in the erotics of design. Imagine the beautiful bodies you are delineating, cutting, dissecting and penetrating. Draw faster, harder, until your drawings start to moan and then finally explode in pure pleasure.

My second objective was to counter the deeply engrained understanding of architecture as a teleological and projective practice – that is, that architecture is always carried out in service to a building project that retrospectively justifies the design activity. I looked instead to develop an architecture defined by its techniques and practices and whose trajectory may be deconstructive rather than constructive.

The final objective was to counter the very deeply held belief not only on the part of students but also on the part of the profession as a whole (it constitutes in this sense a disciplinary fiction) in the benevolence of architecture. Students want to believe, of course, that the profession they are entering into has the possibility of 'making the world a better place' and indeed that this improvement of people's lives is the primary project of architecture. Instead, I look to trouble the naïveté of this position, opening students up to recognize the violence (subjective, objective and symbolic – see Žižek 2008) inherent in any act of architecture – even in the drawings we were producing. While a building project may indeed make some people's lives better, others will inevitably be damaged by the act and indeed even those who are served by a building are inevitably changed – wounded – as a result. More precisely, I hoped to open up understandings of architecture as the production of mechanisms of bodily control.

Steal whatever you can. Not little things: don't break into your neighbour's house or take money from your lover's wallet. Do those things if you want. But first you have to steal yourself. To be queer is to be both thief and stolen property: this is the Law of Architecture and to be queer is to be an outlaw. We are klepto-genetic beings.

We start by identifying a series of architectural concepts that reappear in Genet's work and that start to produce a formal theory of architecture: a formal queer theory of architecture. These klepto-genetic elements are as follows:

Line: It is the fundamental starting point of architecture. It is an essential act of violence and producer of the architectural binary. The line is also unpredictable and dangerous. The line is a tightrope from which we, forced to be funambulists, are always in danger of falling to our deaths. Lines wander off, becoming vagabond or loop around, forcing themselves into neckties and nooses. The line is a trap that we cannot avoid.

Ground: It is unreliable, an illusory convention on which we walk. The ground can fall through at any moment, gravity can fail to hold us down, buildings collapse or fly off into the sky. The ground is built up in the last resort of death, formed from piles of skeletons of our ancestors. Every ground is a stage.

Enclosure: It is the most powerful of the architectural creations, the fictive idea of the interior/exterior separation. Fictive because there is never any real interior: any interior is just another exterior. The architectural enclosure is an act of triple violence: violence to those enclosed, imprisoned, domesticated, subjectified and changed forever and fundamentally by this enclosure; violence to those excluded, who are *othered* and objectified; and the fundamental violence of appropriation, the claim of ownership. As Proudon put it, 'property is theft': enclosure is a primordial act of theft, a primal architectural sin from which we can never recover. The self, the most basic of enclosures, is a fundamental production of architecture. We are both thieves and stolen goods.

Void: as Lacan reminds us, this is why buildings exist: to produce voids. There is a void in every image and in every building that can never be seen. The void is a black hole, powering the machine of image with its massive gravity. Remember what is not seen. The primary voids are the cell, the brothel and the tomb and every human space (including the internal space of the self) is constructed as an amalgam of these.

Machine: Every building and every image is a machine and should be considered using a machinic analysis. What is produced by the machine? What are its inputs, its energy sources and, possibly most importantly, its waste products? The Machine for Living In is at the same time a *desiring machine*, indeed the two formulations, that of Le Corbusier and that of Deleuze and Guattari, are functionally equivalent. Both, in their most basic schematics, are thermodynamic machines, Carnot cycle engines, operating through flows of erotic energy and operating on the structure of the modern world, connected to the other great thermodynamic engines of modernity: steam engines, of course, but also capitalism, Hegelian dialectics, Oedipus, Haussmann's Paris, bourgeois society as a whole.

Ob-scene: The basic architectural vision machine: screen, scene, back-of-house, ob-scene. This is the mechanism by which architecture presents its identity as natural. Architecture presents a reality to the observer, to us, a reality in which the ob-scene, that which sits behind the image, behind the screen, behind architectural reality, is not exactly invisible, but obfuscated. This is the genesis of the uncanny. There is a behind to every image, even architectural images. The purpose of the image is to both hide and expose this behind, which we call the ob-scene, which cannot fail to make itself known. Architecture is the art of the omnipresent front.

These elements become, somehow, both subjects of interrogation and burglar's tools. Although the team is formally organized as a research studio under my supervision, in fact we operate as co-conspirators, breaking down to the largest extent possible the professor/student barrier. Each student agrees to work on a discrete sub-project (see the following paragraphs for examples), with the understanding that projects could move around from student to student and could well outlive any student's participation in the project. In the end I find myself working on most images; the students' work, even if vital, is perhaps best understood as producing raw materials that might propagate in unexpected ways. The attempt is to treat the research group as something of an experimental apparatus, a mechanism that would allow us to develop and test hypotheses.

An expanding collection of tactics is mobilized to waylay students from producing the type of design projects they have been taught to value through their education to this point. The projects are unclear and there is no predetermined end point; rather, they are open questions, open to conjecture and hypothesis, tested through drawing. It is not clear to me what we are looking to produce or where the path is leading; I often have the feeling that we are almost purposefully becoming lost, but it's in the moment when we are most lost, most unsure of our direction, that the miracles happen. Sometimes the tactics are simple, like the introduction of gold leaf and royal purple as a colour scheme. Sometimes it's a matter of asking students to push a known technique past its current limits – do draw the inside of a rectum, to animate it as a galaxy moving in the night sky. Sometimes the task itself seems ridiculous – 3D-print models of the Villa Savoye then wrap them in pages torn from Genet's books so that the Villa can no longer be seen. Sometimes instructions also seem like riddles: draw the rose behind the image, show the void inside the house, draw the house as though it is in love, draw what is inside the empty suitcase and lose yourself in the mirrors as you draw them. And always: push that idea further. Get some real gold leaf. Try putting the suitcase on the bandsaw. How do we make the black void float inside the model of the house?

The projects vary widely although all link in some way to Genet. One group of students redraw the Villa Savoye as inhabited by a thief (a love story), while another perform the wrapping of the Villa Savoye mentioned earlier. One student constructs Mies van der Rohe's Barcelona Pavilion as a hall of mirrors (based on a fantasy that Genet, who was in Barcelona at about this time, spent a few nights sleeping in the Pavilion), while another produces a video of a hall of mirrors being destroyed, based on Genet's *Funeral Rites*. One student draws an image of the funeral of Divine, the drag queen main character in Genet's *Our Lady of the Flowers*, coupled with a rendering of Genet's proposal for a theatre in a cemetery, while another constructs a model of Divine's garret apartment overlooking the cemetery. One student builds dozens of digital models of *abject objects* found in Genet's work, while another produces a video of the prison cell in which Genet wrote his first novel, exploding to become a universe – the *Big Bagne*[4] – and another constructs virtual reality models of a series of quasi-historical brothels, Genet's *houses of illusion*. Another series of videos and drawings explore the fate of the tightrope walker, a line of flight (about a line of flight) that is grounded in an essay by Genet on that theme (and dedicated to Genet's lover, the tightrope walker Abdallah).

Put your life on the line. When you draw a line the line draws you. The line is a thin wire stretched between two worlds: you walk on it as a tightrope walker, knowing that the line could betray you at any moment, you could fall into the abyss. You need to trust the line, even though you know the line is not trustworthy: it is the line that queers you, the line that can easily turn itself into a noose, the line that spells your end.

The work was reviewed collectively in group meetings, at first in person and later online. Of special interest to me were the pandemic meetings that we had online, in which the discussion was always vivid. As the work progressed, ideas started to come to the surface, leading to new opportunities and new projects. Students began to emerge out of the constant destabilization and provocation of the project into a place of extraordinary production. The forced move online as a result of the pandemic produced a significant shift in our production methods, as the work that was considered for traditional gallery exhibition had to be re-thought for web viewing. As a result, the team had to acquire a whole set of new skills that we had not considered previously, such as 3D-scanning, virtual reality rendering, video production and so on. In July 2020 and October 2021, we organized virtual gallery

FIGURE 15.1 That Strange Word *(2020–21). Electronic drawing. Modelling, Photoshop and Illustrator work, M. Orzechowska. Affinity Designer and Photoshop work by C. Ripley. Screen images by C. Ripley and A. Wagle.*

FIGURE 15.2 Sex Fantasy *(2021). Photoshop collage. Contemporary brothel bedroom design. Rhino modelling and rendering, M. Evola. Photoshop composition C. Ripley. Additional Photoshop work A. Wagle.*

exhibitions of the work in progress along with critical peer-review sessions with an international panel of reviewers.

Keep a packed suitcase under the bed. You will need to be able to make a quick escape when the police arrive – the architecture police, the straight police. Because they will come for you. No one can tell you what to keep in the suitcase, except that you will need to have everything necessary to continue on. If you die, the contents of the suitcase should be able to take over your fight.

A few pages ago I claimed that the project attempted to make use of the research group as an experimental apparatus. If that's the case, then it is only reasonable to expect a discussion of outcomes and result of this experiment.

In terms of the official research project, progress has been made. A glance at the project website will show that many *beautiful monsters* have been drawn, drawings that have deepened our understanding of the mechanisms of queerness in architecture as well as its klepto-genetic foundations. What's more, a galaxy of tactics has begun to coalesce that we might employ in the

FIGURE 15.3 Maison Close *(2021). Photoshop collage. Imagined reconstruction of high-class Parisian brothel, between the wars. Rhino modelling and rendering, M. Evola. Photoshop composition C. Ripley. Additional Photoshop work A. Wagle.*

process of queering ourselves as architects (for queering architecture can only ever mean queering architects), a collection that, unlike Le Corbusier's (or Andrew Holder's) five points is never complete, never a totalizing set of prescriptions, but rather an indeterminate and always-changing set of sometimes contradictory and unachievable visions. A certain set of these tactics are represented here through the second text, the wisteria, the italicized paragraphs that interrupt this primary text, a set that is always incomplete and only valid at the moment of their writing and even then only provisionally and even then only for me. This is why we end with failure: indeed, failure is not just the best we can do, it is our goal. Queerness is failure, to resist the totalizing success of straightness. As José Muñoz said, we are not yet queer: the work we do remains constrained and contained, always, by the cell of the normal (Muñoz 2009). *We will never be queer* – this is the primary point, queer is impossible, queering architecture is impossible, all we can do is work towards queerness, work towards an asymptotically distant queer practice of architecture, always on the horizon, always in a distant future, but never within reach. It is within this knowledge of certain failure that *The House of the Thief* operates, from the beginning: the thief

FIGURE 15.4 The Big Bang *(La Santé)* (2021). *Superimposed film stills, Photoshop collage. Imagined reconstruction of cell in Santé Prison, Paris. Modelling in Rhino and Blender, rendering and animation, M. Evola. Affinity Designer and Photoshop work by C. Ripley. Additional Photoshop work A. Wagle.*

can't live in a house, Genet tells us that and yet we must come to grips somehow with the thing that cannot be.

Be a pornstar (we are all sex workers). Embrace drawing as the most intimate of sex acts. Expose yourself for all to see. Be glorious, seduce, ravish. Choose a porn name. Every drawing you make is a drawing of you fucking or being fucked. Draw your deepest, ugliest fantasies and sell them to the universe.

From the point of view of pedagogy, it is considerably more difficult to discuss results. Pedagogic outcomes of the sort this project is looking for don't come into view until years later, if then; so the question at hand is something more like 'how have the participants in the project been changed and how have those changes in turn had effects on the world?' I asked the participating students to send me a sentence or two reflecting on their participation in the project and I will let these statements stand on their own. Abhishek, who wrapped models of the Villa Savoye in the words of Genet and developed the rectum-as-house images, had this to say:

FIGURE 15.5 *La Santé 1942 0206 (2021). Video still, Photoshop collage. Imagined reconstruction of cell in Santé Prison, Paris. Modelling in Rhino and Blender, rendering and animation, M. Evola. Affinity Designer and Photoshop work by C. Ripley. Additional Photoshop work A. Wagle.*

Researching the life and works of Jean Genet required the adoption of an entirely new world view. The study led me to empathize and understand an ethos that was overlooked in my five years of traditional architectural education.

Meanwhile, Michael, who produced virtual reality models of historical brothels as well as the Santé prison, voiced similar ideas:

Stealing Home revealed to me the violence of architecture, as well as the ways in which social organization crafts spatial organization and in turn crafts the subject.

Finally, Maya, who produced stunningly beautiful images of a theatre nestled in Montmartre cemetery, had this to say:

The fearlessness, playfulness and explorative nature of the approach (and the extents to which they were taken) were extremely liberating

FIGURE 15.6 *Untitled, abject object (Marie Antoinette) (2020–21). Electronic drawing. Rhino and Blender modelling and Photoshop work, A. Wagle. Additional Photoshop work by C. Ripley.*

and refreshing. It was great to work with methodologies that inherently question the status quo, even when those can be controversial and uncomfortable. . . . It left me with lots to explore (and ways to explore) as I evolve in this field.

For myself – for after all the pedagogy of the project has acted on me as well – I have become more queer, perhaps, as an architect and educator. Pieces of the project have found their way into my regular teaching (this afternoon I will be presenting 'On Stained Sheets', a paper on masturbation and architecture, to graduate students in my contemporary theory seminar). I've also noticed myself becoming harder, not only less willing to accept the common homophobic micro-aggressions of everyday life but also less tolerant of the closet full of myths and legends that make up most of architectural history and theory, less able to stomach what I see as a naïve belief in the utopian project of architecture. I've come to understand something that I've probably known all along – one of Žižek's *unknown knowns* – that architecture is itself pedagogy, that it is through architecture that we learn how to be ourselves or, as Sara Ahmed puts it, it is architecture that orients us towards certain behaviours, desires, ways of being in the world and away from others (Ahmed 2006). *Architecture is pedagogy:* my project for a counter-pedagogy, then, is not a project against this or that architecture, but a project that seeks to resist, to counter, architecture itself. I have become a traitor.

Betray the things you love. You don't know the depth of love until you betray it. Betrayal is the most intimate relationship between things.

Notes

*   This work has been supported by the Social Sciences and Humanities Research Council of Canada and Ryerson University.

1   Genet spent time at Mettray as a colonist in the mid-1920s and recounted this experience in his first two novels, *Our Lady of the Flowers* and *Miracle of the Rose*.

2   Klepto-Genetics refers to the origins of architecture in theft. This is a restatement of Prouhon's 'Property Is Theft' from 1840.

3   As Bersani puts it, this figure, which Genet likens to the prow of a ship, is a 'fucking of the world instead of each other'.

4   *Le bagne* is a French term (similar to the English term 'the joint') used to describe a penitentiary, especially one that makes use of forced labour. The term appears to have derived from the Bagno of Livourne, a prison built within the ruins of a Roman bath.

References

Ahmed, S. (2006), *Queer Phenomenology Orientations, Objects, Others*. Durham: Duke University Press.

Bersani, L. (1996), *Homos*. Cambridge, MA: Harvard University Press.

Deleuze, G. (1995), *Negotiations, 1972–1990*. New York: Columbia University Press.

Foucault, M. (1977), *Discipline and Punish: The Birth of the Prison*. New York: Vintage Books.

Genet, J. (2003), *Fragments of the Artwork*. Werner Hamacher, Ed. C. Mandell, Trans. Stanford: Stanford University Press.

Genet, J. and Sartre, J.-P. (1987), *Our Lady of the Flowers*. Bernard Frechtman, Trans. New York: Grove, Evergreen.

Halberstam, J. (2011), *The Queer Art of Failure*. Durham: Duke University Press.

Muñoz, J.-E., (2009), *Cruising Utopia: The Then and There of Queer Futurity*. New York: New York University Press.

Preciado, P. B. and Halberstam, J. (2018), *Countersexual Manifesto: Subverting Gender Identities*. Kevin Gerry Dunn, Trans. New York: Columbia University Press.

Ripley, C. (2018), 'Strategies for living in houses'. In Gorny, R. & van den Heuvel, D. (Eds.), *Trans-Bodies / Queering Spaces* [Special issue]. *Footprint*, 21: 95–108.

Ripley, C. (2020), '(Im)proper subversion: taking architecture from behind'. In M. Abrahamson and O. W. Fischer (Eds.), *Dialectic VIII. Subverting—Unmaking Architecture*. Novato: Oro Editions: 68–73.
Ripley, C. (2021), *On the Klepto-Genetics of Architecture*. Doctoral dissertation. European Graduate School.
Žižek, S. (2008), *Violence*. London: Profile.
Žižek, S. (2015) *Organs without Bodies: On Deleuze and Consequences*. Abingdon, Oxfordshire: Routledge.

CONTRIBUTORS

Gem Barton is an author and senior academic, interested in the interrelations between human behaviour, speculation, and spatial design. She teaches and publishes on the subjects of gender and feminism, film and spatial production, futures and fictions, narrative and storytelling, reality and representation, career and enterprise, teaching and learning, interiors and architecture. At the RCA, Gem teaches MA Interior Design and is responsible for steering the research focus of the programme. Gem is co-founder of the Office for Speculative Spatial Design (O-SSD) a ThinkTank for research-led speculative spatial design. Through their work and consultancy, they aim to influence policy towards a more just and inclusive society.

Ben Campkin is Professor of Urbanism and Urban Theory at The Bartlett School of Architecture, co-director of UCL Urban Laboratory, and the author of *Remaking London: Decline and Regeneration in Urban Culture* (2013), which won the 2015 Jane Jacobs Urban Communication Foundation Award. The research Ben leads on *LGBTQ+ Night-spaces* has informed the *London Plan*, local borough provisions for LGBTQ+ spaces, and campaigns to protect LGBTQ+ heritage. He is completing a book on LGBTQ+ venues in London since the 1980s, *Queer Premises* (forthcoming) and is the UK Principal Investigator for the European research collaboration, *Night-spaces, Migration, Culture and Integration in Europe*.

Ece Canlı is an artist and researcher at CECS (the Communication and Society Research Centre) at University of Minho (Portugal), where she is also a guest lecturer in sociology of gender master's programme. She holds a PhD in design from University of Porto. Her work sits at the intersection of material regimes and body politics, more specifically, socio-spatio-material constitutions of gender, sexuality, race, and other identity categories. In her current research titled 'Prison Heterocissexual Complex', she investigates spatial, material and technological conditions of queer incarceration. She is a founding member of the research collective Decolonising Design Group.

Simona Castricum is a multidisciplinary creative and academic working in music and architecture on Wurundjeri land of Kulin Nation. Her approach is one of speculative architectural practice, exploring queer and trans futures in architecture, music, the public realm, and civic life. Simona's work re-imagines radical relationships between the tactile, virtual, and affective conditions of gender and sexual nonconformity. She is also a research fellow in architecture at the University of Melbourne and a musician, DJ and producer, and she runs independent record label Trans-Brunswick Express and is a community radio broadcaster at 3RRR Melbourne.

Adam Nathaniel Furman is a British artist and designer of Argentine and Japanese heritage based in London. Trained in architecture, Adam works in spatial design and art of all scales from video and prints to large public artworks, architecturally integrated ornament, as well as products, furniture, interiors, publishing and academia.

Nicholas Gamso is an associate editor of *Places Journal* and a contributing editor of the *Millennium Film Journal*. He has published widely in the fields of art, architecture, film and media theory, as well as queer and critical race studies. His first book, *Art after Liberalism*, was published by Columbia Books on Architecture and the City in 2022.

Dirk van den Heuvel is Associate Professor of architecture at TU Delft and head of the Jaap Bakema Study Centre, the research collaboration between Het Nieuwe Instituut and TU Delft. His work focuses on the intersection of modern architecture, democratic societies and welfare state histories. His published works include *Architecture and the Welfare State* (2015), *Jaap Bakema and the Open Society* (2018) and *Habitat: Ecology Thinking in Architecture* (2020). He is co-editor of the volume 'Trans-Bodies/Queering Spaces', *Footprint* 21, 2017.

A. L. Hu, AIA, NCARB, NOMA, EcoDistricts AP, is a queer, nonbinary transgender Taiwanese-American architect, organizer and facilitator in New York City. Their practice synthesizes organizing for racial, class and gender justice with design; rethinks the architect's role in facilitating accessible spaces; and manifests in architecture, visual media and collaborative work. Their writing has been published in *Architect Magazine*, *The Architect's Newspaper*, *MAS Context* and *New York Review of Architecture*. Hu writes the *Queer Agenda* newsletter and runs Queeries, a community-building initiative for and by LGBTQIA+ spatial designers. They received a master of architecture from Columbia University GSAPP.

Marko Jobst is an independent lecturer and researcher based in Scotland. He has taught at a number of schools of architecture in London, most prominently as architecture undergraduate theory coordinator at the University of Greenwich. He holds a Diploma in Architecture from Belgrade University and MArch, MSc, and PhD in architectural history and theory from The Bartlett School of

Architecture, UCL. He is the author of *A Ficto-Historical Theory of the London Underground* (2017) and co-editor, with Hélène Frichot, of *Architectural Affects After Deleuze and Guattari* (2020). His forthcoming volume, *Instituting Worlds: Architecture and Islands*, is co-edited with Catharina Gabrielsson.

Lo Marshall (they/them) is an urban studies scholar whose research is oriented around gender, sexuality and cities, with a focus upon LGBTQ+ people's lives and spaces. Lo was named a 'emerging voice in architecture' for the *London Festival of Architecture* and *Design Museum's* 'Manifestos: Architecture for a New Generation' in 2020, and contributed to 'Queer Spaces: London, 1980s–Today' (2019) and 'Electronic' (2020–21).

Timothy Moore is a senior lecturer at Monash University, a founder of Sibling Architecture and the curator of Melbourne Design Week. With Sibling, Timothy has exhibited at the National Gallery of Victoria, Istanbul Design Biennial, São Paulo Architecture Biennial, and Gyeonggi MoMA. At Monash, Timothy is a researcher within XYX Lab that looks at the relationship between gender, sexuality, equity and architecture. Timothy has also worked at architecture offices in Melbourne, Amsterdam and Berlin, and as an editor for three influential magazines, *Volume*, *Architecture Australia*, and *Future West* (Australian Urbanism).

Sarah Nicholus (they and she) is a writer, scholar and queer theorist. Working in gender and sexuality studies across the Americas, Nicholus uses interdisciplinary methodologies derived from media and cultural studies to better understand queerness and LGBT+ sexuality in rural and socially conservative spaces. Nicholus is interested in how transnational queer theorizing can challenge traditional boundaries, including academic, geographic and bodily binaries. Central to their work is dialogue with Brazilian and Latin American scholars, cultural producers and theorists to not only speak to colonial histories and the geopolitics of knowledge production but also to interrogate multiple sites of normativity.

Regner Ramos holds a PhD in architecture from The Bartlett School of Architecture (UCL). A tenured associate professor at the University of Puerto Rico School of Architecture, his research inserts queer spaces into the landscape of contemporary Puerto Rican architectural discourse. Across his different projects, Ramos's design-based research practice unfolds through a variety of methods: performative writing, narration, drawings, video/film and making. His two-year research project 'Cüirtopia' is funded by the FIPI Award (2020–22), on view at the Museo de Arte Contemporáneo de Puerto Rico. Ramos is co-editor of *Queer Sites in Global Contexts* (2020).

Colin Ripley is a professor in and chair of the School of Interior Design at Toronto Metropolitan University (formerly Ryerson University) in Toronto,

Canada, and Director Emeritus of the architectural research firm RVTR. He is author or editor of several books about architecture as well as journal papers on a wide range of topics, including megaregional urbanism, responsive envelope systems, sonic architecture, Canadian modern architecture and queer theories of architecture. He holds a Bachelor of Engineering from McMaster University, a Master of Science in theoretical physics from the University of Toronto, a Master of Architecture from Princeton University and a doctorate in philosophy, art and critical thought from the European Graduate School.

Joel Sanders FAIA is Principal of JSA, an award-winning architecture firm, as well as MIXdesign, a think tank and design consultancy dedicated to creating inclusive design solutions that meet the needs of people of different ages, genders, cultures and abilities. He is professor-in-practice at Yale School of Architecture, where he was formerly the director of post-professional studies. He is the author of three books – *STUD: Architectures of Masculinity*, *Joel Sanders Writings and Projects* and *Groundwork: Between Landscape and Architecture*. His projects have been featured in international exhibitions and the permanent collections of MoMA, Art Institute of Chicago and the Carnegie Museum of Art.

Naomi Stead is a professor in the School of Architecture and Urban Design at RMIT University, Melbourne, where she is director of the Design and Creative Practice Enabling Capability Platform – working with researchers across and beyond the creative fields to engage in high-impact interdisciplinary research for the benefit of people and planet. Over a career of twenty years, Stead has been committed to research-based advocacy – into gender equity and work-related well-being in creative workplaces, and ways in which creative practice and education can respond to the climate and biodiversity crisis. Stead is widely published as a critic and commentator, including as architecture critic for *The Saturday Paper*.

Olivier Vallerand is an assistant professor at Université de Montréal's School of Design, a community activist, architect and historian. His research focuses on how self-identifications intersect with the use and design of the built environment, on queer and feminist approaches to design education, and on alternative design practices. His book *Unplanned Visitors: Queering the Ethics and Aesthetics of Domestic Space*, winner of the 2021 IDEC Book Award, explores the emergence of queer theory in architectural discourse.

Martin van Wijk studies art history at the University of Amsterdam and gender studies at Utrecht University, the Netherlands. His current research focuses on developing a feminist queer reading of the architecture archive at Het Nieuwe Instituut. Martin has recently completed an internship at the Jaap Bakema Study Centre under supervision of Dirk van den Heuvel.

INDEX